unmasking
class, gender, and sexuality
in Nicaraguan festival

unmasking

class, gender, and sexuality
in Nicaraguan festival

Katherine Borland

The University of Arizona Press   Tucson

The University of Arizona Press
© 2006 The Arizona Board of Regents
All rights reserved
♾ This book is printed on acid-free, archival-quality paper.
Manufactured in the United States of America

11   10   09   08   07   06   6   5   4   3   2   1

Library of Congress Cataloging-in-Publication Data
Borland, Katherine.
  Unmasking class, gender, and sexuality in Nicaraguan
festival / Katherine Borland.
    p. cm.
  Includes bibliographical references and index.
  ISBN-13: 978-0-8165-2511-9 (hardcover : alk. paper)
  ISBN-10: 0-8165-2511-0 (hardcover : alk. paper)
    1. Folk festivals—Nicaragua—Masaya. 2. Fasts and
feasts—Nicaragua—Masaya. 3. Folklore—Nicaragua—
Masaya. 4. Masaya (Nicaragua)—Social life and customs.
I. Title.
GT4820.M37B67 2006
394.2697285′14—dc22
                                              2005028395

A los bailarines y peregrinos de Masaya
que crean la cultura del pueblo

Contents

Figures

Note: Unless otherwise specified, all photographs are by the author.

Acknowledgments

I am grateful to Ohio State University, Newark, for providing a seed grant to support my 2001 field research in Nicaragua. I also thank the staff of the Instituto de Historia de Nicaragua y Centroamérica at the Universidad Centroamericana and of the Instituto Nicaragüense de Cultura for graciously assisting me in locating materials for my field study during 2001–2002. I am also indebted to Miguel Angel Áviles Carranza, director of the Centro de Investigaciones Socio-Educativas at the Universidad Nacional Autónoma de Nicaragua, for generously providing me with an academic home during my field studies in 1990 and 1991. The organizations and individuals in Masaya, Nicaragua, who have shared their time, talents, insights, and opinions with me are too numerous to mention. I thank the Colomer and Herrera-Sanchez families for opening their homes to me in 1990 and 1991 and again in 2001. I thank the staff and members of Masaya's Alejandro Vega Matus House of Culture and its Office of Culture, the staff of the Old Market, and the board of the Torovenado del Pueblo for their collaboration.

I owe a profound debt to Monimbó cultural activist Carlos Centeno Gaitán, who provided unflagging support for my research over more than a decade. Without his diplomatic assistance in identifying artists and knowledgeable community members of all backgrounds, I would not have been able to gather the diversity of materials upon which this text and its analysis rest. Mr. Centeno's concern for preserving and celebrating Monimbó's cultural heritage has influenced me deeply, as it has his neighbors and the countless young dancers who have learned their craft from him. I am also grateful for the personal friendship of his wife, Argelia García Soza, and daughter, Samantha Centeno.

I thank my mentors Richard Bauman, Sabra Webber, and Dan Reff for their support and helpful direction at various stages of this project. My colleagues Dorothy Noyes, Elizabeth Bass, and Elizabeth Caldwell read portions of the manuscript, and their thoughtful suggestions have improved the text. Responsibility for oversights and blind spots remains, of course, wholly mine.

Part I The Place of Tradition

Figure 1.1 Saint Jerome atop his mountain, 1991.

1 Living Festival

At 11:00 a.m. on September 30, 2001, Saint Jerome descends from his church atop a mountain constructed of colorful foliage woven on a large wooden frame. Twenty or so men underneath hoist the massive structure on their shoulders and begin to sway backward, forward, and sideways into the street. Half a block ahead a smaller figure bobs above the crowd. Sword in one hand, a pair of scales in the other, and his right foot planted firmly on Satan's head, Saint Michael clears the way for the patron saint.[1] Two groups of elderly men accompany the religious procession. Their staffs, flags, and bongo constitute the regalia of the council of elders, traditional political representatives for the indigenous community on Monimbó.[2] Crowds of devotees and revelers fill the streets, some bobbing up and down in a simple dance of gratitude for a favor granted, a few breaking into a more elaborate carnivalesque shimmy.

The hot white sunlight, the heat of countless bodies packed together, the periodic explosion of fireworks, and the energetic music of brass bands combine in a dizzying assault on the senses. Meanwhile, street vendors push through the crowds, offering plastic baggies filled with water, soda, and *leche* (milk) or cane liquor. A small *torovenado*—masqueraders dressed as animals, ghouls, women, and ragged countrymen—dances vigorously. La Gigantona, a towering effigy of a white lady, also bobs gaily above the surging crowd.[3] Farther along the parade route, a youthful folk ballet troupe from the capital waits in shiny blue costumes to perform for the saint.[4]

When Saint Jerome's mountain approaches Nicaraguan Liberal Party presidential candidate and Masaya native Enrique Bolaños, the saint turns to salute him in a gesture of respect and approval.[5] Bolaños ascends the mountain to place a new cape around the saint's shoulders, then holds up one finger as a sign for the Liberal Party.[6] The saint similarly greets the Conservative Party candidate. When the mountain passes city hall, however, it turns abruptly, showing its back to Liberal mayor Carlos Iván Hüeck[7] and facing instead the home of Dr. Gerardo Sánchez, Sandinista mayor during the late 1980s. There a large group of onlookers noisily support the Sandinista ticket. The saint's generosity to all political parties conceals a tremendous struggle under the lurching mountain, as those carrying him, divided by political sentiments, vie to control his movements.

The living festival not only combines cultural heritage with religious belief, but also constitutes symbolic capital for which various outside interests vie. Performing groups, both local and national, creatively restore cultural practices to the religious procession and thereby strengthen their own claims to authenticity in other venues. Participants express their deeply divided political sentiments, while politicians vie for the saint's favor. At the same time, believers fulfill religious vows; vendors exploit a marketplace; the curious come for the commotion. To add to the complexity, September 30 represents only one moment in the annual celebration dedicated to Saint Jerome. The cultural performances that have migrated from the religious processions to their own festival dates have extended the festival season from six weeks in the 1960s to three months in 2001.

Popular culture or folklore constitutes ordinary people's cultural production. Three cultural performances have taken shape during the Somoza (1936–79), Sandinista (1979–90), and neoliberal (1990–2006) periods as vibrant, evolving forms of this popular culture. The transvestite Negras marimba dances, the carnivalesque torovenado masquerades, and the Lenten-period pilgrimage to Popoyuapa contribute to Masaya's reputation as the storehouse of Nicaragua's traditions. Each is distinct in its aesthetic system, its audience, and its reception and significance at the national level. Together these festival enactments demonstrate that the oppositional power of popular culture resides in the process of cultural negotiation itself, as Masaya continually asserts its uniqueness, deploying cherished traditions to new ends.

The latter half of the twentieth century witnessed an impressive growth in festival activity globally. Scholars have viewed this trend from different locations as the fruit of an advancing tourist industry, as a reaction against the homogenization and erasures inherent in na-

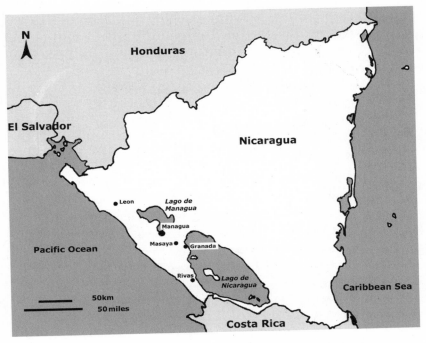

Figure 1.2 Nicaragua. (Adapted from *Maps on File* [New York: Facts on File, 1984])

tional constructions of heritage, as a recurrent method of establishing or contesting the social order within the local sphere, and as a way for provincial communities to negotiate a measure of autonomy within a global cultural economy they cannot hope to influence (Abrahams 1981; Bauman and Stoeltje 1989; Bendix 1989; García-Canclini 1993; Guss 2000; Magliocco 1988; Mendoza 2000; Noyes 2003). Each of these dynamics contributes to the continuing expansion and elaboration of existing festivals, the revival of long-dormant traditions, and the creation of new festivities. Through festival, communities such as Masaya negotiate, incorporate, and resist globally circulating ideas, identities, and material objects. Festival enactments constitute a people's theater, articulating a range of perspectives on the homegrown and the global; on class, race, and ethnicity; on gender and sexuality; and on religious sensibilities.[8] At the same time, they rest on an apparent paradox. Although they derive their authority as assertions of heritage, each performance represents a negotiation of cultural identity, a statement of distinctiveness or difference from the nation and the world that highlights the oppositional power of popular culture.

Masaya lies about thirty miles southeast of Managua and forms a provincial capital for the smaller towns and rural settlements of the Masaya-Carazo region. In contrast to Managua's urban modernity, Masaya cultivates an aggressively traditional identity. Unlike the Spanish-colonial cities of Granada and León, it claims to preserve the nation's indigenous roots, roots that are most visible in the city's southern quadrant, the historically indigenous neighborhood of Monimbó. Masaya's patron saint festival, whose September religious processions signal the beginning of three months of festival masquerades and dances, has become a showcase for this traditional culture, earning the city the sobriquet Capital of Nicaraguan Folklore. Forty years of tumultuous political transformation have contributed to Masaya's drive to construct a unique identity in and through festival.

The Revolutionary Context

The Sandinista revolution powerfully reshaped Nicaraguan identity. Although the Sandinista government ultimately failed to retain its popular majority, the 1978–79 revolution momentarily reversed longstanding power relations: the people prevailed, forcing a ruthless dictator and his army to flee. In the creative opening that followed, all things seemed possible. And, indeed, this small, marginalized nation, then barely 3 million people, suddenly became the focus of intense international interest. Within this context, the country experienced a flowering of the arts, both the new expressions of revolutionary experience and a vigorous folklore revival. Indeed, Sandinista leaders explicitly acknowledged the relationship between revolutionary struggle and cultural production.[9] Commander Tomás Borge, speaking shortly after the triumph, made the now famous observation that the revolution had been achieved "with guitars and poems, and with bullets."

The revolution unleashed high expectations for improvements in everyday life. Yet government rhetoric masked a troubling contradiction: the popular classes were the new leaders of the revolutionary project at the same time that they were deficient—victims of a culture of silence, of an unequal social and economic system that had consistently denied them the tools for self-expression. The revolutionary state therefore launched an intensive education program: in literacy, in political organization, and in new techniques for farming, for artisanal production, and for family life. All these efforts were designed to create a new, more competent, more socially engaged Nicaraguan.[10] Unfortunately, although enthusiastic revolutionaries attempted to reform society by reforming the "people," they were not so successful in transforming themselves. A class-based system of privilege that crossed ideological lines continued to value the urban over the rural, school knowledge over practical experience, men over women, and modernity over tradition.[11]

Sandinista cultural policy was divided between the grassroots, democratizing efforts of the Ministry of Culture, headed by Ernesto Cardenal and Daisy Zamora, and the centralizing, professionalizing approach of the Sandinista Association of Culture Workers, headed by Rosario Murillo. The Ministry of Culture established a number of programs to teach new arts to the people, and it loosely administered grassroots Popular Culture Centers, which sprang up in response to local initiatives throughout the country. In contrast, the Sandinista Association of Culture Workers patronized and promoted performance groups by organizing national festivals, founding the National Dance Academy, and assisting several Managua-based folk ballets. In the intensive nationalization of the dance that followed, regional festival performers, such as those working in Masaya, lost control over the practice and aesthetics of folk dance.

Although Cardenal and Murillo approached the problem of stimulating national culture in different ways, they shared an elite bias that made it difficult for them to recognize and honor the creative independence of popular artists. Cardenal's approach was romantic and patronizing, and Murillo's was exclusive and centralizing.[12] However, critiques from both grassroots and professional artists eventually convinced these cultural leaders to recognize that artists required a certain freedom to develop their own expressive styles and methods (Field 1987, 1999; Wellinga 1994; Whisnant 1995).

At the same time, local communities resisted the heavy-handed influence of Managua cultural planners by investing in their own cultural institutions. Masaya's city government, headed by Sandinista mayor Ernesto Ortega, launched a highly successful, participatory restructuring of the Saint Jerome Festival, which had provided the traditional arena for local cultural enactments. As part of this effort, the city government developed a very successful fund-raising program in order to assist performance groups financially. Consequently, the number of organized festival performers from popular neighborhoods grew, and the festivities themselves became the liveliest and most colorful that residents can remember. Financed by *local* government initiatives, Masaya's cultural recovery constituted a direct reaction against cultural nationalism (Borland 2002).

During the politically transitional years 1990 and 1991, the Saint Jerome Festival was contested terrain. City residents had already heatedly resisted the national appropriation of their prized performance form, marimba dancing, during the Sandinista period. Indigenous-identified Monimbó residents struggled against dominance by mestizo, town-center dancers in the local festival arena. Members of the newly elected Union of National Opposition (UNO) political party battled to wrest neighborhood cultural and religious symbols forcibly from what they regarded as unworthy Sandinista hands.[13] Yet the partisan polarization so evident at that time partially obscured even larger forces that were transforming both daily life and festival practice.

During the postrevolutionary decade of the 1990s, Masaya's cultural recovery continued to gather force, even though the city government no longer offered financial assistance to performers. The number of organized marimba dance groups performing in the Saint Jerome Festival increased steadily among all social sectors, as did membership in the Catholic *cofradías* (brotherhoods) responsible for religious processions. The nighttime Procession of the Ahuizotes now rivals the older carnivalesque masquerade, the torovenado, in popularity. Moreover, participation in the Lenten pilgrimage to the nearby sanctuary of Popoyuapa increased eightfold between 1991 and 2001.

What has fostered this vitality? The city government remained financially strapped. National cultural policy favored the restoration of colonial rather than indigenous heritage.[14] Tourism remained sluggish. Moreover, the economic belt tightening of the neoliberal period resulted in a decline in real income among the popular classes.[15] All of these factors suggest minimal returns for festival expenditures. Even so, ordinary Masayans have refused to relinquish their identity as artists and culture producers.[16]

How do Masaya's cultural practices incorporate and at the same time resist global influences? How do they simultaneously promote community integration and express community tensions? To understand the living festival one must move beyond an analysis of Nicaraguan culture that regards post-1990 developments as a return to pre-1979 relations. Indeed, popular culture is the property of nationalists on neither the political right nor the left. Instead, it constitutes a historically changing set of practices that are intimately related to, but never subsumed by dominant political or cultural formations.

Guss (2000) has elegantly demonstrated that festival constitutes a privileged arena for articulating the struggles between local and larger-than-local social formations. Yet local social formations are themselves complex and multifaceted. The contests that festivals enact, the arguments that individuals make through bodily performances and parodies of identity, always imply multiple audiences. Moreover, the larger-than-local now exists within the local community as part of its daily experience. Therefore, the cultural work that festival enactments accomplish may involve the incorporation and perhaps even the cannibalization of global trends and influences.

Modernization

In Latin American studies, *modernization* has been conceptualized in a variety of ways. Economically, it refers to the shift to large-scale export agriculture that began in the late nineteenth century. This change promoted infrastructural development, state encroachments on rural and often indigenous communities, and state curtailment of the power of the Catholic Church. Politically, then, modernization is associated with the growing power of the state. Within the development paradigm, *modernization* refers to the spread of services and technologies to underserved communities and simultaneously to the concentration of populations in urban communities. In worldview, modernization refers to the spread of reason, or science, over magic.

However, as in other parts of Latin America, modernization in Nicaragua has been uneven, fragmented, and impermanent, so much so that the country exhibits an emphatically postmodern juxtaposition of incongruous and even contradictory technologies, systems, lifeways, beliefs, and practices. Rowe and Schelling (1991) have argued that the current globalizing transformations in Latin America approach the intensity of those experienced five hundred years ago at the time of the European Conquest. Just as the conquered populations then creatively incorporated Spanish novelties into existing cultural systems (Harris 2000), so too are contemporary communities such as Masaya selectively digesting the goods, beliefs, systems, values, and information that emanate from powerful global networks. Popular culture both reflects and responds to these larger changes *without* necessarily being eradicated by them.[17]

Folklore and Folklorization

Folklorists have long noted the complex and contestatory nature of popular culture (Lombardi-Satriani 1974), in particular festivals (Abrahams 1981; Cohen 1993; Harris 2000; Magliocco 1993; Noyes 2003; R. Smith 1975; Turner 1986). Field studies have repeatedly challenged Durkheim's ([1912] 1961) model of festivals as specially marked occasions for individuals to participate in a unified, collective, transcendent experience that is somehow set apart from everyday life (Eade and Sallnow 1991). Instead, social boundaries continue to operate even in the most liminal types of festival. Moreover, when asked, participants express widely varying motives for attending festivals. Such diversity challenges the notion that festival provides an experience of a unified collectivity.[18]

Festival growth and transformation, moreover, often occurs within the context of a transfer of cultural heritage from one group to another. This process, which has most often been linked to nation building, has been labeled *folklore revival* in the United States or *folklorization* in Latin America. Folklorization is the means by which usually urban, privileged intellectuals revalue the cultural enactments of often marginalized groups in their society, refashion them as regional or national folklore, and project them into new media and performance spheres (Kirshenblatt-Gimblett 1998; Mendoza 2000). Although those who reshape popular culture may exhibit a range of intentions, the effect of their effort is often to sanitize or domesticate popular practices that once threatened the elites. Moreover, folklore revivals can enshrine degrading stereotypes about marginalized groups. Therefore, any discussion of festival growth and meaning must consider how elite adaptations and interpretations of folklore affect popular practices (Guss 2000; Mendoza 2000).

In Masaya, the folklorization of Indian ritual dances and masquerades began in earnest during the 1960s within the context of new Central American interest in folklore on the part of voluntary organizations such as the Lions Club. In the 1970s, a countercultural youth movement revalued and deployed Indian culture against the social elitism of an Americanized dictatorship, and in the 1980s the Sandinista government identified these forms with resistance to foreign domination. In the 1990s, the neoliberal governments of Violeta Barrios de Chamorro and Arnoldo Alemán praised folklore as an expression of the nation's fervent Catholicism.

On one hand, folklorization constitutes a kind of transcultural borrowing, the constant appropriation and reappropriation of cultural elements between and among groups. For instance, if indigenous communities had centuries ago adopted and adapted Spanish performance forms, then the late-twentieth-century mestizo recuperation of these traditions as national heritage simply demonstrates how cultural practices continually move from popular to marginal groups and back, from one ethnic group to another. However, such a formulation ignores the persistent structures of inequality that elevate the aesthetic performances of one group over those of another.[19]

On the other hand, if we characterize folklorization as the incorporation of alternative cultural formations into the existing hegemony by more powerful social sectors, we must admit that not only distant national intellectuals, but also local popular groups participate in this process, for they continue to be subordinated within and affected by the dominant hegemony (García-Canclini 1993). Resistance to hegemonic incorporation will be found in the emergent, innovative aspects of festival performance, those that have not yet been codified or fixed as heritage. Aspects of a festival enactment that provoke anxiety and uncertainty among outside observers may offer a new kind of community integration or distinctiveness for participants. Such aspects of festival performance serve to redraw or reinforce the local boundaries that keep an alternative position viable. In this way, participants resist hegemonic definitions of their artistry while at the same time proposing their own alternate definitions.

Gender and Sexuality

Gender and sexuality constitute two dimensions of performance that intersect the local-global, class, and ethnic oppositions that produce the politics of festival. These dimensions have become increasingly marked as transnational civil rights movements and mediascapes transform contemporary social life, trespassing on patriarchal performance domains and reconceptualizing local traditions (Kugelmass 1991; Sawin 2001; Ware 1995, 2001). In Latin America, self-styled traditionalists equate women's active shaping of festival performances with the destructive influence of folklorized national styles on *authentic* local heritage (Guss 2000; Mendoza 2000). The danger to established performance codes and to the underlying sexual order becomes even more troubling when signs of homosexuality cease to be contained within grotesque masquerades and begin to assert themselves boldly in the classic or elegant festival genres. Theatricality and performativity, to use Diana Taylor's (1998) distinction, become intertwined, producing the anxiety and excitement that accompany counterhegemonic forms. In spite of local claims to the contrary, gender, sexuality, and the heightened awareness of them in festival enactments represent challenges that emerge from within the local collectivity, rather than hegemonic intrusions from without. Women and gay men exist within the local sphere. In the past, their participation in festival may have been ignored, constrained, or defined in particular ways. Today, they are active meaning makers within the popular arena.

Embodiment and Social Structure

Festival, as Dorothy Noyes astutely points out, is a "total social fact" (1997:140), a cultural production that is difficult, perhaps impossible, to comprehend in its entirety. This book does not attempt to explain all the dimensions of the Saint Jerome Festival, of Masaya's popular culture, or of indigenous Monimbó's lifeways and worldview. Nor do I pretend to advance theoretical understandings of embodiment. Instead, I build on the foundational insights of dance scholars who have shown that everyday bodily practices and specially marked dance events are mutually constitutive of both ethnic (Ness 1992) and gendered (Cowan 1990) identities. The bodily training for residents of a particular place who embrace a particular form of festive expression begins in infancy and continues through a lifetime of instruction and experience. Indeed, Noyes argues, the individual's internalization of a community identity can be imagined as "the traces in the body of what you've taken in through performance" (2003:256). In this way, an experience often described in essentializing terms as a blood inheritance can be articulated as an effect of repeated exposure or immersion.

In traditions where dance provides a vehicle for religious communication, it remains a source of *authentic* embodied experience even when subsequently deployed as a sign of local or national culture. Thus, residents of Cebu City in the Philippines find the different styles and choreographies of ritual (singular), troupe, and parade *sinulog* unimportant, regarding all three as manifestations of the same essential form. In fact, Ness argues that in this case the rise of explicitly cultural displays of the dance reinvigorated a moribund ritual tradition (1992:226). In Cuban Santería, Hagedorn argues, staged performances aimed at tourist audiences nevertheless continue to evoke a profoundly religious response in believing, enculturated members of the faith (2001:107–35). Therefore, the loss of the sacred in modernized forms of festival presentation and entertainment cannot be assumed for all cases.

A critical question in festival scholarship is the degree to which symbolic performances of identity carries over into dancers' everyday life. In other words, can artistic performances shape or reshape social structure? Those who identify continuities between the symbolic and social performance of self argue for a strong effect: social hierarchies and sexual identities are made and remade through performance (Mendoza 2000). I adopt a more cautious position, recognizing breaks as well as continuities between staged performances and everyday acts. Such a position acknowledges a range of performance effects: performance as an escape, as a compensatory alternative, as an exploration of what might be, as a temporary transcendence of social and personal limitations, and as an opportunity to mask (Limón 1994; Noyes 2003). It continues to recognize the fervent attachment of communities and individuals to specific forms of festive expression.

Masaya Festival Innovations

In her influential work on dance in the Philippines, Ness (1992) identifies three perspectives through which one can productively analyze traditional dance: the semiotic, the historic, and the ethnographic. I adopt the medium-range lens of the ethnographic description in order to consider festival as a people's theater, an arena in which participants negotiate questions of cultural and geographic location, gender, sexuality, and traditionality. I introduce a historic dimension in order to trace both the growth of festival participation and changing meanings over time.

I begin with an exploration of how Masaya earned its reputation for traditionality, examining the history of the place and its veneration of Saint Jerome. Masaya constituted the largest indigenous settlement in Nicaragua from the Conquest to the early twentieth century. It has been Nicaragua's most popular ritual center for at least two centuries. Indian culture, however, did not provide the content for national identity until the early Somoza era, when folklore enthusiasts identified the Dance of the Inditas as an enactment of the national myth of mesticization. More specifically, the Inditas Dance told the story of the birth of the Nicaraguan people through the harmonious union of inferior Indian women with arrogant but gallant Spanish men. This nationalist interpretation of the origins of the dance remains uncontested. Yet the *practice* of marimba dancing departs significantly from this script, underlining the way in which a dominant discourse paradoxically defines yet fails to contain popular enactments.

The book includes studies of three cultural enactments as they evolved during the revolutionary and neoliberal periods. Two enactments take place within the context of the Saint Jerome Festival (chapter 2). The third occurs during the week prior to Holy Week and marks a shift toward the veneration of another miraculous image, Jesus the

Redeemer. The torovenado and Ahuizotes masquerades (chapters 3 and 4), the Negras marimba dances (chapters 5 and 6), and the Monimbó pilgrimage to Popoyuapa (chapter 7) speak eloquently yet differently about the performance of social identity, about revivals and folklorization, about the politics of culture, and about the motivating force of belief in cultural enactments.

The playful masquerade dances of the torovenados represent the carnivalesque aspect of Masaya's traditional repertoire. This festival enactment was revived and transformed in the 1960s by better-off residents of the indigenous-identified neighborhood of Monimbó, where about thirty thousand people now reside. In the 1980s, the torovenado was celebrated and supported by Sandinista government officials who viewed it as a forum for popular social critique. Nevertheless, modernizations of both the means of festival production and the masquerade imagery provoked vehement local opposition among residents who viewed these changes as a deformation of the tradition. In the 1990s, torovenado organizers struggled to maintain the festival's contestatory and integrating functions. They recognized two conflicting purposes for the masquerade—to express a changing identity and to invoke nostalgia for a vanishing past.

The beleaguered torovenados were gradually overshadowed by a new festival masquerade, the Procession of the Ahuizotes. The Ahuizotes focused on recuperating through performance the indigenous neighborhood's supernatural inhabitants, who had been banished by the advent of streetlights and other community improvements. Yet if the Ahuizotes Procession represented a conservative, nostalgic turn and lacked the critical bite of the torovenado masquerades, it attracted the participation of women and in that way challenged a previously unacknowledged gender barrier in masquerade performances. Although the Masaya community embraces this new tradition, Nicaraguan cultural nationalists view it with anxiety as the intrusion of a North American festival form, Halloween. This nationalist reaction suggests that the Ahuizotes constitutes a potentially destabilizing cultural practice.

As with the torovenados, the growth in the Negras marimba dances can be traced to the 1960s folk dance revival in Masaya, which was influenced by similar movements throughout Central America. Whereas mixed-sex marimba dancing became Nicaragua's national folk dance, the transvestite Negras dancers remained rooted in the Saint Jerome Festival. They acquired a preeminent reputation in the local dance scene, for they claimed to have brought the form to artistic perfection. Their stylistic innovations reflect an elitist turn in the tradition, however, as a professional group of town-center mestizos appropriated this formerly Indian tradition as their own. As a consequence of this elitism, some Negras dancers refused to participate in the Sandinista folk dance revival.

More recently, the greater acknowledgment of sexual difference in civil society has prompted a reconceptualization of the Negras dances as a homosexual expression, a development that has provoked a range of responses from dancers of different sexual identities. All the Negras groups artfully deploy claims of traditionality to present novel performances. Their nuanced performances preserve the parodic qualities of earlier mixed-sex marimba dances in ways that the unmasked Inditas Dance, now firmly established as heritage, no longer does.

The pilgrimage to Popoyuapa, like the Ahuizotes Procession, grew out of the insurrectionary and early revolutionary period of the late 1970s and early 1980s. The newer festival enactments reflect a nostalgic desire to re-create through festival aspects of community life that have been transformed with modernization, but that remain useful and relevant to neighborhood residents. Both the pilgrimage and the Ahuizotes flourished during the 1990s and have been quickly accepted as beloved traditions that are specifically associated with the indigenous neighborhood of Monimbó. Whereas the Ahuizotes playfully invoke the neighborhood's now displaced supernatural inhabitants, the pilgrimage to Popoyuapa attests to the strength of popular belief in miracles.

Conclusion

Each of these cultural practices shows that popular assertions of identity do not neatly line up along a single progressive or conservative front. For instance, torovenado organizers embrace these carnivalesque masquerades as an arena for social critique, but at the same time they anoint themselves as the festival aristocracy within Monimbó. The

Ahuizotes provides both a creative opening for female (and family) masqueraders and a cover for male gangs' destructive play. Transformations in the Negras dances challenge a stigma against homosexuals, on the one hand, but claim the superiority of middle-class, mestizo dance groups, on the other. The pilgrims to Popoyuapa become a model group by conforming to the orderly vision of the Catholic hierarchy, but they identify the power of their enactment as an expression of their distinctive ethnic identity.

At the same time, the festivals exhibit certain partisan affinities. Whereas Sandinista revolutionaries gravitated toward the liberatory playfulness of the torovenados in the 1980s, the neoliberal governments favored the religious seriousness of the pilgrimage in the 1990s. Yet neither political tendency has fully harnessed the form and meaning of these popular events. Indeed, when they have attempted to do so, popular enthusiasm for the events has waned.

In each tradition, organizers and performers produce festival enactments for a variety of purposes and sometimes are even at cross-purposes. Far from providing a unitary statement about the people, these enactments—dances, masquerades, and processions—demonstrate how complex and multifaceted popular identities are. Moreover, if it is true that these enactments evolve as continuous responses to outside appropriation or attempted incorporation, if they constitute a reiteration of distinctiveness, an emphatic embodiment of local difference, then they also owe their capacity to accomplish this work to the generative forces within the local community, its ability to create new forms to fit changing circumstances. In turn, the strength of this generative principal rests, somewhat paradoxically, on the community's traditional reputation.

2 The Capital of Nicaraguan Folklore

The Saint Jerome Festival Through Time

On October 23, 2000, Nicaragua's National Assembly passed a measure declaring Masaya the Capital of Nicaraguan Folklore. Such a designation raises a host of questions. How can the traditions of one place represent the nation as a whole, and what are the consequences of such a declaration for the people who enact these traditions? Appadurai reminds us that a community is shaped not only by how it produces and reproduces itself through internal socializing practices, but also by how it contrasts with other places (1996:191). What does it mean to be Nicaragua's premodern center in contrast to Managua, the nation's artistic, intellectual, political, and economic capital?

On one level, the legislative decree constitutes a marketing ploy to attract tourists. In the 1990s, Lorenzo Guerrero, Nicaraguan minister of tourism, developed a series of tourist venues in different regions of the country. Thus, the Spanish colonial city of Granada became the place to hear musical concerts, and Matagalpa became associated with the natural environment and ecotourism. In Masaya, the recently reconstructed Old Market provides an elegant outlet for quality crafts. The market also presents folk music and dances at its Thursday evening Verbenas throughout the year. Such performances commodify local culture, transforming it, as García-Canclini (1993) has pointed out, into stage shows removed from the ritual calendar and aimed at an audience of strangers. However, cultural displays packaged for outside consumption at the Old Market in no way replace the traditional dances that unfold in Masaya's church plaza, city streets, and private living rooms from September to early December each year.[1]

Moreover, historical circumstances have fostered the strong identification of Masaya with folklore. Masaya was an important ritual center prior to the Spanish Conquest. Its harvest festival, converted to a Catholic saint's day, has been the most popular in Nicaragua for centuries. The city itself constituted the largest indigenous settlement from the Conquest to the nineteenth century. Subsequently, the neighborhood of Monimbó retained that identity even as a discourse of *mestizaje*, or a mestizo national identity, erased other Indian communities from the national consciousness. Monimboseños cultivated distinctive performance arts as well as practices they shared with other popular communities. In the mid–twentieth century, middle-class cultural promoters refashioned these traditions, interpreting them as the cultural heritage of the mestizo nation. With the 1979 revolution, this heritage took on an oppositional character as the people's arts were wedded to a project of political liberation. Yet the revolutionary celebration of Masaya popular arts as national culture had contradictory consequences for the Masaya community.

The folklorization of cultural practices is a recurrent aspect of nation building. Throughout the twentieth century, Latin American intellectual elites attempted to forge a common national culture by reframing local, indigenous, or popular beliefs and practices as quaint displays of culture, thus taming and rendering acceptable these once-disdained cultures of difference (Van Young 1994:367). In countless folklore revivals, ethnic or social elites defined, transformed, and sometimes even enacted their newly discovered patrimony, establishing criteria of authenticity and appropriating representational authority (Borland 1994, 1996, 2002; Field 1987, 1999; Largey 1991; Nájera Ramírez 1989; Scruggs 1994, 1998). Elite definitions forcefully influence popular practice. Nevertheless, the living culture of a place continues to unfold in all its complex dimensions of meaning. Thus, Masaya's traditional identity continues to grant residents the authority to identify what they do as culturally significant. Local performers challenge national constructions by drawing on a rhetoric of authenticity even when their own practices are clearly influenced by national revivalist models. Masaya artists are folklore authorities not because they faithfully preserve the tradition. Rather, their authority stems from their ability to generate new cultural practices in response to the transformations effected by outside cultural agents.

The Mangue Subtext

The origins of Masaya's Saint Jerome Festival remain shrouded in mystery and local legend. An uncooperative priest at the Church of Saint Jerome has little to say about local festive practices, and the city itself retains no archives.[2] Curiously, Saint Jerome is not the original patron of the city. That honor belongs to the Virgin of the Assumption, who is also the patron of Monimbó and Nicaragua. However, it was not uncommon in colonial Latin America for a community to change the Spanish-imposed patron for a saint they preferred (Mendoza 2000).

In Europe, Saint Jerome was venerated as one of the four doctors of the church until the fourteenth century, when a cult arose celebrating his miraculous healing powers. This was one of a number of cults of the saints that spread through early Renaissance Europe, inspiring popular devotion and a proliferation of images, relics, and miracle legends. The ascetic, penitent Jerome, pictured as a hermit, dominated during the fourteenth century. Orders of Saint Jerome, including the Spanish Hieronymites, emerged in the second half of the fourteenth century and became particularly powerful in the fifteenth century. Yet both Dominicans and Augustinians were influential in the early popularization of the cult. By the fifteenth century, Erasmus and the Italian humanists sought to expunge the legendary fictions and accounts of miracles that had by then accrued to Saint Jerome's biography. They propagated an image of Jerome as a scholar and man of letters. By the end of the sixteenth century, however, Saint Jerome's popularity waned, and subsequently he became more a figure for research than for veneration (Rice 1985; Walsh 1991:307–10).

In Masaya, Saint Jerome appears only as an ascetic hermit. The pale, blue-eyed figure is naked save for a pink loincloth and flowing white beard and hair. He kneels, grasping a stone in one hand; a lion crouches at his side. This figure recalls Jerome's four-year withdrawal into the desert wilderness of Chalcis, an iconography well represented in sixteenth-century Latin American *retablo* painting. Masayans affectionately call him Tata Chombo (Grandpa Jerry), the Doctor of the Poor, or the Doctor Who Cures Without Medicine.[3]

Given the Masayan emphasis on Jerome the penitent rather than on Jerome the scholar, as well as the considerable influence of the Hieronymite and Dominican Orders at the inception of Spanish Nicaraguan history, it seems likely that the saint arrived in Masaya during the early colonial period. Nicaragua's second bishop, Francisco de Mendavia, was a Heironymite who succeeded Father Diego Álvarez Osorio in 1536. The Heironymites were invited to the New World to carry forward Fray Bartolomé de Las Casas's work of protecting the Indians against the worst abuses of the conquerors (Remesal 1964:151–59), but what they did specifically among the Indians of Nicaragua's Pacific Coast is not known. Two Royal Orders in 1537 charged Mendavia with the tasks of constructing churches in both Christian and Indian settlements, "giving them the ornaments and things brought from Spain," and with visiting the Indians and following up on their complaints of mistreatment by *encomenderos* or settlers (Molina Argüello 1957:122, 121).

Mendavia constructed the cathedral in León, the city that became the ecclesiastical and governmental center for the colony, and this cathedral also contains an image of Jerome the hermit. Mendavia was succeeded by Father Antonio Valdivieso in 1544, the Dominican priest who fought against the abuse and enslavement of the Indians so energetically that he was beheaded by the Spanish colonists in 1550.[4] From 1551 to 1576, the Nicaraguan bishopric reverted to Heironymites Gómez Fernández de Cordoba and, briefly, Fernando de Mendavia. After that, the Heironymites were not represented in Nicaragua's highest religious office.[5]

Early accounts of the indigenous populations of the Masaya-Managua area and their religious rituals provide fascinating but ambiguous traces of the current veneration of Saint Jerome. Before the Conquest, the area between the two great Nicaraguan lakes was heavily populated by Mangue or Chorotega settlements.[6] A little lower down in the Rivas Peninsula and farther north in the vicinity of El Viejo, the Nahua or Nicarao people represented a more recently arrived culture group from central Mexico, with a distinctive language, political organization, and religious pantheon and rituals. Both groups constituted settled, well-fed communities with temples, priests, and extensive markets. Both exhibited a number of beliefs and practices that were common throughout Aztec-influenced Middle America. Each group venerated a number of gods associated with particular landmarks by performing human sacrifice, ritual cannibalism, bloodletting, and elaborate dances. Both groups also indulged in heavy drinking during ritual occasions.[7]

Chronicler Gonzalo Fernández de Oviedo (1976), who visited Nicaragua in 1528 and 1529, provided the earliest and most extensive descriptions of indigenous Nicaraguans. He reported that both the Mangue and the Nahua engaged in a number of games and dances, the songs for which often contained a historical subtext (León-Portilla 1972:57). He was most impressed by the acrobatic feats of the Nahua Voladores, or Flying Men,[8] but he also described several other festival dances, including large-group *areitos*, where men and women danced in separate concentric circles, and couples dances that sometimes included male cross-dressers (Oviedo 1976; see also Chapman 1974). These kinds of performances appear to have been common throughout Mexico and Central America. Oviedo was also impressed by a distinctive gender order that appeared to prevail in Nicaragua. He reported that "the indians who speak Chorotega are the older indigenous group of those parts and they are a crude and quick-tempered people, and very subject to and directed by their women" (1976:362). Likewise, chronicler López de Gómara found it curious that the Nicaraguan warrior Diriangen consulted his women before launching his attack on the conquistador Pedrarías Davila in 1522 (Incer 1990:139). Such behavior contrasted sharply with the patriarchal views of women held by sixteenth-century Spaniards.

When the Spanish arrived, the Masaya volcano was still active, and several chroniclers noted that it illuminated the night sky as far away as Granada. The Mangue "took this inferno as their god," according to Friar Blas de Castillo, reporting on the experiences of Friar Tomás de Berlanga (Incer 1990:229). Oviedo remarked that the volcano was surrounded by a wilderness populated by lions, tigers, and other wild animals. The cacique Lenderí of Nindirí, an indigenous village immediately northeast of Masaya, informed him that an old prophetess lived within the volcano. Oviedo reported, "she was really old and wrinkled, and her tits to her belly button, and very little hair, which stood up on her head, and long sharp teeth, like a dog's, and her color darker and blacker than the indians; and her eyes sunken and blazing; and finally, [Lenderí] painted her in his words as if she were the devil" (1976:392; also quoted in Incer 1990:219). According to the chronicler, the indigenous priest consulted this prophetess on matters of warfare, crop planting, and weather. After the prophetess had delivered her message, the priest would sacrifice a number of willing victims by throwing them into the volcano.[9] Oviedo also noticed a great pile of plates and bowls beside the altar at the volcano's mouth. He wrote that the Indians told him that they brought the prophetess food to placate her because she was also responsible for tremors and bad weather (1976:393; see also Incer 1990:220). Another observer, Fray Toribio Benavente (Motolinia), added that children were thrown into the volcano during droughts to bring rain (Incer 1990:264).

The belief that mountains were responsible for both rain and illness appears to have been widespread throughout Middle America. Franciscan chronicler Juan de Torquemada reported that a Mexican festival of the mountains was celebrated in October as a petition both for bringing rain and for avoiding illness (Mace 1970:27 n. 8). Mace adds, "Durán makes it clear that it was a harvest ritual, but he, Sahagún and Torquemada all point out that it was primarily designed to prevent and cure illness. Their descriptions differ in some respects but a reading of all reveals that the most important part of the rite was the offering of miniature mountains made from a hardened dough" (1970:28). Although the mountain of the Saint Jerome procession is neither miniature nor made of dough, the symbolism of placing the curative saint atop a mountain is suggestive of pre-Columbian ritual.[10] A historical connection between the worship of Saint Jerome and the preexisting cult of the volcano may also explain why he is portrayed in his seminaked hermit aspect (like the naked prophetess), accompanied by a lion (an animal found at the volcano), rather than in his aspect as a church scholar.

Indeed, Nicaraguan scholars Alejandro Dávila Bolaños (1977:22) and Jorge Eduardo Arellano (1986:43) have suggested that the early Spanish clergy substituted Saint Jerome for the Mangue volcano prophetess. Palma reports a Nicaraguan legend that Saint Jerome retreated into the wilderness to cleanse himself from an earlier life of sexual debauchery (1988:41). During his seclusion, he was tempted by a devil in the guise of a woman. He succumbed, but he then repented and was sanctified. This legend might be read as the story of how Saint Jerome vanquished and simultaneously replaced the earlier prophetess. It might provide a model for Masayans to follow as well. In this way, a pagan figure was Christianized, the color of the divinity was transformed from black to white, and its gender from female to male. Yet today few devotees of Saint Jerome recognize any pre-Columbian subtext in the religious festival, nor do activists in contemporary indigenous political organizations connect their communities' religious practices to those of their pre-Columbian predecessors. Instead, they argue that the Saint Jerome Festival is a nineteenth-century popularization of an earlier elite practice.[11] These claims remain unsubstantiated. Nonetheless, indigenous beliefs and practices were clearly transformed over centuries to produce a new popular understanding shaped but not entirely dictated by new relations of power.

Indian Masaya

During the initial years of conquest, the indigenous population of Nicaragua declined precipitously. An estimated six hundred thousand Indians in 1524 were reduced to a mere forty-two thousand by 1548. Illness, warfare, and the massive enslavement and exportation of Nicaraguans to work in Peruvian mines contributed to the population decline. As a consequence, Nicaragua remained chronically underdeveloped during the colonial period. Lacking the workforce necessary to support economic growth, many Spanish settlers remained relatively poor, small landholders (Newson 1987:118–24).[12] Indians lived apart from other ethnic groups and were required to provide portions of their crops and service to the new authorities. While Granada and León quickly became the two centers of Spanish government, trade, and culture, the pre-Columbian settlements of Masaya, Nindirí, and Managua retained a distinctly indigenous tone.

As in other areas of Latin America, Catholic cofradías became the primary form of Indian religious expression. These religious organizations were segregated by race and were dedicated to venerating a particular saint by purchasing statues and ornaments for the local church, celebrating special masses, and financing processions in the saint's honor.[13] The cofradías owned lands and cattle, and far from being a drain on the community, they provided a mechanism for capital accumulation.[14] In fact, many indigenous Nicaraguan cofradías amassed considerable wealth, providing loans to members and subsidizing public projects. The cofradías kept careful accounts and reported annually to the church authorities on their conduct. Cofradía wealth, however, was ultimately controlled by Spanish religious authorities and was often pilfered by the local clergy and even by indigenous cofradía leaders (Peña 1998).

Nevertheless, the relative autonomy of the cofradías provided an alternative space within which the indigenous residents could maintain and develop their own beliefs and practices. Preserving a separate cultural-religious identity in a situation of general subjection to a racially distinctive ruling class also provided psychological escape from that subjection.[15] Spanish officials were well aware of the danger such an alternative posed to their authority. Historian Germán Romero Vargas notes that the Spanish religious and political leaders objected to cofradía organized festivals: "In 1662 the investigator for the Spanish Crown, Frasso, declared that the Indians in their festivals made huge feasts, became drunk and danced to 'recall the memory of their antiquity.' In 1793, governor Aysa shared this opinion" (1988:104). Thus, government functionaries did not entirely approve of the colonial-era popular Catholicism of indigenous Nicaraguans.

The indigenous tradition of burlesquing the new Spanish authorities in dance drama marks another cultural development of the colonial period. When Irishman Thomas Gage traveled through Chiapas, Mexico, in the 1620s, he noted that the Indians imitated the Spanish in music and dance ([1648] 1958:145; 243–46). The oldest known instance of this cultural mimicry in Nicaragua is El güegüense (The honored elder), a play written in a combination of Nahuatl and Spanish, the two languages of government and missionizing in seventeenth-century Nicaragua.[16] In the play, an indigenous merchant dupes various representatives of Spanish authority. Drawing on the theatrical devices of misunderstanding and deafness that often appear in dual-language traditions, the merchant plays verbal tricks on his superiors.[17] Comedy, dance, and drama were well-developed forms in pre-Columbian Middle America, but much of this tradition was lost or destroyed during the Conquest (Harris 2000; Mace 1970). During the colonial period, however, new festival performances combined with religious processions to form the indigenous popular religious expressions characteristic of the area. One might argue that these new performances not only functioned to recall an Indian past, but also challenged Spanish domination.[18]

Indians of the colonial period retained a measure of political self-rule. The *alcalde de vara*, or indigenous mayor, and the counsel of elders, made up of eight assistants to the mayor, were responsible for handling disputes within the community. They also acted as intermediaries between the community and the Spanish authorities. They collected tribute and enforced Indian labor obligations to the Spanish, on the one hand, and presented Indian complaints to the authorities in cases concerning land disputes between Indians and non-Indians, on the other (Romero Vargas 1988:82–83). The adult males of the indigenous communities held land communally, and their leaders, also male, were responsible for the purchase, sale, and rental of these lands. Indian families cultivated staple crops and fruit trees in small plots surrounding their *chozas*, single-room homes of cane and thatch. Family parcels were protected by low walls of thorny piñuela bushes (Romero Vargas 1988:30–32).

Provincial Masaya

From 1522 into the mid–nineteenth century, Granada and León represented the two centers of *ladino* or Spanish-colonial culture and the axis for elite Nicaraguan history. Masaya, which constituted the second-largest population center after León, remained overwhelmingly Indian.[19] The town was composed of four indigenous sectors, each with its own indigenous mayor. As late as the eighteenth century, 80 percent of six thousand Masayans were Indian. On his pastoral visit to Masaya in 1751, Bishop Morel noted that only twenty-eight families lived in adobe houses, a mark of higher social status and a Spanish cultural orientation (Morel de Santa Cruz 1962).

Whereas Indian customs strongly influenced Nicaraguan popular culture in the early nineteenth century, Indian languages rapidly declined (Burns 1991). By midcentury, ethnologists such as Ephraim Squier (1852) could find few competent Mangue speakers. Nevertheless, foreign visitors regularly commented on Masaya's indigenous character (Bovallius [1883] 1977; Lévy [1873] 1976; Squier [1853] 1990). After the political center of the country shifted to Managua in 1851, however, a new contrast developed between Managua's urban modernity and Masaya's provincial traditionality. In the late 1800s and early 1900s, the mestizo populations in both cities grew rapidly. In

Masaya, a split formed between Monimbó, which was oriented toward the small towns and rural settlements of the Masaya-Carazo region, and the northern part of the city, which was oriented toward Managua and Granada. Monimbó retained its strong indigenous identification, but the Church of Saint Jerome, once located in the indigenous sector of Los Guillenes, was surrounded by an increasingly mestizo downtown.

Jerónimo Pérez, a Masaya ladino who became mayor in the 1850s, regarded the city as rife with immoral and criminal behavior. He described the Saint Jerome Festival of the mid-1800s as a rowdy, sometimes violent affair that attracted delinquents and included weeks of public gaming (1977:779). In 1871, European traveler Pablo Lévy reported that "The patron saint's festival of certain towns is very popular, as, for example, in El Viejo or in El Sauce; attendance is even greater when the image of the Saint is reputed to be miraculous, as, for example, in La Conquista. But there is no festival in the whole Republic more popular than Saint Jerome in Masaya, where more than 40,000 people attend" ([1873] 1976:245). Considering that the entire estimated population of the country (which did not then include the Atlantic Coast) was 206,000, and that of Masaya was only about 18,000 (Squier [1853] 1990:373), attendance was indeed substantial.[20]

Neither Pérez nor Lévy described the festival dances in any detail. Lévy noted only that Indian dancers dressed in a uniform, Spanish manner and that the dances of the popular classes were indecent.[21] The first real description of festival dancing came from Daniel Brinton in 1883. Never having seen the dances himself, Brinton relied on Dr. C. H. Berendt's field notes. An ethnologist, Berendt had lived for some time in Nicaragua. Brinton reported that several kinds of dances and dance dramas were offered in fulfillment of a religious promise:

Frequently a number of persons join in the dance. Such is one, still occasionally seen, called Las Inditas, the Little Indian Girls. The period of its celebration is on the day of St. Jerome. The women are masked and wear a loose mantle, a skirt with lace edging, a sash of rose color, and a hat with feathers. They carry bouquets and have a silk handkerchief fastened around the waist, the ends meeting over the hips. The men are in grotesque costumes, with ugly masks.

They dance in couples, but without touching each other. The music is the marimba and the guitar. The songs usually turn on some matter of local interest. ([1883] 1969:xxv–xxvi)

According to this description, masked, formally dressed women danced with grotesquely costumed men. This gendered distinction between elegant women and ugly men is completely absent from marimba dancing today. If we put aside the question of how accurate this description might be, the scarcity of nineteenth-century descriptions of festival performances and the foreign, ethnological tone of those that exist indicate that Monimbó's festival dances were not yet regarded as the stuff of national cultural patrimony.

During this same period, Masaya's economic base and ethnic composition were changing. Indians in the southern Pacific areas had retained control of their lands for much of the nineteenth century, with incoming mestizos renting from the indigenous communities. Yet by the 1870s the new agro-export business in coffee, a business that required additional land and a substantial temporary workforce, prompted local elites to encroach on common landholdings (Dore 2000). Nevertheless, the shift to export agriculture was not as extensive here as in the North, and Masaya remained a center for both crafts production and for the agricultural trade of small independent farmers. In the early 1880s, the Swedish naturalist Carl Bovallius described Masaya as a bustling yet rustic market town of about twenty thousand. He emphasized both the continuing indigenous character of Masaya and the apparent strength of the local economy, commenting that even the animals appeared well fed ([1883] 1977:294). Field has suggested that the cheap goods produced in the towns of the Masaya-Carazo region supported the more extensive proletarianization of the North (1999:87).

At the same time, the city benefited from infrastructural improvements. Writing in the 1870s, Jerónimo Pérez remarked that Masaya had shifted from an indigenous hinterland to a crossroads for commerce. The Indians Pérez had once described as easily aroused by bandits to commit atrocities against municipal authorities were now "as peaceful as they are industrious, and so amalgamated with the ladino that far from maintaining a racial hatred, they favor each other mutually. With little savageness, the Indian here lives and tranquilly enjoys—working, eating, and dancing—when the ladino perhaps suffers from a conflict" (1977:782). According to Pérez, then, Masaya Indians retained a distinctive lifestyle that presented certain advantages over that of their non-Indian neighbors. The onset of modernization appears to have lessened interethnic tensions in the city. Yet this celebratory view of Masayan race relations was not to last.

The José Santos Zelaya government (1893–1911) brought even greater infrastructural development, including a national railroad that linked Masaya and many smaller communities in the region with the capital. Zelaya dissolved the cofradías in 1899 (Arellano 1986:71), freeing up lands formerly belonging to the church for export crops. In 1906, he legally abolished the indigenous communities (Rizo 1999:43), turning communal lands over to the municipality for distribution.[22] In this way, the emerging state divested Monimboseños and other indigenous groups not only of their lands, but also of the religious and political institutions that supported their distinctive identities. At the same time, elite ladinos developed a powerful myth of Nicaraguan mestizaje to rationalize their sometimes violent assaults on Indian communities.

The Myth of Mestizaje

Ladinos asserted that the Nicaraguan people were a homogeneous group of mixed-race individuals. They had been born during the initial period of contact between the Spanish and Indian cultures as the offspring of indigenous women and male Spanish conquerors. The mestizo proudly inherited the best qualities of each racial group: the Indian legacy of valiant resistance to outside invasion, on the one hand, and Spanish civilization, on the other. The myth worked powerfully on the popular consciousness in part because mestizos were becoming the majority population in Nicaragua by the turn of the twentieth century. Moreover, the myth contested the view prevalent among nineteenth-century foreigners that mixed-race individuals and cultures were inferior to the racially "pure" Spanish and Indian communities.[23] What the myth obscured, however, was the continuing existence of indigenous-identified people (and, on the Atlantic Coast, of African-descended people as well) whose loyalty to the mestizo nation was at best conflicted. It also ignored continuing social disparities based on race. Consequently, the language of equal and undifferentiated citizenship provided the means for stripping minority communities of their historical privileges (Field 1998; Gould 1993, 1998).

In the early twentieth century (around 1916), North American traveler Dana Munro observed the unacknowledged racial distinctions in the mestizo nation that continued to permeate the society:

> The upper classes, especially in Nicaragua and Salvador, are for the most part of European ancestry, and the laboring population, although there is but a small part of it which does not also show an admixture of Spanish blood, is distinctly Indian in features and customs; but only in a few places is there a sharp line between either of these classes and the half-breed, or *mestizo*, element, which is perhaps the most numerous of the three. Social distinctions seem to some extent to coincide with, but they can hardly be said to depend upon, racial lines. (1983:72)

In this fluid system, indigeneity could as easily provide the foundations for national identity as it could offer the ground for an oppositional and oppressed otherness. Munro clearly observed that despite the rhetoric of mestizaje, Nicaraguan society was divided into three hierarchically organized racial and social groups.

To be Indian, then, was to remain an undigested, socially subordinate part of the mestizo nation. Indian Masaya was now reduced to Monimbó, but the lines of identification remained porous, and, as Field (1998) has pointed out, being Indian in fact encompassed a multiplicity of cultural experiences. Numerous scholars have attempted to specify why Monimbó remained Indian, pointing to social stigma, internal social networks, a preference for endogamy, and occasional opposition to the state (Breso 1992; Field 1998; Gould 1993, 1998; Membreño Idiaquez 1994). What is clear is that the community's identity is relational. Monimboseños remained Indian in contrast to their urban mestizo neighbors, even though their cultural practices blended with those of their rural neighbors. Moreover, their recognized indigeneity concealed a variety of perspectives within the community as well as the waxing and waning of the intensity of difference between Indians and non-Indians over time.[24] In the twentieth century, as in past centuries, Monimboseños alternated between peacefully coexisting with other

Masayans and maintaining an uncommunicative, sometimes hostile distance in response to social stigma. At times, they supported the state, succumbing to the same partisan divisions that divided the nation as a whole; at other times, they spearheaded popular resistance to intensified economic and political oppression.

When Zelaya was ousted in 1909 by a Conservative coalition backed by U.S. Marines, civil war followed (Walker 2003). By 1912, the Conservatives had returned to power, providing the indigenous communities a brief respite from the national elite assault on their material and cultural heritage. Monimbó successfully sued for the restoration of its legal status, for the right to conduct a census, and for the return of its lands. Nevertheless, cofradía lands were not recovered. The formerly powerful cofradía institutions became voluntary organizations dedicated only to sponsoring festivals. At the same time, indigenous Masayans abandoned the practice of communal ownership. Instead, they distributed their lands to the community's six thousand members. A Granada landowner expropriated the remaining communal lands in the 1930s (Gould 1998:151).

Popular disenchantment with emerging monopolies owned by U.S. and oligarchic interests in Nicaragua soon surfaced after the U.S.-backed Conservative restoration. Interestingly, it was the indigenous communities of the urban Pacific Coast who led the popular classes in protests against monopoly rate hikes, disruptions of informal commerce, and gross negligence in operations in the early 1920s. In Masaya, Monimbó's charismatic and authoritarian alcalde de vara Vital Noriongue led two attacks on the U.S.-owned railroad in 1919 and 1922. Yet Noriongue and his followers downplayed the ethnic dimension of these uprisings, identifying themselves as aggrieved citizens of the nation rather than as Indians (Gould 1998:147–55).[25] Early twentieth-century Monimboseños both resisted and capitulated to continued assaults on Indian lands, institutions, and cultural identity brought on by a modernizing state.

Nationalizing the Inditas

Masaya was christened the Cradle of Nicaraguan Folklore in this period, when the distinctions between Indians and the popular classes were be-

Figure 2.1 Youthful dancers celebrate the arrival of the Monimbó Wagon Pilgrimage in Popoyuapa, 1991. These contemporary dancers exhibit none of the "absolute racial distinction" that López Pérez posited in 1939.

coming less marked (Gould 1998:172 n. 53). Simultaneously, Monimboseños stopped performing some of the larger dances and dance dramas they had once organized. This contraction of the festival repertoire was perhaps a consequence of the weakened cofradías. Smaller groups of torovenado masqueraders and marimba dancers, however, continued to perform at the Saint Jerome Festival. These groups were sponsored for the most part by individual Monimbó households. With indigenous performances on the decline, mestizo Masayans began to take an active interest in the festival dances as national heritage (Borland 2002; Scruggs 1998). In 1939, Masayan Manuel López Pérez published a description of the Monimbó Inditas Dance, which quickly became the authoritative historical account of Masaya folk dance practice. Unlike earlier ethnological reports, this text demonstrates a new interest in the "story" that the dance enacts. In fact, instead of describing an actual performance, López Pérez provided an elaborate plot summary that is heavily indebted to the myth of mestizaje:

When the marimba begins to play, "the Inditas" are seated peace-fully. It's the Viejo (old man) who, from the first notes, has been set in motion, with elegance and poise, advancing from the extreme of the circle that the spectators form towards the place where one finds the woman. He moves gracefully, with agility and passion, with variation but without the frenetic lewdness of the dances of the Blacks and mulattos. The sonorous bells enhance the agitation of the masculine body. When he faces the "Indita," he redoubles his activity. Opening his arms he invites her to dance with him. At last the lady rises to her feet, opens her fan and enters the dance. (quoted in Peña Hernández [1968] 1986:77)

López Pérez sexualized the dance while at the same time differentiat-ing the Nicaraguan racial crossing from Black sensuality. This need to distinguish between Afro-Nicaraguan and Indian bodies points to an underlying silence about the African contribution to the nation in the myth of mestizaje. The mulatto is a peculiarly absent presence in Pacific Coast Nicaraguan culture, having been largely absorbed into Indian and ladino ethnic communities.[26] Nevertheless, the marimba is an African contribution to Nicaraguan culture, a fact that Masayans acknowledge but do not celebrate (Scruggs 1994).

López Pérez contrasted the movements of an Indian female with a white male:

The movements of the lady are monotonous and simple. Truly, they don't attract the attention of the spectator. They correspond to modesty, honesty, but even more than this to the manifest inferior-ity of the Indian woman before the white man, in whose presence she cannot unfold her personality. The Viejo, on the contrary, goes along with the Indita, now pursuing her, now cutting in front of her, now circling her, with lively, insinuating, passionate, but al-ways gentlemanly gestures. Sometimes with his towel forming a tense arc between his arms, either in front of the chest or behind the neck, he approaches the Indita offering heat and intimacy. At others, his feet move with attractive agility in the complicated za-pateos and compases. The movement of the waist is extremely clear in its insinuations. (quoted in Peña Hernández [1968] 1986:77)

The "mixing" that occurs in the Inditas dance becomes one between a series of neatly organized oppositions: Spanish/Indian, complex/simple, interesting/monotonous, male/female, old/young, arrogant/humble, rich/poor. Conveniently absent from this description are details that would complicate López Pérez's reading of the dance. For instance, until the 1960s both male and female Inditas festival dancers were likely to be indigenous Monimboseños, and both wore whiteface or pinkface wire-mesh masks to hide their identities.[27] Thus, the dance retained the colonial-era parody of Spanish authorities, and "absolute racial distinction between the two dancers" was not, in fact, "reflected in even the minutest detail of the costuming," as López Pérez insisted (quoted in Peña Hernández [1968] 1986:78).

López Pérez concluded his description by drawing parallels between the dancers' attitudes and the mythical history of the Nicaraguan nation: "The dance ends as it began. The Viejo sits the Indita back in her place, and another old man begins the formation of another pair. Seeing the development of the dance we think of an idyll, more than between two human beings, between two cultures: the one barefoot and oppressed, the other rich and arrogant, but both as if they were in the amorous task of creation" (quoted in Peña Hernández [1968] 1986:77). By calling the interaction of the two dancers or cultures an "idyll," López Pérez indicated that from the elite perspective at least, social, racial, and gender inequalities ultimately result in happy union.

By providing a reading of the dance as a romantic conquest, López Pérez also distanced the mythical creation of the Nicaraguan people from the historical Conquest: "Certainly, the dance does not correspond, in truth, to the conquest era when the brutal male, like a centaur, raped and violated the woman and then abandoned her" (quoted in Peña Hernández [1968] 1986:78). He hypothesized that the dance originated in a later period. But in so doing he once again appropriated the "indigenous" dance for a nation of mestizos, even though Monimboseños, the performers of these dances, continued to be identified as Nicaraguan Indians.

To complete the process of nationalizing an Indian dance or folklorizing popular culture, López Pérez distinguished the Nicaraguan form from all other Indian dances in Latin America. He declared that although many mestizo dances can be found in other countries: "The

Inditas dance on the contrary tells us how the mestizo race was formed: by a sexual crossing of two races of unequal culture in which America provided the oppressed and timid egg, and Spain the free, superior, masculine element" (quoted in Peña Hernández [1968] 1986:78). It is, therefore, the dance of mesticization.

As Mendoza (2000) and Guss (2000) have pointed out, understanding how elite adaptations and interpretations of folklore affect popular practices is crucial to understanding the politics of festival production and reproduction. López Pérez's description of the dance was the first to identify it as an enactment of national identity, and it remains the standard explanation for the original meaning and style of the dance. It has been reprinted at least four times in the popular press, including the Sandinista Party newspaper of the 1980s, *La Barricada*.[28] That none of these publications challenged López Pérez's description or offered counternarratives attests to the continuing power of its rhetoric. Even Monimboseños accept the description as the "traditional" form of the dance, though they point out that contemporary female dancers do not dance in this way. Thus, in the absence of any other extended historical account, López Pérez has succeeded in providing an authoritative storying of past practices that is clearly based on the myth of mestizaje. To the degree that Monimboseños approximate this "original" model for the dance, they participate in pejoratively stereotyping themselves.

Indian Marginalization under Somoza

Nicaraguan society continued to exhibit strong class divisions during the Somoza dictatorship. Wealth and power were concentrated among a small elite, and the rural populace lived in poverty. In Masaya, Monimboseños enjoyed the lowest social status, even when they surpassed their mestizo neighbors in actual wealth. During this time, the indigenous mayor became a mere figurehead. His authority was reduced to organizing volunteers periodically to clean the community cemeteries.

After World War II, Nicaragua experienced some economic growth, largely due to the mechanization of agriculture. A subsequent social transformation occurred, with the upper classes prospering, the urban middle class expanding, and the rural middle class entering a decline (Ryan et al. 1970:75–80). Large-scale cotton plantations began to eat up land around Masaya, although, again, the shift to export agriculture was not as extensive as in the northern region around León (Paige 1997). Monimboseños continued to produce hand-crafted goods for the national market, yet the shrinking size of family farms and a flood of cheap, foreign manufactured goods resulted in the community's steady economic deterioration.[29]

Meanwhile, Monimboseños continued a lifestyle that visibly differed from that of working-class residents in adjacent neighborhoods. Most residents lived in chozas, the Indian thatch-roofed homes, furnished with locally made furniture, appliances, and utensils. The majority of residents were small farmers or artisans who worked either for themselves or with other non-Indian laborers at larger farms and workshops. Market women, always a powerful group, took advantage of the stable, growing economy. Less-affluent residents often worked as carters or maids and cooks for affluent families in the center of town. Some got seasonal work picking cotton at the edge of the city or in the northern regions of León and Chinandega. Festival expressions that combined religious observances with dance, drinking, and feasting continued despite the negative attitudes of some town leaders, who viewed these practices as excuses for Indians to absent themselves from work (Peña Hernández [1968] 1986:38).

The Saint Jerome Festival remained the most well attended of all the country's patron saint festivals and now lasted approximately thirty days, from the saint's procession on September 30 to the last Sunday of October. However, from the 1950s on, Masayan festival practices were influenced by the globally developing tourist industry, which encouraged countries throughout the world to cultivate popular arts and crafts as symbols of national distinctiveness. Voluntary organizations such as the Lions Club began to organize regional folk dance competitions and other forms of cultural exchange. Thus emerged a new performance space for marimba dances outside the context of the religious festival, where youthful dancers represented their nation. They discarded the characteristic whiteface, wire-mesh masks and donned "folksy" costumes based on the apparel of early-twentieth-century Indian servants. The ensuing folklore revival, promoted largely by middle-class schoolteachers, encouraged mestizo and even elite Masayans to learn and perform Indian dances as their national cultural tradition.

In addition to participating in staged folkloric events, elegant marimba groups from the city's town center began to participate in the Saint Jerome Festival. Yet although revivers revalued the Indian *dance*, Monimbó *dancers* remained marginalized. Monimbó *marimberos* retained control of the musical performances, hiring themselves out to Masaya and Managua folk dance aficionados, but even in this area the transformations at work constituted a form of social domination through cultural appropriation. Ethnomusicologist T. M. Scruggs notes of the newly emerging urban dance groups, "the presence of Monimbó musicians serves as a touch of authenticity, an iconic link with the roots of the tradition, seated to one side, playing the requested piece upon demand" (1998:8). Thus, the myth of mestizaje continued to exert hegemonic control: elites disdained modern Indian practices even while they "revived" a historical Indian dance, "improving" it with elite styling. This revival allowed both conformist and oppositional sectors of the middle and ultimately the upper classes to revel in their Indian heritage without being confused with living Monimboseños. As a consequence, marimba festival dancing was transformed from an Indian dance in whiteface into a Ladino dance in Indian garb. Within a decade or so, dance groups even abandoned the Inditas costume for fanciful imitations of folk costumes from around the world.

While residents of the town center increasingly adopted marimba dancing as their own practice, a group of young, Indian-identified professionals in Monimbó initiated their own revival. These neighborhood activists selected the more carnivalesque form of the festival tradition, the torovenado masquerades. Their aim was to recover an oppositional Indian identity at a time when the Hispanic contributions to Nicaraguan culture were consistently elevated over the Indian contributions. Thus, the new cofradía of the Torovenado del Pueblo was born. Even as the town-center revivalists recognized their marimba dances as symbols of a mixed Spanish and Indian heritage, the Monimbó *torovenaderos* attempted to peel away a perceived Spanish overlay to expose the tradition's indigenous roots. Both Masaya and Monimbó revivalists shared a vision of festival dances as cultural rather than religious obligations. Both claimed to improve upon the existing model with new aesthetic and organizational styles.

Monimboseños had remained relatively quiescent during their community's long decline under the Somoza dictatorship.[30] Thus, their spontaneous insurrection in February 1978 came as something of a surprise to both the dictatorship and the revolutionary movement. The local insurrection was sparked during a community mass commemorating murdered opposition leader Pedro Joaquín Chamorro. The National Guard arrived and fired tear gas into the crowd just as a nearby grade school was being dismissed, injuring several children. In response, Monimboseños barricaded their main roads, declared their neighborhood a free territory, and kept the National Guard out for two weeks. Resisters turned the neighborhood's visible signs of government neglect to their advantage. They used the uneven terrain to ambush the guard from above and the intricate network of narrow walkways connecting one house to another to avoid detection. Moreover, they invented a powerful homemade bomb in local fireworks factories, which they called a *cuajada*, "homemade cheese." They wore festival masks to disguise themselves when confronting the guard. Finally, Monimboseños "recovered" their reputation as "savage" Indians to intimidate the guards and dissuade them from entering the neighborhood at all.[31] Somoza subsequently ordered aerial bombing, which devastated the neighborhood and brought international attention to the insurrection.

As a consequence of these actions, the popular conception of Monimboseños as backward rustics changed radically. Now, to be Indian was to be heroic, resourceful, and at the forefront of the revolutionary struggle. At the same time, Monimboseños had formed a powerful link between resistance and traditional festival arts. With the revolutionary victory, they were filled with a new and heady sense of pride. But even as the revolution was celebrating Monimbó's tradition of resistance, it sought to incorporate the neighborhood into the nation after the long abandonment during the Somoza period. Physical improvements were accompanied by social transformations as Monimboseños became more aware of and connected to the larger spheres of the nation and world. The various mass mobilizations that characterized the 1980s—including the literacy campaign and the military draft—made participants (willingly or unwillingly) part of something larger than

Figure 2.2 Youths practice throwing contact bombs in woods surrounding Monimbó, 1978. The use of festival dance masks to hide the insurgents' identities helped conflate traditional and revolutionary symbolism. (Copyright Susan Meiselas/Magnum Photos)

their home community. Finally, the fact of the revolution brought formerly marginal Nicaragua to the world's attention. Although Monimbó and Nicaragua had never been isolated from world events and processes, the local consciousness of and attention to extralocal spheres intensified dramatically in the 1980s.[32]

Revolutionary leaders' promises to rebuild Nicaraguan culture on a more egalitarian basis fell far short in practice, however. In the intensive nationalization of culture that followed the revolution, Monimbó's oppositional symbols were appropriated for national purposes. Folk ballets in the nation's capital presented choreographed versions of marimba and other regional dances to the world, robbing Masaya dance enthusiasts of their authority in the dance (Scruggs 1998). In response to this challenge, the Masaya city government and grassroots cultural organizations shored up the traditional context for folk dance performances: the Saint Jerome Festival. They successfully enlarged the festival, adding a series of benefit social dances to raise funds for festival performances, reviving a festival queen contest, and selling the square to vendors of carnival amusements. At the same time, they initiated a forceful effort to popularize festival performances, providing financial support to new and existing groups of performers. As a consequence, Monimboseños and other working-class groups increased their participation in the festival cultural enactments. Masayans remember the Saint Jerome festivities of the mid-1980s as the largest and merriest ever. By the close of the decade, about forty-five performance groups from all city sectors participated in the Saint Jerome festivities, which now spanned three months, from early September to the last Sunday of November (Borland 2002).

The Neoliberal Shift in Popular Culture

With the defeat of the Sandinista program in the February 1990 elections, state support for popular culture evaporated. The Institute of Nicaraguan Culture, which inherited some of the responsibilities of the Sandinista Ministry of Culture, lacked an adequate budget for cultural programming.[33] This retreat from the popular terrain reflected both a general reduction of the state bureaucracy and a new emphasis on the Catholic foundation of Nicaraguan popular culture.[34] Arguing that the festival dances were originally presented in fulfillment of a religious vow and therefore represented a personal sacrifice, the city Office of Culture resisted subsidizing performing groups. However, despite the loss of state support and the worsening economic environment for the popular classes, the Saint Jerome Festival performances continued to multiply. By 2000, more than sixty groups from all city sectors participated in the festival.

Far from marking a religious return, the growth in festival dancing reflects a continuing concern for reviving, celebrating, and enacting a local cultural identity. The national threat to Masaya's cultural authority that had enlivened the festival in the 1980s has now given way to a transnational assault. In Managua and to a lesser degree in downtown Masaya, North American–style convenience stores and video rental establishments feed the appetites of an Americanized elite, many of whom had spent the 1980s as refugees in Miami. In Monimbó, the flood of foreign goods has deprived artisans of their local markets, and the neighborhood's internal economy has suffered. Debt, joblessness, physical and mental illness, delinquency, and despair—all symptoms of social disintegration—now plague the neighborhood. Festival enactments of all kinds continue to grow, however, providing opportunities for sociability, instruction, collaboration, innovation, and competition in an otherwise bleak era. The community's resilient insistence on sponsoring and performing festival enactments subordinates profit to artistic expression in the service of community integration.

The festival calendar now officially begins with a queen contest in early September. Three religious processions follow: the Bajada on September 20, the saint's day on September 30, and the Octava on October 7. Each procession marks a progressively larger and longer circuit, and each draws a specific audience. At the Bajada, Saint Jerome travels through the streets immediately contiguous to his church, stopping at the homes of those who are known to be particularly devoted to him. On September 30, he processes to the Parochial Church of the Assumption about six blocks away, attends a mass, and returns by the same route. This procession attracts participants from all over Nicaragua. On October 7, the saint circulates throughout Masaya in a tour that can last more than twenty-four hours. This is the rowdiest procession, as those carrying the saint sometimes resort to alcohol to maintain their stamina. Young Masayans may test themselves to see how long they can stay with the procession. On the Sundays in October, torovenaderos and children's marimba dancers make their own processions through the city. On the Sundays in November, adult marimba dancers and the transvestite Negras groups perform. On the final Sunday of November, el Domingo de Apante, the Diablitos dancers close the festival with their large, circular masked dance.[35]

Clearly, the legislative decree that christened Masaya the Capital of Nicaraguan Folklore represents a technique of incorporation—the state recognizing, domesticating, and commodifying a site of difference. Yet Masaya's reputation for traditionality rests on a history of continuous ritual and performance practice. Other Nicaraguan cities and towns annually reenact ancient performances in their patron saint festivals as well. Yet Masayans have actively cultivated a folklore revival in response to repeated threats to their cultural authority. Performing a cultural identity in effect produces it, and in Masaya producing and performing in festivals are what people do. From late August, when group rehearsals begin, to the last dances in November, throughout the city, over the shoulders of an encircling crowd, through the doorways of the humblest and the most elegant homes, in yards and patios, one glimpses dancers and masked figures, dancing now not to placate volcanic deities or to reenact the mythical formation of the national body, but largely for themselves, to produce and celebrate their own distinctiveness.

This dynamic departs sharply from the "indigenous" Nights of the Dead in Mexico, which, after being advertised by a national tourist bureau as the authentic version of national tradition, were overwhelmed by camera-toting tourists and television crews. There, the local observances became spectator sports, emptied of any transcendent content (Brandes 1998; García-Canclini 1993:96–98). In contrast, the Saint Jerome Festival provides the anchor for the performance of local, popular culture that resists limiting hegemonic constructions of the tradition. Even if the national legislature hopes to encourage tourism to Masaya by naming it the folklore capital, and cultural activists contrive ways to accommodate festival arts to tourist schedules, the dances remain most significant for Masayans themselves. As Bendix (1989) has argued, tourism does not, in fact, constitute the primary motive for heritage or traditional enactments in all contemporary small communities. Rather, residents demonstrate an enduring need to conjure themselves to and for themselves.[36] What meanings Masayans convey to one another through their evolving cultural enactments are the subjects of the following chapters.

Part II October Masquerades

3 When a Little Tradition Modernizes

Torovenado Masquerades of Masaya

Carnival has long been identified as at least a temporary site of popular resistance to hegemony. For example, Scott identifies carnival as an "ambiguous political victory wrested from elites by subordinate groups," as a place to voice otherwise repressed antagonisms toward the authorities (1990:178). Turner (1986:138) and Gilmore (1987) note the propensity of propertied residents to leave town during Brazilian Carnival, the popular classes literally taking over the streets. Natalie Davis (1975) observed that carnival in early-modern Europe provided models for the kinds of disorder subsequently employed in peasant revolts. Bakhtin, who is perhaps the most influential proponent of carnival's liberating spirit, views premodern European carnival as a time and space that privileged the commoner's voice, dissolved artificial hierarchies, and unleashed an inclusive, regenerative laughter.[1] In these constructions, carnival becomes a privileged space of popular expression.

Ethnographers working in contemporary rural communities, however, view the Bakhtinian carnival of pure possibility and unlimited license as a characteristically modern form. They distinguish modern festival, which they locate in urban centers or tourist destinations, from contemporary festivals of rural, ethnically distinctive groups, where license is carefully scripted and controlled (Lechuga 1988).[2] In Middle American indigenous communities, carnival masqueraders impersonate evil and chaos in order to purify the community (Bricker 1973). Many festivals still retain pre-Christian ritual features such as petitioning for rain (Dow 1988) or for protection from illness (Mace 1970). Maskers often portray the mestizo, who for many indigenous groups represents the immoral other (Brandes 1988; Dow 1988; Esser 1983; Lechuga 1988). In this way, masqueraders challenge larger hegemonies by critiquing the moral authority of cultural outsiders. Nevertheless, the critical license masqueraders enjoy does not always extend to their unmasked audience. In fact, these festival participants may experience the humor as repressive rather than liberating.

Lindahl (1996a) cautions students of carnival to note the highly conservative, anachronistic features of masquerade as well as the emergent features that push observers to think in new ways. He observes that when rural Louisiana Mardi Gras performers play at stealing from their unmasked neighbors, they carefully channel their rowdy acts of license into time-honored routines. Ultimately, the rural Mardi Gras symbolically reconstitutes the community. Despite their transgressions during the day, masqueraders prepare an evening meal for everyone, thereby reasserting mutual interdependence and fellowship. The carnivals of small communities, then, provide an opportunity for certain members of society to criticize both cultural insiders and outsiders, dominators and dominated, while at the same time they make the community visible, harmonizing disparate, perhaps conflicting elements in a final act of collective integration.

In Masaya, many small carnivalesque masquerades used to participate in the Saint Jerome Festival. During the 1980s, two large processions centered in Monimbó, the Torovenado del Pueblo and the Torovenado de Malinche, eclipsed the smaller masquerades. What happens when a small community's self-referential carnival becomes a popular celebration of license, critique, and creativity, exceeding the bounds of the traditional script?[3] What happens when a revolutionary state supports and celebrates these festivals? And what happens to the carnival when the revolutionary project unravels? As Masaya's carnivalesque torovenados grew in popularity, they lost their ability to represent, distinguish, or integrate the host community effectively. Although the interests of neighborhood revivers momentarily converged with those of the Sandinista government, the resulting bacchanalian celebration soon provoked discontent among local residents. During the conservative reaction of the 1990s, torovenado organizers scaled back on the license and excesses of the previous decades, but this partial return to a community aesthetic was accompanied by a general creative decline. Throughout these transformations, masquerade sponsors and participants expressed their anxiety about capitalist incursions in festival production and imagery.

The 1990 Torovenado del Pueblo took place on the final Sunday of October. Throughout the central streets of the town, individual and group masqueraders paraded in a rather disorderly fashion toward the Saint Jerome Church. Onlookers mingled with the costumed participants, drinking and dancing to the festival music of small brass bands. Uncle Sam and several Violeta Chamorros ambled past. From a truck decorated with palm leaves, a group of young men dressed as exotic dancers announced they were "Las Chicas del Can," an all-female Latin dance band. Devils and spooks of various kinds charged through the crowds of onlookers, scaring small children. Old-style ox-drawn carts wound down the street, a fat market woman slapping tortillas in one, a barber pantomiming his trade with a machete in the other. Scores of men dressed as stylish women tottered down the street in high-heels alongside scores of ragged campesinos, their faces covered with carved gourd masks.

One of the most noticeable masquerade groups in the Torovenado de Malinche, held a few weeks later, was a band of former contras in heavy black beards and green uniforms. Instead of carrying guns, they squirted water on onlookers from hoses attached to portable pesticide packs. A sign explained that they were waiting for the president to fulfill her promise and give them land to work. The masquerades and the materials used in both torovenados were a mixed assortment of native and foreign elements, representing, as I would find during my year's stay, contemporary cultural life and concerns in Masaya. Nevertheless, a large number of residents voiced discontent with these torovenados, charging that they had exceeded the limits of appropriate masquerade. Faced with a rapidly changing environment in everyday life, where more and more families owned televisions and wore imported tennis shoes, these residents looked to the torovenado as a way of reaffirming a distinctive cultural past. This desire to limit the festivals to nostalgic evocations of an indigenous past registers the complex and unstable relation between hegemonic and popular culture.

The Older Torovenados: Structure and Form

Although no written descriptions of the torovenados of earlier eras exist, Masayans agree that they once served as an indigenous form of

Figure 3.1 A traditional parody of the poor in the Torovenado del Pueblo in 2001. The sign reads "The farmer of El Mojón."

venerating the saint through a spontaneous display of masqueraders who paraded through the streets, led by a small statue of Saint Jerome, carried on a miniature replica of the mountain used in the religious procession. Brinton mentioned that a dance called the Toro y Venado (Bull and Deer) was performed in the Saint Jerome Festival during the 1870s ([1883] 1969:xxvii). At that time, the dance involved dialog or songs expressing topical or local themes.⁴ Abelino Eskorcia Zúniga (1979) wrote an account of its origins based on the oral tradition. He claimed that the first torovenado was performed in the 1850s after a wealthy landowner sent a bull to kill a "tigre" (jaguar) that had been killing his cattle.⁵ When the bull succeeded, the landowner asked his farmhands to commemorate the event in masquerade for the patron saint festival. One masquerader dressed in the dead jaguar's skin; another imitated the bull. The rest donned old clothes that the landowner provided—some as men, some as women. They wore grotesque masks and masks of bearded foreigners, and they carried stuffed wild animals—squirrels, iguanas, and small monkeys—that they used like marionettes. Periodically during their procession, the jaguar and bull masqueraders (which Eskorcia described as demonstrating the agility of a deer) feigned combat, while the chorus cried "Hey little bull, the jaguar hunts you!" (1979:4–6).

Although there may be some truth to the report, the evidence that this was the first or original torovenado is insufficient. Indeed, many elements in Eskorcia's description suggest a preexisting indigenous model. Though no earlier accounts of Masaya's torovenados exist, indigenous Mexican and Central American masquerading traditions display a common set of characters, including the Tigre, or Jaguar; men impersonating monkeys; male transvestites; and "uglies" or grotesque figures. With the arrival of the Spanish, dances and dance dramas featuring bearded white men and bulls also became popular among indigenous groups. These stock characters take on different roles in different locales, but scholars have generally agreed that they represent successive layers of mythical, historical, and topical allusions.⁶

Moreover, early Spanish accounts identified a vibrant pre-Columbian performance tradition that included dances, acrobatics, theater, song, animal masquerades, female impersonation, the ridiculing of foreigners, and mock battles. Because Spaniards engaged in similar masquerade performances, they reinforced an already sophisticated performance tradition, substituting Christian images and holidays as the occasion for dance and theater performances (Harris 2000; Mace 1970). The torovenados may be connected to a group of deer dances, or *bailes del venado*, found throughout North and Central America. Like the torovenado, these dances or dance dramas are humorous, with characters imitating old people, sick people, and animals. Mace reports that one such dance among the Quiché of Guatemala was a bawdy comedy involving a deer, a jaguar, an old man, his dog, and a man suffering from malaria (1970:61). The old man sets out to kill the jaguar, but instead the jaguar, now joined by a deer, turns on the hunting party, causing havoc. Another dance drama from the Quiché, called the Patzcá, consisted of a group of dancers wearing old, dirty clothes and grotesque masks simulating goiters. This dance petitioned the mountain deity, who was responsible for both rain and health. By pantomiming illness, the masqueraders attempted to avoid it, and, curiously, the dance was known as "the dance that made the divinity laugh" (Mace 1970:19–31). Saint Jerome's association both with curing illness and with the mountain or volcano that the Mangue worshipped before they were converted to Christianity suggests that perhaps the torovenado also functioned as a humorous plea to supernatural beings for health.

In the living memory of Monimboseños, only two traditional masquerade figures continued to grace the processions: the jaguar and *la vieja del torovenado*, perhaps a reference to the pre-Columbian volcano priestess. Most torovenado masqueraders conveyed purely topical meanings, making fun of particular people, groups, or personalities by imitating them in costume, mask, and gesture. Accompanied by brass bands, the masqueraders cavorted through the streets of the city, visiting Saint Jerome at his church and then winding back to the home of the torovenado host. When the band played, the masqueraders broke into a free-form dance characterized by the rapid shimmying of torso and hips.

Before 1960, torovenados were organized by a particular household in order to fulfill a vow. Alternately, a Saint Jerome devotee who owned a small statue of the saint might host an annual torovenado in his honor. The host family would announce to the general public its intention to sponsor a torovenado eight days before the procession was to take place. This form of veneration was strongly associated with the indigenous-identified community of Monimbó and adjacent rural communities.[7] Anita Vívas López, whose mother and grandmother hosted a torovenado, related that up to the 1960s the announcements were made by a specialist who walked through the streets beating the *tuncun*, an indigenous drum. Anyone who wished to participate was welcome, and masqueraders generally threw together a costume of old clothes and household utensils for this purpose.

In fact, the masqueraders often parodied campesinos and poor people. José del Carmen Suazo, a Monimbó mask maker, remembered people using gourds or cardboard for masks: "And they went out in old torn-up clothes. For example, the Iguana hunter, the Iguanero, with an old, faded hat, the clothes full of sticks, pure campesino, the clothing of the true campesino, but old. And the floats were ox-drawn carts. And they went out imitating, caricaturing the most typical characters of Monimbó."[8] Vívas López remembered that cross-dressing was particularly popular: "And they put on old dresses, they came to ask for a loan or to rent a dress, or if it were my brother, he borrowed a dress of mine. And so he made himself up as a woman, a particular person and went out. Or if there were a recent wedding, then they went out burlesquing them, more or less as the wedding party."[9] Because weddings were rare in the neighborhood, burlesquing them challenged a couple's claims to social superiority. However, another popular burlesque was of the campesino family, with a man dressed as a pregnant woman leading a trail of small children.

On a given Sunday in October, the masqueraders would assemble at the host family's house and hold a formal Catholic prayer.[10] They would then wind through the streets, dancing and cavorting to the Church of Saint Jerome, then back to the house. There, the family would distribute festival foods and drink to all who had participated.[11] Many residents used to have small plots of land outside the city, where they grew their own crops and raised farm animals. The organization and production of a torovenado, then, relied on a household's available resources. Although a few festival items—fireworks and music—might be purchased, most of the materials necessary for the party were from a sponsor's own farm or from rural friends and supporters who donated materials to the host.[12]

Torovenado hosts came from a variety of social and political backgrounds. An elderly resident of rural Quebrada Honda, José Cornelio, worked as a young man on a large estate outside Masaya. He remembered the landlord treating the workers to cane liquor if they would dress up and dance to venerate the saint. Despite this patronage, José Cornelio said, "in the torovenado they made fun of everyone, but mostly of the rich people, or of the people who set themselves up as superior to the rest."[13] One very famous torovenado in Monimbó was sponsored by Somoza supporter Carmelito de García.[14] But Rogelio Toribio also recalled that in his mother's Torovenado de Malinche, which began in 1938, masqueraders caricatured Somoza and the National Guard. These performances were risky, he noted, and masqueraders displayed themselves only briefly, later discarding their costumes. Thus, the torovenados were not related to any particular ideology, even though they tended to be arenas for social and even political criticism.

Suazo gave an example of the kind of criticism a masquerader might make: "So, when they realized that a lawyer was robbing a piece of land or some question like that from someone, and he left those campesinos, those poor people, crying, and so they came to caricature that lawyer and the poor woman who—that's how the woman went out, crying and fighting with the lawyer, 'give me my deed, he's taken away my deed!' And she breaks into tears. And so, it's a representation of what they had done in reality." The pre-1960s torovenados thus provided specially marked occasions for Monimboseños to burlesque both their humble and self-important neighbors and outside agents of social repression. Masqueraders utilized degraded and grotesque elements—dirty, old, broken-down things—to fashion their critique. This choice is a common one among oppressed groups, who risk retaliation if they adopt the costumes of the privileged classes. By dressing down, however, they can potentially launch a powerful, veiled critique of their superiors while at the same time reinforcing that group's stereotypical expectations of the poor Indian.[15] The small torovenados of the pre-1960s era, in spite of their contestatory potential, were largely ignored by the local and national governments.

The Torovenado del Pueblo Recovers Roots

Masaya's folklore revival in the 1960s gave birth to a new organization, the Torovenado del Pueblo. Manuel Villagras, one of its founders, explained that the idea for this festival arose among a group of young graduates of the Salesian High School.[16] These young Monimbóosenos—teachers, lawyers, professionals—came from families that were able to finance their higher education. Through their own reading, they had become aware that the education they had received had never addressed issues of their indigenous identity. One afternoon in 1960 the young men witnessed a traditional torovenado pass through the streets:

> We were drinking, it's true, all of us always drank together, the neighborhood friends. So: "We're going to take out a torovenado that's better than that one there! But we're going to give it *this* sense! We want this sense—if not, we're not going to take it out—to revive our own roots. Someday we're going to initiate this question. Where did we come from, who are we, who were our forefathers, who are our families, who were our people, where was the original city, what happened to our people?"[17]

The decision to improve the torovenado was, from the beginning, conflated with a notion of reviving indigenous roots. Revival always implies a certain distance from the living tradition, either temporal or psychological. Indeed, although the Torovenado del Pueblo founders consider themselves indigenous Monimboseños, several appear more European, a characteristic that provided them with social advantages vis-à-vis their more indigenous-looking neighbors. Yet their community affiliation alienated them from the Spanish-mestizo culture to which they had gained partial admittance.[18] These young Monimboseños wanted to strip the Spanish veneer from local popular culture.

Donald Ortega, another founding member of the Torovenado del Pueblo, states that the purpose of the new torovenado was to preserve the tradition. He told me, "It was dying out, one hardly saw this anymore. So we organized ourselves in 1961, so that this popular expression wouldn't die, so that it would be maintained always."[19] Preservation arguments, however, often served to mask the appropriation of a traditional form by a new group for new purposes. Villagras remembered, "There were other torovenados, but they were organized by people who had made a religious promise. Juan Telico, Manuel 'Culito' [Ortíz], [and] Paz Rodriguez of the Four Corners—they hosted torovenados. But these were more or less from a Christian perspective. Religious—Christian. And so within this field, we see the influence of the church. And within Christianity, that brings the mestizo identity. But we gave another turn to the torovenado, looking for our roots: we revealed ourselves." For these youthful torovenaderos, the question of identity was a question of getting beyond the church, which had been imposed on an indigenous culture by the Spanish Conquest.

Ironically, the return to indigenous roots constituted a modernizing move, for the torovenaderos could not restore the pre-Christian practices of their Mangue ancestors, which involved human sacrifice and bloodletting. Instead, they secularized the torovenado by removing the religious core. They did not organize the torovenado to pay a religious promise, and they dispensed with the preprocession house prayer. Moreover, they set up the new torovenado as a cofradía. Unlike the house-based torovenados, this torovenado financed itself by taking up collections door-to-door and holding fund-raising parties prior to the festival. As the Torovenado del Pueblo's popularity grew, the city government expressed an interest in financing it. Subsequently, members of the cofradía living in San Miguel and San Juan neighborhoods tried to move the festival downtown. In response to these threats to neighborhood control, Monimbó lawyers wrote up eighteen articles governing the organization and its purpose. They determined the official boundaries of Monimbó and required proof that all potential members were Monimbósenos by blood from at least three generations back.

Moreover, The Torovenado del Pueblo invented *mayordomos* or orders named after traditional neighborhood products—the mayordomo of the *nacatamal* (Nicaraguan tamale) or of *cususa* (cane liquor), for example. As in a *mayordomía* or traditional festival organization, they asked people to make a donation by becoming a mayordomo of a specific festival item. Unlike in a traditional mayordomía, however, the donors gave money instead of wood or fireworks. By targeting wealthy Masayans, the young festival organizers became very successful fundraisers. Villagras added, "The idea was to take money from the rich with these mayordomías of ours to underwrite a popular activity, an activity for the people." The organizers' professional standing made it easier for them than for farmers and craftsmen to gain access to the town's wealthy citizens, and soon they were able to generate much greater income for festival production than any house-based torovenado could.

In its second year, the Torovenado del Pueblo sponsored a public feast, as a religious cofradía would, in the plaza of the Magdalena Church the day before the torovenado. The cofradía also began to give prizes, collected from local craftsmen, to the best-costumed masqueraders on the day of the procession. For the organizers and donors, they held a *parada del banco* (literally "close the bank"), or dinner party, the day after the torovenado. And they claimed the last Sunday of October as the official calendar date for the Torovenado del Pueblo.

Restructuring the Torovenado del Pueblo, however, compromised the integrative function of festival organizing. The mayordomía system practiced in Monimbó enacts community and ideally renews social bonds by creating a complex web of social and material obligations that require much visiting and "face time."[20] As mayordomos accumulated and redistributed goods, they also cemented social relations. Torovenado del Pueblo organizers had discovered a more efficient means of producing the festival, but by taking from the rich to give to the poor, they had altered the existing communitarian model for festival production.

The structuring of the Torovenado del Pueblo as a cofradía, the organization of fund-raising work, and the specifically cultural focus of the festival marked this torovenado as different from the house-based torovenados that had preceded it (and that continue to perform, albeit less visibly). Although it remained a fiercely localist, indigenous-identified group, the masquerade it sponsored was open to anyone, and participation grew quickly among all neighborhoods in Masaya through the 1960s and 1970s.

The Revolutionary Torovenados

With the revolution in 1979, the ideals of new government leaders and of Torovenado del Pueblo organizers converged. As nationalists, the Sandinistas looked to folklore to combat the cultural imperialism of the United States and the servile imitation of foreign models that they identified with the Somoza period. The Torovenado del Pueblo founders had already conceptualized their torovenado as an exploration of autochthonous cultural identity. They now conceptualized the masquerade as a form of resistance, historically to Spanish domination, more recently to the National Guard, and generally to assaults on self-determination from all quarters. When two Monimbó Sandinistas lost their lives in conflicts with the National Guard, the cofradía changed its title to the Elías and Reyes Rodriguez Great Torovenado of the People to honor them.[21]

Given Monimbó's participation in the revolution and the festival's contestatory potential, it is not surprising that revolutionary leaders enthusiastically embraced Masaya's torovenados. High-ranking government leaders personally donated money to support the Torovenado del Pueblo, for under revolutionary circumstances the cofradía relaxed its rule against accepting money from government. Felipita Cermeño, coordinator of Masaya's Popular Culture Center, became the first female member of the cofradía. Miguel Bolaños remembers that there was so much money at that time, fund-raising became redundant. With this dependable financial backing, the cofradía expanded its activities beyond the Sunday of the event to include various preprocession activities. It developed internal rituals, modeled loosely on the community's traditional political organization, the council of elders. It multiplied the number of bands and the amount of fireworks used during the procession and offered masqueraders more and more expensive prizes, now from the city's large commercial houses. Finally, the postfestival dinner party for cofradía members gained a reputation for being an extravagant bacchanal.

These transformations in the festival, however, led to public outcry that the tradition was being distorted by capitalist influences. Although many traditional mayordomías held a parada del banco, the increased luxury of this event in the Torovenado del Pueblo created a perception that cofradía members were profiting from the festival. In 1991, Flavio Gamboa complained, "So, of all the money they requested, they gave out part, and they kept part for their own personal extravagances. And that's what began to destroy the true folkloric development that had developed over the years."[22] Moreover, Gamboa viewed the introduction of prizes as a kind of payment for masquerading. Finally, he criticized the way the organizers had given themselves titles and invented ceremonies for the transfer of leadership from one year to the next. The passing of the staff, modeled after the transfer of the symbols of community leadership in the council of elders, became a way for organizers to celebrate their own leadership in festival production. In Gamboa's view, they had made themselves into a torovenado aristocracy.

Whereas the innovations in the Torovenado del Pueblo became a target for criticism, Masaya's other great torovenado, the Torovenado de Malinche, retained a reputation for traditionality. Carmen Toribio, the festival's sponsor, was a marketwoman who participated in several neighborhood religious mayordomías. From 1938 to 1979, her torovenado had been one of Monimbó's many small house-based festivals. Over the years, this torovenado grew to include an *alborada* (opening ceremony or preparty) with fireworks, music, and traditional games the evening before the day of the masquerade.[23] With the revolution, the Toribios also received financial support from government agencies and politicians. Soon the Torovenado de Malinche approximated the Torovenado del Pueblo in size. The Toribios' son, Rogelio, remembers serving five to six hundred plates of food at the *requirimiento*, the festival meal at which those who have pledged support confirm their willingness to participate in festival production. To accommodate this larger festival, a formal committee was constituted to assist the Toribio family and friends.[24] The Torovenado de Malinche also began to award prizes to masqueraders, but they limited them to objects manufactured in the neighborhood. The humble origins of this torovenado, its organizers, and its prizes contributed to its reputation as a more *authentic* alternative to the Torovenado del Pueblo.

Nevertheless, Torovenado del Pueblo organizers continued to take the lead in defining the tradition for the outside world. Increased outsider attention to the Torovenado del Pueblo, including coverage on television news programs and in newspapers, prompted Donald Ortega to write a brief explanation of the significance of the masquerade, which was printed in the festival program, repeated in annual newspaper reports, and borrowed by the organizers of other torovenados.[25] This text has crystallized what the torovenado symbolizes for the community and the country: "It's a mythicoreligious syncretism, composed of two symbols: the Bull and the Deer. The Bull symbolizes domination, force, imposition; the Deer, liberty, cleverness, agility. Spain and America. The Bull is tamed, domesticated; the Deer remains untamable, like our race"

(Cofradía del Gran Torovenado del Pueblo 2001). This statement soon became the authoritative interpretation of the festival's underlying meaning. Ortega's explanation moves from syncretism to opposition. In the end, the bull and the deer are not united; they are contrasted as tamed and untamable, and the race Ortega claims is not the mestizo Nicaraguan, but the Indian, who remains free from foreign influence. Even though Ortega's exegesis attributes greater weight to the Indian contribution to Nicaraguan culture, this locally grounded, community perspective remains easily subsumed by the Nicaraguan myth of mestizaje, which makes Indian resistance to domination part of the collective heritage of all Nicaraguans. During the revolutionary era, the assumption of a rebellious Indian identity by the mestizo body politic obscured the continuing existence of disadvantaged Indian communities, just as revolutionary rhetoric obscured the continuing class bias evident in many areas of Sandinista practice (Colburn 1986; Dore 1990; Field 1988, 1999; Gould 1998; Saldana-Portillo 1997; Vilas 1992).

Whereas Ortega created a new definition of the torovenado, Miguel Bolaños contributed a physical symbol: a mask of a bull with deer antlers that now also graces the procession. Thus, the syncretic symbol of the torovenado was born. The organizers' imaginative reworking of the traditional symbols allows us to see more clearly what was missing in earlier constructions, for Eskorcia's origin story fails to account adequately for the reference to the deer in the dance's title, Toro y Venado. In fact, one might argue that Eskorcia's wealthy nineteenth-century landowner, like Catholic clergy elsewhere in Middle America, had replaced the indigenous deer with a Spanish symbol, the bull, who fought and vanquished the indigenous predator, the jaguar.

And yet the older torovenado masquerades as they were performed by Monimboseños avoided the limitations of a particular script and instead exploited the topical. It was this aspect of the traditional masquerade that also dominated in the two great torovenados of the revolutionary decade in spite of organizers' public requests that masqueraders explore their cultural roots. The emphasis on people's culture and people's creativity, fostered by the revolution and combined with excellent prizes and the presence of national television, inspired some elaborate and unusually artistic skits during the 1980s. One notable float, mounted by musician Gustavo Espinosa, re-created the Nahuatl

Figure 3.2 A man directs traffic in the 1983 Torovenado del Pueblo. His sign reads "Reagan and His Gorillas." Skits like this expressed the dominant anti-imperialism of the time. (Photo from *La Barricada*, October 31, 1983; printed with permission by the Instituto de Historia de Nicaragua y Centroamérica)

myth of the Plumed Serpent;[26] another celebrated colonial-era Rafaela Herrera's defense of the San Carlos fortress after her father was killed by marauding English pirates. Oscar Marenco explained how he and his friends designed the float in 1987:

> I made a ship with some friends. It was on a trailer, but just dragged behind a truck. It was such a beautiful number. We were imitating Nicaraguan things. So, we made the castle on a truck bed, Rafaela Herrera, just as it was. She was there with her wick and a cannon and the people there calling that they had killed her father, and now they were going to make havoc. And so, she set off the cannon, boom! And you should have seen the explosion it made, but it was only smoke. Boom! And the pirates who were the English. So they responded with their cannons.
>
> Boom!
>
> That was . . . Look, it made such an impact on Masaya that ev-

erybody had to come and see it. And the Sandinista, the one who died recently [Luis Carrión], thought it was so beautiful that he got up onto the truck and said, "This number is so good, repeat it for me!" And we were all making gestures, rah, rah! There goes Horacio Perez, and then fighting and falling down.

We made the cannon of big long tubes like this with stones around them and the wick was big like this, so that Rafaela could light it—Piss! Bwah! We've thought of doing it again, but the problem is [money]. You have to rent trucks, a lot of things. We won first place. They gave us a television, other things.[27]

Like other Masaya torovenaderos with whom I spoke, Oscar emphasized the homemade quality and the historical and cultural focus of the display. Yet this skit drew on Nicaragua's national history of resistance rather than on local themes. It could easily be read as a metaphor for Nicaragua's defense against U.S. incursions during the 1980s. Thus, it reflected the intense nationalization of popular culture of the period.

Reaction and Nostalgia

By the close of the 1980s, many Monimbó residents, including some Torovenado del Pueblo organizers, were deeply troubled by changes in the content and style of the masquerade: a preponderance of political and associated religious satire, the intrusion of "foreign" objects and themes, the increased visibility of homosexual masqueraders, and a shift in the costuming aesthetic from rags to finery. Oscar Marenco lamented in 1991, "When they captured the American Hutchinson, there they were, not just one but a lot of people [masquerading as Hutchinson].[28] But these are things of the war! There they were, some white boys, disguised as the National Guard. But for me, that's not a torovenado! That's all you see now. Now the torovenado is disintegrating." In Marenco's view, the contestatory element of the torovenado was directed at the Sandinistas' enemies, indicating that the form had become politicized. However, he did not argue that the festival had therefore lost its critical edge. Instead, he articulated a nostalgia for the self-referential humor of the older torovenado: "It's better when they go out

Figure 3.3 Lascivious transvestism in the Torovenado de Malinche in 1991.

making fun of the women who sell gum, of those people who shine shoes, but shoes all broken and worn out." Such sentiments imply an exhaustion of the nationalistic impulse and a simultaneous desire to turn inward to familiar community themes.[29]

Other critics charged that the torovenados had become vehicles for disseminating an exclusively Sandinista ideology. Donald Ortega strongly contested this view:

What we say in the publicity is that they should respect morality, truly, in the loudspeaker announcements and in the newspapers. But the people go out to make fun of the devil himself in reality! A torovenado went out here with a little bag of dirt—the Agrarian Reform had given a little land to someone. And when ENABAS was created, [they showed] what they gave them was a few drops of cooking oil.[30] Well, they're bandits! And you can't stop them. You can't say anything to the people, nothing. With the question of the Russian aid, a barbarous masquerade goes out. "Russian Aid to Nicaragua," it says—a bunch of old things, old shoes. Right there is the thing, the criticism. On that day, there's no law, nothing. Here the police leave, and everybody goes dancing through the streets making fun.

Thus, Ortega argued that the masquerade had always provided an arena for political critique, among other things. Nevertheless, he acknowledged that carnivalesque license has its limit:

The people enjoy being merry, with the music, the fireworks, and all, everyone in costume. But there was one year [1980], the war had just ended, that they started to denounce the Sandinista Front. And a cart went out filled with frogs and some toads. They called those who were in the Sandinista Security toads. So they brought a bunch of frogs in a cart, a frog farm, with slogans and all. We had a problem there.

So we had to talk to them; we intervened there because, well, there could have been a fight over that. And it was better for them to desist from presenting that masquerade. Because it was right after the war, and the city was all stirred up. And we told them there might be someone killed, because that had never happened, that people had already gathered together on the corner and they were going to attack them and who knows what. So they understood, and they took it away.

This masquerade directly targeted the Sandinista military, arguably the most powerful governmental organization at the time. Although Ortega emphasized the organizers' responsibility to ensure the masqueraders' safety, this particular group seemed to have encountered the limit to free expression.

Religious masquerades, too, assumed a political dimension when in the 1980s and 1990s the Nicaraguan Catholic hierarchy sided with the counterrevolution. And yet critics who complained about masqueraders' disrespect for religion were often motivated to do so by their own political agendas. In the 1990 Torovenado de Malinche, for example, Bosco Canales, an active participant in Monimbó's numerous mayordomías as well as an outspoken Sandinista, represented the mayordomía of the Virgin of the Assumption, patron of Monimbó. In a float-style masquerade, Canales and a group of homosexual friends depicted the Virgin lying down and covered with a gauze cloth, just as she is displayed the evening before she is taken out in her procession. The cross-dressed "devotees," caricatures of local women, were gathered around this central figure. By midday, like other masqueraders, they were quite drunk.

The reaction was explosive. Even though most of the women caricatured had worked closely with Canales in numerous neighborhood mayordomías, they were not amused. Instead of viewing the skit as an exploration of heritage, the members of the Virgin of the Assumption mayordomía, all of whom were ardent UNO supporters, chose to interpret the burlesque of the Virgin in the context of a *Sandinista* torovenado and thus as a challenge to the new political order. They claimed the masqueraders had attacked Monimbó's most sacred image. They urged the parochial priest to denounce them, which he did in church the following day. Canales had seriously misjudged the prevailing political atmosphere in 1990, just as earlier satirists of the Sandinista security had misjudged it in 1980. Although religious caricatures had long been part of the torovenados, they were now viewed as serious distortions of the tradition.

Evelyn Montoya, UNO Masaya Office of Culture employee, explained, "We now want to revive all those beautiful practices, revive them without mistreating our religion. We are very Catholic because of our parents, because of our traditions, so we don't like the way they ridicule our religious images, our churches, our priests. Here we respect these things. We want our customs to continue as before, healthily, humbly, always respecting our Catholic leaders."[31] Whereas Office of Culture workers attributed the disrespect for religion to the 1990 Torovenado de Malinche Sandinista organizers, the organizers insisted that they discouraged such masquerades. Donald Ortega argued:

> They dress up as priests, they dress up as nuns, they dress up as virgins. There was one year [in the 1960s] when all the saints of the church went out. Every one of the saints, the twelve apostles, craziness. The people here, I don't tell them to go out. We don't want them to engage in these vulgarities, but since they are crazy things, we can't tell the people not to. Sure, that's not what we wanted. We would rather that the folkloric spectacle go out—legends, myths, old memories. Some of this kind of thing is presented, but the majority are religious and political masquerades. Denouncing things, things like that.

Even as Ortega denied an anti-Catholic bias, he recognized that the 1980s marked a shift in the tenor of masquerades toward the contestatory.

Disenchantment with the great torovenados in Masaya did not simply derive from political or religious antipathies. Although the torovenados had always provided opportunities for male cross-dressing, a new kind of female impersonation had emerged in the large torovenados of the 1980s, in which gay men donned stylish and sexually provocative female attire, such as skimpy bikinis or showgirl outfits. Indeed, for many nonresident observers of the festival, the torovenados of that era presented opportunities to go see the *cochones* or gays on parade. For sympathetic analysts, these gay masquerades combined a ludic expression of sensuality, a restoration of pre-Columbian gay identity, and a subaltern homosexual alliance against hegemonic class and sexual oppression. From this perspective, male homosexuals had colonized a Bakhtinian space of pure possibility in order to express their difference and in so doing had expressed solidarity with all oppressed social sectors (Blandón 2001; Lancaster 1992b:295, 1997).

This emerging nonlocal view arises also in Bolt's influential 1990 allegory of Sandinista Nicaragua, *El libro de la nación Qu*. In the fictional narrative, the first of a series of oral traditions, recorded and handed down from generation to generation, is the story of a pair of brothers-in-law, Xuitzal and Tlotzín, who go off to divert themselves one evening. Having become intoxicated, Xuitzal penetrates Tlotzín anally in a celebration of phallic pleasure. Their wives arrive and chastise Xuitzal, saying:

> Xochipilli, Lord of the Dance
> Lord of the Great Toro-Venado
> Xochipilli this man celebrates your rites
> Out of time.
> Let the punishment of the community come
> For this man, Lord. (Bolt 1990:142)

The next day Xuitzal is walking alone when he meets a neighbor, to whom he recounts his crime. The neighbor asks if Tlotzín had ever had relations with a man before. Xuitzal believes not. The neighbor then jokes that he should marry the man to keep people from talking (141–45). Through literature, then, Bolt artfully projects into the ancient oral tradition a relatively recent notion that the Saint Jerome Festival offers license for otherwise censured male homosexuality. For many Masaya residents, however, the explicitly homosexual masquerades transformed the torovenados into a species of carnival, which they understood as a foreign form. Homosexual licentiousness was part of the bacchanalian excess that exceeded local notions of appropriate masquerade.[32]

In the earlier torovenado of living memory, poverty had been highlighted. During the 1980s, many masqueraders chose the opposite extreme, using elaborate, expensive costumes and props. In 1991, Gamboa related, "Today you see people dressed in exorbitant finery, and in Monimbó and surrounding areas nobody dresses in such a high style." Evelyn Montoya concurred: "Here culture and civilization have arrived gradually, and the folkloric customs have changed. But before, things were more rustic, without these exotic costumes, without stockings, without all those things. The masks, yes. The masks, a few elegantly tailored costumes, but old and worn out, dirty." José del Carmen Suazo added, "There weren't any floats like you see in the Torovenado del Pueblo. Now it's like a carnival. Now one sees stranger things, foreign things, foreign masks of plastic and rubber—synthetic materials. No, before it was pretty. The masks were of native trees, all rustic, abstract, deformed, made by the masqueraders themselves." A mask maker and artist himself, Suazo lamented the loss of a native aesthetic. The images being presented in the torovenados had become strange, foreign, unsettling; they conflicted with the community's view of the masquerade as an investigation, representation, and celebration of Monimbó's cultural heritage.

Clearly, the festival had responded to the community's incipient urbanization, modernization, and globalization. Manuel Villagras explained:

> [It] has been transformed, motivated by the interrelation that exists in the modern world, through the communications system. Now it takes one minute to receive the news with a parabolic antenna or with short-wave radio transistors. We can listen to Rome; we can listen to Spain; that is, the world is interrelated. And this related, communicated world has also influenced the torovenado. For example, Norwegian culture has nothing to do with the torovenado—Eric the Red—and Eric the Red has gone out here. We do not approve of Eric the Red. And so on. Roman soldiers. We do not approve of Roman soldiers.[33] Because these are cultural elements with their own traditions, their own ideologies, and we do not approve of this. We approve of the historical and political context of our own identity.

As Villagras pointed out, the organizers really had limited control over what the masqueraders chose to present in the Torovenado del Pueblo. On the one hand, they retained an ideal for the torovenado that would exalt the neighborhood's distinctiveness. On the other, they recognized that residents' cultural experience increasingly included elements from the world outside the neighborhood.

The nostalgia for a lost community, however, also contained a desire for neighborhood integration in a period marked by sharp political polarization. As residents explained, self-referential caricature need not be critical or degrading. Sometimes it simply displays the idiosyncrasies of a well-known resident. Mask maker Norlan Briceño recalled, "There was a woman, Margarita Alemán—she's now an old lady—who used a motor scooter to give injections. Someone caricatured her."[34] In his narrative reconstruction of a masquerade of this kind, Roberto Augustín Marenco expressed both the risks such masquerades entail and the conviviality they produce when they are successful. In 1986, a

Figure 3.4 Political critique remains evident in the Torovenado del Pueblo in 2001. Loosely translated, the signs read (from left to right), "Party of Corrupt Thieves," "If Alemán was a doer, Bolaños covers up better," and "To continue bank failures, vote PLC."

large, white-skinned woman asked Marenco to help her portray doña Irma:

> La Irma is the fat woman from the restaurant, a good little bar located in front of the Red Cross, a fat woman. Have you ever passed by there? Really fat. That's Dona Irma "Melona."[35]
>
> "So I'm going to go out," she [the masquerader] says.
>
> "Okay," I say, "if you're going out, I'll get you the dress of that fat lady, and since I'm going to make the dress," well, I made the mask. Well, she went out in the Torovenado del Pueblo.
>
> Dr. "Sompopo"[36] says, "Look, I want you to go to Irma's bar." "No," I say, "I'm afraid she might treat me badly, because I was out making fun of her."
>
> "Go, go," he says.
>
> And I go, smartly dressed, with Irma "Melona," me behind. [Marenco pantomimes anxiety.]

"Ay, my sister," she says, and the woman in the bar comes out. I didn't know it, but the woman who disguised herself was a friend of Irma's. And so, what does she say? "Ay, my sister." And she went and got a big liter [of rum] and gives it to me and says, "Take it!"

And the doctor was waiting, and he said, "What happened?"

"She gave me a gift."

"You see?" he says.

That's the story of Irma.[37]

Such caricatures index the inclusive regenerative laughter that Bakhtin associates with premodern European carnival as well as the social cement produced through joking relationships.

Contemporary torovenados, however, do not simply provide opportunities for Monimboseños to engage with one another playfully. Instead, they register the neighborhood's increasing connections with larger arenas of national politics and international mass markets. In the 1980s and 1990s, they expressed an intense political experience of real events in the real world, just as they did in an earlier period when they satirized the ruthless lawyer dispossessing campesinas. Now, access to foreign materials and foreign cultural models is greater than it was in an earlier time when Monimbó was more self-sufficient than it is today. Yet global interconnectedness provokes a corresponding impulse toward distinctiveness—if not in ordinary life, then in festival. Community residents, including the torovenado organizers themselves, have turned once again to an exploration of their cultural roots.

Creative Decay

Whereas in the 1960s the Torovenado del Pueblo organizers had modernized the festival by reconceiving its structure and purpose, and in the 1980s the Sandinistas had celebrated its contestatory symbolism, the neoliberal governments of the 1990s retreated from the popular, leaving folkloric groups to their own devices. In contrast to the open, participatory model for festival planning developed during the Sandinista period, in the subsequent decade the city Office of Culture became less and less responsive to the community organizations and performance groups that essentially produced the patron saint festival. Nicaragua's new cultural policy under the UNO and subsequent Liberal Party governments strongly emphasized the country's Catholic tradition. Festival enactments were "authentic" only if they represented a religious promise, which was essentially a personal sacrifice. Therefore, city government workers argued, the state should not support performance groups financially. Nor did the newly formed national cultural organizations, the Nicaraguan Institute of Culture or the Ministry of Tourism, provide financial assistance to the festival sponsors.[38] With one notable exception, politicians' personal donations now provided only token support to festival organizers. Leaner economic times required significant adjustments among torovenado sponsors and masqueraders, leading to a period of expressive decadence.

The Torovenado de Malinche continued to enjoy a reputation for greater traditionality in the 1990s. At the same time, its sponsors strenuously highlighted their identification with the Sandinista Party. When presidential candidate Daniel Ortega expressed a desire to become the first non-Masayan mayordomo of the Torovenado de Malinche in 1993, the Toribios were thrilled. When he lost the 1996 elections, however, they feared their festival was ruined. Throughout the decade, Ortega and his partner Rosario Murillo continued to support this torovenado economically and to participate in festival events when they were able. Nevertheless, Rogelio Toribio admitted that the torovenado suffered from its association with a political leader who repeatedly failed to regain the presidency. Toribio insisted that unsympathetic neighbors began to boycott his festival, while the neoliberal city government ignored it.

Indeed, the 2001 Torovenado de Malinche appeared smaller and less vibrant than the festival of a decade earlier.[39] The two-block-long procession included small groups of men dressed as market women and numerous neighborhood spooks, but there were no organized skits like that Canales mounted in 1991. Instead, several full-size models of mountains dominated the procession. Carrying the Saint Jerome mountain is a physically grueling task, regarded as a form of devotion, penance, or sacrifice when performed as part of a religious procession. It also provides an opportunity for male camaraderie. In Masaya, the mountain bearers often drink heavily and have even been known to become forgetful of the saint they are carrying. In the 2001 Torovenado de Malinche, the mountain bearers appeared to signal the bodily aspect and rough play of carnivalesque forms[40] as they charged down the street knocking into other masqueraders. But the cognitive message of this masquerade remained unclear for most observers. Residents shook their heads, unable to comprehend the meaning of the sign. Commentators writing in the national newspapers were scathingly dismissive of both the mountain bearers and the event.[41]

In contrast to the Toribios, the organizers of the Torovenado del Pueblo identified their close association with the Sandinista Party during the 1980s as a mistake. In 1991, they strenuously asserted their independence from partisanship, proclaiming their politics were cultural, not partisan. They held a public ceremony in Magdalena Plaza to induct into the cofradía UNO mayor Sebastián Putoy, who was, incidentally, the first Monimboseño ever to serve as mayor of Masaya. They also formally prohibited satires of saints, bishops, and cardinals in a gesture of respect toward Catholic religious sensibilities.

As a consequence of these adaptations to changing times, the Torovenado del Pueblo has retained its reputation as Masaya's most important torovenado. Organizers complain of the difficulty of raising funds to support festival activities and the city government's lack of interest. Yet hard times have also forced them to return somewhat to earlier forms of festival production. Dolores Ortega, mayordoma of the cofradía in 2001, explained that organizers now contribute their own funds monthly to ensure an account balance. When they hold festive events for themselves, those who drink pay for their own liquor because all donated funds and goods go toward the expenses of the festival proper. Thus, Gamboa's earlier assertion that the organizers profited from their festival no longer resonates with the community. Moreover, the cofradía no longer gives out fancy prizes for the best masqueraders. Instead, they distribute basic food baskets,[42] a practice that more closely approximates that of former household-based torovenados that rewarded masqueraders with a festive meal. Although the number of participants and onlookers has diminished somewhat, the Torovenado del Pueblo continues to sponsor popular performances of biting political commentary, self-referential humor, and neighborhood history.

In 2001, an election year in Nicaragua, the Torovenado del Pueblo

Figure 3.5 The jaguar masquerade from the traditional torovenado, September 30, 2001.

masqueraders took on the candidates. A husky man in a pink caftan, a whiteface, wire-mesh mask, and a Sandinista Party hat and scarf approached a group of onlookers and offered them small baggies filled with dirt. When someone asked him what they were, he quipped, "Estoy dandote tierra para que no me echen tierra" (I'm giving you dirt/land so you don't talk trash/dirt about me). The caricature of presidential candidate Daniel Ortega was richly resonant, building on political symbolism that already resonated contradictions. The Sandinistas in 2001 had discarded the red and black of the confidently revolutionary party and now sported pink, what Nicaraguans jokingly refer to as *color chiche* after the popular corn beverage, but also slang for a woman's breast. Eleven years earlier Ortega had unsuccessfully run for president as El Gallo Enavajado, the Fighting Cock, against Violeta Chamorro, who had posed as both the nation's mother and its patron saint, the Virgin Purísima. Now he was revealing his feminine side amidst serious allegations of sexual abuse by his adult step-daughter, Zoilamerica Narvaéz. The packets of dirt the masquerader distributed to the crowd represented the new Sandinista land-reform plan that would provide start-up materials for those who wanted to make a go at food self-sufficiency. And so his performance drove home a cynical message that land-reform promises were a bribe.[43] Many onlookers, not immediately sure what to make of the mock candidate, were hesitant to accept his "gift," adding yet another dimension to the humorous critique. Not far behind, a luxurious car carried caricatures of outgoing president Arnoldo Alemán and his cronies, pantomiming in dress and gesture the profligacy and corruption that made these national leaders infamous. Two bands of turbaned Al Qaeda members marched through the street, registering the recent tragedy in the United States. Oddly, they stopped every block or so to "execute" one of their members by shooting him in the head. Thus, the national and global issues of the moment were playfully represented.

These skits were surrounded by a swirl of local references. In a horse-drawn buggy sat two elegantly attired masked "ladies" with long gowns, wigs, and broad hats. A sign on their gig announced that they represented Alfredo Montalván's Negras marimba dance group. This skit cleverly parodied the elitism of a town-center marimba dancer by imitating his own customary torovenado masquerade. A group of young men in cardboard masks painted bright blue presented a traditional Monimbó funeral party. One masquerader filmed the whole procedure with a cardboard camcorder, while another pantomimed a hysterical mourner who had to be revived periodically by the rest of the group. Another young man impersonated a pregnant high school girl, with the unfortunate's name pinned to the back of his denim jumper. Men in high heels and elegant evening gowns, men dressed as beauty queens, men dressed as market women, and scores of devils and spooks danced energetically to the brass bands.

The 2001 Torovenado del Pueblo thus represented Monimbó's heterogeneous reality. The masquerades were both critical and conservative, playful and aggressive, with local, national, and international referents. Men, boys, transvestites, and even a few women danced not to supplicate the volcano deity or to help a friend pay a religious promise or to defend the nation, but for the joy of going out, of representing themselves and their concerns in the dance. By participating in an enactment of Masaya's cultural uniqueness, torovenaderos insert their community within the larger field of national and global cultural production. Through celebration, they continuously produce their own difference from these larger fields.

Miguel Bolaños regards the essence of the torovenado as "to have a creative idea, to express it creatively," and in this sense he sees the 1990s as a period of decline.[44] In 2001, he observed that participation slackened when people realized they would no longer win big prizes. Only the drag numbers and those who wish to express a strong political idea now invested in their masquerades. He concluded, "So that made us realize that the event is not a true expression of culture, that without realizing it, we had converted it into something that we were paying them to do. So we maybe confused things there, and we were deteriorating the popular expression." This view recalls Lombardi-Satriani's (1978) assertion that capitalism corrupts folklore. However, such a view posits an ideally pure or authentic popular culture existing outside of capitalist relations, a view that most contemporary folklorists reject (Bendix 1997:143).

In a contemporary setting, hybrid cultural forms seem not only legitimate but inevitable. As Rosaldo points out, all cultural traditions are the product of transcultural borrowing and lending, so that positing a space of purity becomes in effect an ideological exercise (1995:xv–xvi). Emphasizing that the popular exists always in relation to the hegemonic as both an alternative and an oppressed field of cultural production, García-Canclini (1993) identifies the real challenge for cultural activists not as how to preserve the pure products of a premodern subculture, but as how to empower the popular subject to take control of the means of his or her own production within the larger capitalist system. Paying people for their creative efforts does not distort their creativity unless one also robs them of their agency. However, leaner economic times may have restored to the festival the aesthetic of poverty that many in the neighborhood identify as central to the masquerade tradition.

In this generally depressed period, a new torovenado arose in the heart of Monimbó, entitled the Thirtieth of September Traditional Torovenado: Revival of Customs. Like the founders of the Torovenado del Pueblo in the 1960s, organizers of the Thirtieth of September Traditional Torovenado wanted to restore the torovenado to an *original* model. This time, however, the founders were Monimbó laborers rather than professionals. In September 1991, as the date for the religious procession approached, cofounders Bismark Suazo and Sebastián Gaitán Ortega lamented the fact that masquerades and dances had become separated from the procession itself and were now performed on subsequent Sundays in October and November. They decided to restore the torovenado to the procession on September 30. Both men quickly surveyed friends and managed to organize twelve for their first masquerade. This skit revived the torovenado that Abelino Eskorcia Zúniga had described in his 1979 pamphlet as the original torovenado from circa 1850. Suazo found a jaguar skin and made the mask. He mounted stuffed squirrels and monkeys on poles for other dancers to carry. And he recovered a beautiful wooden mask that Juan Herrera (b. 1900), a noted neighborhood dancer, had carved in his youth. In the first year, the group walked to the Saint Jerome religious procession accompanied by indigenous flute and drum music.

Because both Suazo and Gaitán were in recovery at the time, they implemented the Alcoholics Anonymous policy of not aligning with any other group in order to maintain their independence and singular purpose.[45] By the second year, they had invited a number of neighborhood residents who enjoyed masquerading, including Bosco Canales, to join them. The group eventually grew to about thirty masquerad-ers. Year after year they reenact their core values of enlivening the religious procession, mounting the jaguar masquerade, and emphasiz-ing poverty rather than finery. By collecting donations from neighbors, they embellish their procession with brass band music and fireworks, and they host a house prayer the evening before the masquerade. Yet the very low economic standing of most of the founding members and their commitment not to collaborate with any other organization have kept this torovenado small. In 2001, nine years after their first mas-querade, the group walked to the religious procession without musical accompaniment because they had not succeeded in raising the neces-sary funding.

The Thirtieth of September Traditional Torovenado attracts neither criticism nor strong participation from Monimboseños, for it consti-tutes a folklorization of a previous practice in order to *represent* the tradition. For example, although the sponsors host a religious prayer and therefore more closely approximate the form of a pre-1960s toro-venado, they do not perform the masquerade in order to fulfill a reli-gious vow. Rather, they perform to demonstrate what the torovenados used to look like. But this demonstration involves fixing one histori-cally documented topical caricature as the traditional form. The Thirti-eth of September Traditional Torovenado did not succeed in becoming the laborer's alternative to the Torovenado del Pueblo. In fact, sponsors of this torovenado continue to participate in the larger torovenados be-cause, they say, they enjoy dancing. Instead, as a literal reenactment of a former torovenado, it works as a historical skit, curtailing popular participation.

If during the Sandinista period the government supported and cel-ebrated the torovenados for their contestatory potential, the neoliberal insistence that folklore be self-supporting privileges a more conserva-tive, limited kind of masquerade. Monimboseños—festival sponsors, masqueraders, and neighborhood observers—now embrace a limiting definition of the popular. They identify strongly as the nation's tradi-tion bearers, an identity that reflects both their difference with respect to Managua and their revaluation of a previously maligned indigenous identity. Poverty, in this construction, carries the positive values of self-reliance, independence, and expressive authority. Yet their neighborhood is more urban, more divided by class and political polarization, less self-sufficient, and generally poorer than it once was. All these factors contribute to the transformation of the community that many experience as disintegration. By attempting to limit the torovenado masquerades to a nostalgic re-creation of a lost community, where money does not motivate creativity, festival organizers and participants have reproduced oppressive social relations in which Indians perform the nation's culture at their own cost. Moreover, the burden of creating culture without remuneration is greater than it once was. Ironically, all the torovenados are now resolutely modern because their primary purpose is to provide a cultural expression rather than to enact a religious ritual. Instead of engaging supernatural agents, who were once seen as the primary shapers of natural and social life, the modern masqueraders engage each other, the state, and even global human networks of exchange.

4 Spooks, Nostalgia, and Festival Innovation
The Ahuizotes of Monimbó

Although it is certainly true that a revolutionary state celebrated the torovenado's contestatory character, the festival's changing structure, style, and meanings reflect the underlying influence of increasing national integration and globally circulating goods and ideas. Discomfort with festival changes among some residents indicates not only differences in partisan ideologies, but also interests rooted in variously entwined class, ethnic, and sexual identities. Concern about the loss of local distinctiveness reveals an underlying anxiety about community disintegration. Yet the partial realignment of the torovenados to local notions of appropriateness has produced a sense of expressive decay. Nevertheless, as one might predict from the experiences of small communities elsewhere (Guss 2000:24–59; Magliocco 1988), local alienation from the larger torovenados resulting from the intrusion of foreign elements stimulated the creation of a parallel festival exclusively for indigenous-identified Monimbó, which succeeded in redrawing the line between local and other, autochthonous and alien forms of celebration.

The Procession of the Ahuizotes emerged from the Torovenado del Pueblo in 1981 as a nighttime masquerade of neighborhood spooks. By 1990, Monimboseños unanimously approved this new event as a positive innovation in festival practice. And in 2001, the Ahuizotes Procession, which now embraced all of Masaya, outstripped the Torovenado del Pueblo in popular participation. The enthusiastic acceptance and rapid growth of this new neighborhood tradition was a consequence of three interrelated features: the procession initially restored the masquerade to the neighborhood of Monimbó; it embraced a neighborhood aesthetic; and it avoided divisive issues of politics, religion, and sexual orientation. Moreover, as a new form it attracted women's active participation in a way that the torovenados had not, making visible the gendered nature of older masquerading traditions. Thus, the Ahuizotes Procession exhibited both conservative and progressive social impulses. At the same time, it fulfilled the neighborhood's need for symbolic integration, something the torovenados no longer accomplished effectively.

By the new millennium, however, this procession came under attack from two sides. Managua-based intellectuals, regarding the Ahuizotes Procession as an alarming invasion of the North American Halloween, began to voice the kinds of objections that Masaya residents had earlier lodged against the torovenados. This nationalist perspective, however, exaggerated the foreign elements of the masquerade. In Masaya, a growing number of youth gangs presented a much more tangible threat to the festival, as the playful invocation of horror carried over into all too real acts of violence. For the moment, residents continue to regard the Ahuizotes Procession as a nostalgic restoration of the neighborhood's supernatural past even as they incorporate more contemporary experiences with the supernatural in their masquerade imagery.

Monimbó's Supernatural Legacy

As is true elsewhere, supernatural phenomena in Masaya are associated with dark, isolated places. Before the 1980s, "había mucha cochinada" (there were a lot of evil/dirty things going on) in the neighborhood, Monimboseños say. The neighborhood maintained a rural ambience that was distinct from the rest of the city. Residents recall that it was sparsely populated, with only a few dim streetlamps lighting the way through uneven terrain. La Calle del Calvario, a major street, and Cailagua, a particular street corner just opposite the old National Guard post, were particularly popular with spooks—or, the doubters assert, with people impersonating spooks in order to frighten their neighbors.

The word *ahuizotes* generally means "strange, frightening phenomena" (winds, lights, noises) or signs of impending misfortune (*malos agüeros*). It also refers to a group of Nicaraguan phantoms, witches, and legendary figures. In Masaya, the most often mentioned are: La Mona (the monkey woman), Los Cadejos (a pair of black-and-white dogs with matted hair), La Carreta Nahua (the Death Cart), La Cegua (a horse-faced or skull-faced woman), and La Taconuda (a white woman with cavernous eyes who wears high-heel shoes and peers into people's windows). All of these characters can be found under other names throughout Mexico and Central America, indicating a shared cultural heritage and roots in pre-Columbian mythology. For instance, *cihua* means woman in Nahuatl, and the Cegua may be linked to the Aztec goddess Cihuacoatl—the woman with the serpent skirt, Quetzalcoatl's consort, who is both the progenitor and consumer of humans (León-Portillo 1972). Spanish Catholicism introduced the red-and-black devils Las Ánimas (three souls in purgatory) and El Condenado (the condemned man) to this regional stock of supernatural creatures.[1] Moreover, La Muerte Quilina (the skeleton), perhaps a universal symbol of death, holds a prevalent place in Monimbó's supernatural pantheon. What is important locally, however, is that the ahuizotes are autochthonous figures as opposed to foreign-identified ones, such as leprechauns, vampires, and witches on broomsticks.

Milagros Palma (1984), the only Nicaraguan author to collect supernatural legends systematically, asserts that these legends embody the terror of history. She argues that ordinary people retained the memory of the Conquest as a collective trauma and transmitted it in supernatural legends. This reading, which has become standard among Nicaraguan intellectuals and journalists, is suggestive for some figures. For instance, the Padre sin Cabeza (the Headless Priest) may represent Bishop Valdivieso, beheaded in 1549 for opposing Governor Pedrarías Dávila. In addition, the Carreta Nahua, a driverless cart filled with skeletons, may represent the genocide of the Conquest period. However, the most frequently mentioned traditional spooks in Masaya, the Cegua and the Mona, are not legendary phantoms at all, but human beings who have altered their appearance magically.

Nagualism, the notion that certain people have the ability to turn themselves into animals, remains current in local popular thinking. Therefore, a Monimboseño who encounters a peculiar animal while out late at night may consider it to be a real person, often female, who has shed her human form and adopted an animal form for malicious purposes. The Cegua is also understood to be a real person who has either vomited up her soul (Peña Hernández [1968] 1986) or shed her skin and flesh in order to transform herself. Usually, the flesh comes off from head to toe, and she leaves it in a tray or bowl, where her husband sometimes finds it and wittingly or unwittingly salts it so that she cannot resume her former shape.[2] Today, debates about the Cegua concern whether the figure is truly a transformed person or simply a woman in disguise. For instance, seventy-three-year-old doubter Rosa Colomer recalled that her father, a policeman in the pre-Somoza era, came across a Cegua one night. When he unmasked her, he discovered a neighbor woman who was trying to scare her husband.

However, many Monimbó men describe having met the Cegua when they were out late at night inebriated and alone. Their first-person accounts follow a common narrative pattern. The Cegua beckons to her victim, enticing him to follow her into graveyards or wild places. When he is disoriented and lost, she turns on him, revealing her hideous countenance. The fright can bring on high fever, insanity, and even death. The Cegua remains real enough in the modern imagination for wandering men to take precautions. In 1991, I went to a party in the countryside with a group of Monimboseños. We returned quite late, walking along a very dark dirt road. When we came into the lighted town, I noticed one man (who had gone to the party to see a woman who was not his wife) had turned his shirt inside out to ward off the Cegua.

That same year two teenage literacy workers reported that someone had caught a Mona and tied it to a tree in Valle de la Laguna, a rural settlement east of Monimbó. The Mona had escaped by the time I arrived to see her with my own eyes, but residents assured me that she had been real, a woman who had used magic incantations to transform herself into a monkey. In 2001, I visited María Bernabéla García, a Monimbó artisan in her sixties, to ask her about the ahuizotes. García, like Colomer, assured me that the Ceguas were human beings who disguised themselves to frighten wandering men. She herself had had several experiences with the Mona, however. One night her son came home inebriated and fell into his hammock. Soon he started complaining loudly, so his wife, who was sleeping naked in the next room, got up to see what the matter was. She found a Mona rocking him violently. Picking up a broom, she smacked it, and the creature ran off. A few days later the young wife noticed that a neighbor woman had a bandage on her shoulder and front just where the broom had caught the Mona. She surmised that it had been this neighbor who had caused the mischief. In this account, the Mona functionally replaces the Cegua as a transformed woman who threatens inebriated men.

García also recalled that her husband had come across a Mona sleeping with a bunch of chickens. He gave the creature a nudge with the wooden end of his machete and said, "Come, friend, it's almost daylight, wake up." The Mona rubbed its eyes just like a waking person, gathered up the chickens, and ran off. A week or so later a stranger came looking for García's husband. The stranger introduced himself by name and thanked him. "What for?" asked García's husband. "Another man would have killed me, having found me sleeping there. Thank you for not killing me." At the end of her story, García turned to me and said, "You see? It was the Mona." Finally, García related her own encounter with a Mona on a street nearby. The Mona was herding a bunch of chickens, but the chickens didn't make a sound because, García said, the Mona had enchanted them. García emphasized that she wasn't afraid of these creatures because she knew they were "Christians like us." Thus, for her, the Mona is a real person, not a phantom, and should not be feared.[3]

Certainly, contemporary Monimboseños exhibit a range of beliefs in and attitudes about ahuizotes, just as contemporary North Americans display a variety of interpretive stances with regard to the supernatural. Nevertheless, Monimboseños generally agree that recent physical changes have reduced the frequency of supernatural phenomena in the neighborhood. Indeed, during the last quarter of the twentieth century, Masaya urbanized rapidly, both as a consequence of internal population growth and of in-migration from the surrounding rural areas.[4] From a population of 31,000 in 1971, Masaya grew to 89,000 in 1995 and then to 114,000 in 2002, and Monimbó consistently housed about one-quarter of the city's population until 1995.[5] The densely populated neighborhood now houses 30,000 people and is no longer visibly distinct from other parts of Masaya. With the revolution, community-improvement brigades, international development projects, and government initiatives leveled the cliffs, paved the major streets, extended streetlights, replaced thatch-and-cane housing with more closely spaced cement block units, and built new housing on open fields. As a consequence of such development, residents explain, encounters with ahuizotes have diminished considerably in Monimbó.

Nevertheless, technological transformations do not so easily transform habits of thought. As Linda Degh has pointed out with regard to North Americans, people adapt remarkably easily to change even as they "hang onto their hereditary values and keep stubbornly to their traditions" (2001:425). Indeed, she argues that legends and supernatural beliefs emerge from internal human needs that remain fairly constant over time.[6] The Cegua, for instance, may embody feelings of guilt or at least ambivalence on the part of men. Although a prevailing machista ideology encourages drinking and philandering as a means of demonstrating one's masculinity (Lancaster 1995), this behavior also strains relations within one's primary household and family, creating a cultural double-bind. My own sample of stories is too small to be representative; however, it suggests, first, that only men encounter the Cegua and, second, that women are more likely than men to reject her authenticity. Thus, first-person accounts of the Cegua appear to represent, at least in Monimbó, a stable narrative performance form based on an experience that is limited to men.[7] Although beliefs in these figures are dispersed over a wide geographic area, Monimboseños consider them to be autochthonous to the neighborhood.

In Monimbó, encounters with ahuizotes also include experiences with shadowy figures, frightening noises, and shimmering clouds of light. Traditional wisdom dictated in the past that if one observed something unusual, it was better not to investigate for fear of attracting evil. Therefore, many ahuizotes, such as the Carreta Nahua, were recognized only by the sound they made as they passed because no one dared look at them.[8] Each individual was left to imagine the identity of the shape in the shadows. Luís Méndez, a laborer in his forties, demonstrated to me how such beliefs become manifest in narrative, when the narrator does look. He recalled walking along a country road one night and finding his way barred by a dead man covered with flies. Remembering his father's advice to confront anything that won't let you pass, he found a club and moved toward the carcass. When he got there, Méndez recalled, the ahuizote had transformed into a harmless pile of leaves. Thus, Méndez's discovery did not lead him to doubt his earlier vision. Rather, it confirmed that what he had seen was, in fact, an ahuizote.

Moreover, in contemporary legend-telling sessions, encounters with traditional spooks are often mixed with those of more contem-

Figure 4.1 Masked youths in the 2001 Ahuizotes Procession.

porary figures, such as mass murderers and Satan. In 2001, Adolfo Colomer recalled a narrow escape from murder at the hands of a wartime
psychopath, known only as M-16, shortly after the revolution. Significantly, M-16 harbored a special hatred for Monimboseños. Thus, the
internationally recognizable figure of the insane serial killer became lo-
calized, dressed in the historical particularities of Masaya, and person-
alized as part of the narrator's direct experience. Internationally recognizable supernatural figures also appear to take on the characteristics of
local embodiments of evil. For instance, Méndez described a harrowing
encounter with Satan while he was sleeping in his own bed and how
he was forced to wrestle repeatedly with his visitor. However, when he
correctly identified and named his opponent, "the man, his face—his
flesh began to peel off, the flesh fell to the ground from his head to his

feet, and all that was left was a skeleton standing in front of me. Then he disappeared from my sight. I'm narrating this because it's a real-life experience, something present just as I am here, you and I are present."[9] In this narrative, Satan changes from human form to a skeleton much as a Cegua would. Clearly, Monimbó's supernatural tradition represents a mixture of indigenous, Catholic, and contemporary images and ideas that combine in various ways. The ahuizote comprehends at least four distinct classes of phenomena: (1) unusual, frightening sounds or sights, (2) legendary phantoms, (3) real people who have transformed themselves into nonhuman forms or are dangerously insane, and (4) evil apparitions.

Impersonating the Ahuizotes

The Festival or Procession of the Ahuizotes began in 1981 with the formation of the Ahuizotes Jurídicos, a group of lawyers from Monimbó, younger associates of the Torovenado del Pueblo organizers. Donald Ortega's daughter, Dolores, remembered that the organizers affectionately nicknamed them Los Cadejos because they tagged along after the organizers wherever they went.[10] These young people had mounted a successful torovenado skit representing Monimbó's supernatural inhabitants. In 1981, they sponsored a nighttime procession for the Friday before the Torovenado del Pueblo that would circulate only through Monimbó. Their masquerade immediately caught on with community residents, who formed a parallel festival, the Ahuizotes Populares. Like torovenado masqueraders, ahuizotes cavort and dance to *sones de toro* (literally, bull songs) played by local brass bands. In 1991, neighborhood resident Roger Muñoz explained, "The ahuizotes go out only in Monimbó. At the level of the neighborhood people go out spontaneously. They make their own costumes, and they go out of their own accord. That Friday, the day of the Ahuizotes, I prepare my costume without anyone having invited me. While the Ahuizotes Jurídicos are organized, and so they have to go out in this parade through the streets of Monimbó."[11] In spite of its recent origin, the festival was quickly approved as a tradition in Monimbó because it responded to the localist, community aesthetic for festival masquerade.

Until 1998, the paraders did not descend to the town center to visit

Saint Jerome. Instead, they confined their wanderings to the neighborhood of Monimbó. Participation was and remains open and spontaneous. A core group of organized individuals form a parade, neighborhood residents join them at will, and when the parade ends, they all continue on through the streets until late at night, making mischief. Moreover, participants employ simple costumes that, in their emphasis on the ugly and the grotesque and in their reliance on homemade or locally produced materials, approximate the local masquerading aesthetic that neighbors regard as appropriate for a torovenado. Masqueraders typically wear a loose-fitting, long-sleeved, white or black Dacron hooded gown that covers their entire body. They may drag a string of tin cans behind them, wear chains, or carry wooden staffs, crosses, machetes, or plastic baby dolls. Local mask makers produce the inexpensive papier-mâché masks most participants wear. Most popular are masks of bloody ghouls, skulls, and horned devils. This kind of masquerading capitalizes on the grotesque but avoids overtly sexual imagery. The category confusion the Ahuizotes Procession exploits is that between the living and the dead rather than that between genders. The procession itself functions to recall nostalgically a not so distant past, as one day a year the spooks that used to frequent the neighborhood return. At the same time, connections between contemporary experience and nostalgia remain strong, for residents continue to relate and debate supernatural encounters in their everyday conversations.

Once established, the Ahuizotes Procession rapidly accreted festival activities. Thus, on the Thursday prior to the procession, sponsors hold a *vela*, or a candlelight vigil, with food, drink, music, and the *palo lucio*, or greased pole (a traditional festival game), for anyone who wishes to attend. Here the organized Ahuizotes display the costumes they will use on the following day, imitating *la vela del vestido*, a neighborhood tradition that town-center residents disparage.[12] The group also elects an Ahuizotes queen, a teenage girl dressed ghoulishly, who leads the procession.[13] However, even as the Ahuizotes Procession has grown larger than the Torovenado del Pueblo from which it emerged, it lacks the formal structuring of its parent. Miguel Bolaños remarked in 2001, "We think it's easier to organize an Ahuizotes [Procession] than a torovenado, because the Ahuizotes is spontaneous, and we're not wasting money on giving out prizes, this and that. People come, their mothers come disguised with the children. We don't have to do as much. In contrast, the torovenado on Sunday, it's more complicated because we have to organize them, we have to direct them, we have to keep them going. It takes time. With the Ahuizotes, they go on their own." Thus, the Ahuizotes Procession remains a popular manifestation with minimal intervention even by the festival organizing committee. The prizes that some had viewed as distorting the popular character of the torovenados were never introduced.[14] Even so, the event grew, demonstrating that other motives besides mercantilism, on the one hand, and religious fervor, on the other, support festival performance. The Ahuizotes Procession attends not to discarded performances, but to the tradition in the form of celebration itself, with content that, if not confined to historical imagery, speaks to community members' present needs and imagination to represent for themselves a cultural past.

Whereas the torovenados began to overwhelm the community with masquerades that some found objectionable on ideological or moral grounds, the Ahuizotes Procession, with its more strictly defined representational purpose and scope, has avoided conflict and fulfills Monimbó's need for a festival of its own. Ahuizotes dancers carry no signs or other messages expressing partisanship. Some may dress as nuns and priests, but they do not masquerade as identifiable religious leaders or images that other community members venerate. Moreover, the costumes the masqueraders employ are concealing rather than revealing. The lascivious transvestism that alienated some residents when it emerged in the torovenados is absent in this event. In some ways, then, the Ahuizotes Procession was the response to a conservative social impulse after the liberatory excesses of the torovenado.

By 1998, the procession had gotten so large that Torovenado del Pueblo organizers conceded to the Ahuizotes Jurídicos' wishes and allowed the procession to leave Monimbó. It descended to the Church of Saint Jerome and returned to the Magdalena Plaza in almost as large a circuit as the torovenado processions. Thus, the Ahuizotes Processions embraced all of Masaya, and some residents even claimed that youth were now arriving by bus from nearby towns to participate. Masqueraders now process through the streets accompanied by large crowds of unmasked supporters—the maskers, in effect, carrying their audience. Youth delight in lighting aerosol sprays on fire, brandishing small dead rats or iguanas in the faces of unwary bystanders, or shaking chains to menace onlookers. Throughout the four-hour procession, the lively brass bands provoke occasional spontaneous dancing. When the masqueraders ultimately return to the Magdalena Plaza in the heart of Monimbó at about midnight, all the masqueraders dance to a rousing final number, suggesting the kind of collective group performance one finds in a Caribbean Mas'. Then the crowds disperse into small groups that melt away into the night.

Masquerading Women

As a new form, the Ahuizotes Procession also responded to progressive impulses. Participation by women who had played largely a supportive role in the torovenado masquerades actually increased. Indeed, although men continue to outnumber women in all masquerades, substantial participation by women distinguishes the Ahuizotes Procession from the traditional torovenados. Residents argue that women and families prefer the nighttime masquerade because it is cooler. The dark and the costumes also conceal them from too much public exposure. Dolores Ortega suggests that the evening is a time when women are generally free from household tasks that might limit their participation in a daytime masquerade. But the most convincing reason for women's greater participation in the Ahuizotes is that it provides an opening for women that the already male-defined torovenados do not.

Indeed, although participants rarely acknowledge the predominantly male character of torovenados, these masquerades have a reputation for roughness, with their arduous route in the hot sun, heavy drinking, rude themes, and, in the larger torovenados, fierce jostling for prizes. From an outsider's perspective, the torovenado is a carnival of homosexuals (Lancaster 1997:19), and the few women who do participate are marginal—drunks or prostitutes. Yet Monimboseño Carlos Centeno was surprised when I asked why women didn't participate in the torovenados because he had never thought of this community tradition as limited to men. As in carnivalesque festivals in other Latin American towns, the masculine character of torovenados may be the consequence of unintentional exclusion. For instance, Dow reports that some Mexican Sierra Otomí masqueraders "were especially excited because of a rumor that a young woman was going to dance with them; however, she did not appear. As usual, the atmosphere of revelry was a little too rough. The drinking might get heavy, lewd language and gestures might be used, and women are reluctant to associate themselves in public with these particular male excesses" (1988:176). This reluctance, of course, is related to real social consequences for a woman whose reputation is compromised, even though, in Masaya at least, the small number of women who have participated in the torovenado have been neither prostitutes nor drunks. Instead, they are women of higher than average education whose families are heavily involved in either organizing or participating in the Torovenado del Pueblo.

Estela Rodriguez, sister of the Torovenado del Pueblo martyrs Elías and Reyes Rodriguez, participated in the Torovenado del Pueblo as an ahuizote before the Ahuizotes Procession became a separate event. However, she recalled that her mother objected strongly to women taking part in the masquerade:

> My mother said it was vagrancy. All of my brothers went out, and of my sisters, I'm the only one who likes these things. None of my sisters has gone in these processions, only me. Then when I had children, I went out with them—the Ahuizotes at night and in the Torovenado masquerading. No one recognized me. In *that* torovenado [the Ahuizotes Procession], men and women go out. But for my mother it was taboo. So watching the people go out, I loved it. "Ah," I said, "some day I'm going to go out." And the opportunity to go out presented itself the first time. And afterwards—all this has happened after I grew up—my children all go out, as ahuizotes.[15]

Rodriguez emphasized that the strength of the social taboo against women's participation initially thwarted her own desire to join the torovenado and continued to dissuade other women—her sisters, for instance—from participating. Masquerading as an ahuizote in the Torovenado del Pueblo provided her initial break from tradition, and it is interesting that she mentioned others' failure to recognize her as an important factor in the experience. Once Rodriguez became an ahuizote, however, participation in both masquerades became a family activity that both the male and female youth of her household enjoy.

Dolores Ortega, who became the director of the Torovenado del

Figure 4.2 Ninoska Jarquín performs a traditional parody in 2001 while playing with the audience's assumption that festival transvestism represents male shamelessness.

Pueblo in 2000, had participated in the torovenado masquerade since childhood because she liked it. Insisting that women always masqueraded, she recalled in 2001, "The person who taught me marimba and torovenado was my mom. And my mom traditionally participated in the torovenado every year, and she went out secretly. Since my father [Donald Ortega] was going out in his organizations, he didn't know, and my mom went out with her female neighbors."[16] Although Dolores insisted the Torovenado del Pueblo has included both male and female masqueraders, she emphasized that her mother engaged in a double deceit in order to participate. This kind of secret masquerading strongly contrasts with the open environment of the contemporary Ahuizotes Procession, where mothers are recognized participants.

Recent studies of festival change point to women's increasingly active roles in festival enactments globally, but describe different dynamics for women's inclusion in different places. In the Cuzco region of Peru, for example, youth imported a mixed-sex dance from another region into their Saint Jerome Festival because the local traditional dances excluded women (Mendoza 2000:207–32). In Venezuela, after the mixed-sex Tamunangue dance was nationalized in the 1940s, the new stage presentations that followed allowed women to take a more active, assertive role in the dance. Women now perform all aspects of the dance and music, those traditionally delegated to women as well as those formerly reserved for men. Indeed, some contemporary female performers have turned the dance on its head to assert women's power over men (Guss 2000:129–72).

Similarly, as female masqueraders entered rural Cajun Mardi Gras celebrations, they took greater liberties with the masquerade leader than men would (Ware 1995). As late as 1977, Lombardi Satriani could argue that the absence of women and women's perspectives in popular cultural enactments provided a strong qualification to the notion of folklore as culture of contestation. More recently, Patricia Sawin (2002) has pointed out that an aesthetic model of performance that does not take into account the complex interaction of emotion and desire in performer-audience interactions obscures barriers to women's performance. Competence in performance is always already a gendered concept, and, for women, performing one's gender competently can be directly at odds with taking responsibility for an act of cultural representation. Contemporary studies of women's festival participation suggest that women performers use traditional arts to critique and contest male dominance. The entrance of women masqueraders into formerly all-male traditions can be seen as the most revolutionary of all transformations in popular culture, reflecting not only the global broadening of women's participation in all aspects of society, but also a move toward self-representation and self-definition.

Yet one must not overstate the oppositional nature of women's performances, at least with regard to spontaneous popular performances such as the Ahuizotes Procession of Monimbó. Although emerging Nicaraguan women writers and artists developed a strong feminist voice in the 1980s and 1990s, artistic and sexual liberation was restricted largely to the most affluent or politically connected sectors, who participated in a global circulation of progressive ideas about the artificiality of the sexual double standard (Beverly and Zimmerman 1990:87–94, 104–7). Feminists continued to push for social change during the 1990s as the movement shifted from state-controlled organizations to independent groups operating within civil society. Nevertheless, entrenched attitudes and the social disarray that accompanied the deepening poverty of the neoliberal 1990s hampered this important work (Babb 2001; Chávez Metoyer 2000; see also Howe 2003 and Whisnant 1995:383–433).

In fact, women's participation in public playfulness remains constrained in various ways. In 1991, Carlos Centeno remarked, "In the Ahuizotes, children, youth, adults, women, everybody participates. Although the woman goes out, she has to ask her husband's permission because machismo exists here. If a man likes the tradition or simply if he likes it, he goes out with a couple of drinks in him, and he puts on a costume with an idiotic rag, and he goes making mischief. But the young girls also go out. In other words, it's a popular festival in which everybody participates."[17] Centeno's description indicates a gradual loosening of strictures against women's frivolity, with young women participating more freely than those who are already matrons.

The performance history of Monimboseña Ninoska Jarquín, nineteen years old in 2001, illuminates how some women negotiate a more active role in festival enactments. A student of economics at the national university, Jarquín actively participated in the torovenados, the Ahuizotes Procession, and a marimba youth group, Los Chorotega, from 1997 to 2001. Her decision to marry in that year provoked her retirement from the marimba group, as it would be unseemly, she explained, for a married woman to continue dancing with unmarried youth.[18] However, she viewed her participation in the torovenado as a family inheritance from her father, who has participated since childhood. Before agreeing to marry, she insisted on the right to continue participating in the torovenado with a group of gay male friends, a condition to which her future husband acceded.

Qualifying Dolores Ortega's claims that women have always participated in the torovenado, Jarquín asserted that female masqueraders remain rare. In fact, she delighted in the shock value of her performance:

I don't take my mask off during the whole route of the torovenado, but people, now people know who is a man and who is a woman. And so the people say—the majority, as you know, are cochones who go out—the people say, "She's not a man, she's a woman." And so, inside my mask that I'm wearing, I'm enjoying that because it's true. So, when the torovenado ends, when we get to the San Sebastian Church and the parade is over, so, I decide to take off my mask, so that people realize that I'm not the same as the rest. And so the people say, "Oh look, eeeh [breathes in], that girl isn't embarrassed to go out in that, look! And look how she dances!" Because I like to dance and all, but I feel proud to inherit this tradition because I feel it in my blood.[19]

Jarquín's delight in the evident failure of her masquerade seems paradoxical on the surface, but it reveals how gender impersonations are and are not the point of torovenado masquerades. Interestingly, she does not engage in cross-dressing. Even so, she challenges gender categories, for the underlying assumption in the tradition is that masquerading is a male activity that requires a characteristically male shamelessness. However, like other Monimboseños, Jarquín regards the torovenado as a nostalgic display of identity, not the radical challenge to *natural* identities that some carnival scholars identify as the form's major contestatory thrust. She participates because she likes to carry on neighborhood traditions and because she delights in the dance. The skits she and her friends have represented—"Monimbó Indian Women Adorning the Lord of Miracles with Flowers," "Monimbó Indian Women Candy Sellers," "Indian Women Selling Vegetables in the Streets of Monimbó," and "Monimbó Indian Women Visiting a Wake"—all emphasize traditional characters from the neighborhood. Rather than ridiculing these characters, the parody becomes a humorous homage to them.

Moreover, Jarquín insisted that her identity as a woman, even within the context of a largely gay male display, is easy to spot. Likewise, Dolores Ortega believes that torovenado masquerading creates little confusion among audiences about the participants' genders. She told me, "Behind a costume, one never knows if it's a man or woman. But we distinguish her by the detail. If the dress is short, in the legs, and if it's long, in the dance. Women dance more sedately; the man is more rapid and agitated. And she stays quiet, the man no. He stops dancing, and he goes messing around, greeting people, yelling. Even at night, with the Ahuizotes, we know it's a woman." Thus, women's limited entrance into the torovenados and greater presence in the Ahuizotes reflects both a loosening of restrictions on women's public playfulness and a continuation of gendered interaction styles in which men are active and at home in the public sphere, whereas women, even masquerading women, are more restrained.

National Anxieties and Halloween

Even though Monimboseños celebrate the Ahuizotes Procession as a return to tradition, nationalist intellectuals in Managua question the festival's authenticity, partly as a consequence of how they frame the cultural practice. In 1998, Wilmor López, Nicaragua's leading folklore documentarian, asserted that Nicaragua has no informed, critical culture because everything has become adulterated. The problem resulted not from the adoption of foreign customs such as Halloween, López argued, but from a failure to know and value Nicaragua's autochthonous traditions. He interpreted the Ahuizotes Procession as a display of ancestral indigenous spirits, the gods of the Chorotega, the Nagrandans, and even the Caribs.[20] This view, of course, extends Monimbó's nostalgia for the neighborhood's recently departed supernaturals several centuries backward and identifies the Monimbó innovation as nationally important to the preservation of cultural memory in a time of global change.

Soon, however, Halloween became the enemy of the Ahuizotes Procession. In October 2000, scholar Edgard Escobar decried the popularity of North American Halloween in Nicaragua, which he viewed as not only foreign, but Satanic, a blood rite that breeds hatred in youth. Escobar mounted a library exhibit of traditional ahuizotes at the Central Bank Library to instruct Nicaraguan youth in their own supernatural tradition.[21] These figures, he asserted, were neither pagan nor bloodthirsty.[22] When a television reporter questioned the importance of Escobar's effort, writer Julio Valle Castillo came to his support, branding as neocolonialists those who would scorn what were now described as Nicaragua's national spooks.

Valle Castillo further identified Masayans' Ahuizotes Procession as a confusion of the autochthonous torovenado with the foreign Halloween and warned that all hybrid forms are sterile.[23] Such sweeping journalistic pronouncements reflect anxiety about U.S. cultural imperialism in a period when North American social, political, and business influence in Managua is palpable. In fact, in the October 25, 2001, issue of *La Prensa* an advertisement for a Halloween party at the upscale Cocibolca Jockey Club appeared immediately below the coverage of the Masaya torovenados. The close relationship between Managua and Miami and the steady stream of people moving back and forth between the two metropolises since 1990 has contributed to a marked American cultural influence, particularly among middle-class residents. Yet such anxiety has not led to the growth of Ahuizotes Processions in Nicaraguan cities where Halloween is currently practiced. Instead, it has resulted in criticism of the Monimbó festival enactment.

Brandes (1998) reports similar disquiet among Mexican intellectuals with the appearance of Halloween symbols and customs in Mexico. In this case, Mexico's structural equivalent—the Day (or Nights) of the Dead—has acquired a new political meaning as something very Mexican in opposition to U.S. cultural imports. Brandes notes that state tourist agencies actively promote the Day of the Dead in certain indigenous communities. This has led to elaborations of the tradition and even to invented traditions in these areas. Thus, Mexican nationalists project onto indigenous communities the responsibility for maintaining and displaying national culture for both Mexican nationals and foreigners.

Similarly, Managuans care about what Masayans are doing because Masaya has long been conceived as a repository of national traditions. Thus, what Masayans do signals the health of traditional culture generally. However, with regard to its underlying form, the Ahuizotes is not even a structural equivalent of North American Halloween, for Halloween is essentially a form of ritual begging, whereas the Ahuizotes remains fundamentally a processional dance. Moreover, the festival date is dictated by the date of the torovenado, which bears little connection to All Saints' or All Souls' Day.[24] Nor does the masquerade symbolism reveal much specific Halloween imagery. In 2001, the most obvious foreign influence was a plastic mask from a Hollywood horror movie, *The Scream*, modeled after Edvard Munch's famous painting of the same name. One group of teenagers had decided to dispense with masks altogether and simply paint their faces ghoulishly with black and white grease paint, a choice that some Monimboseños considered Halloweenish. However, these individuals were far outnumbered by those sporting beastlike, skeletal, devilish, and pustuled, blood-dripping ghoul masks, the majority of which are produced by local mask makers.

In fact, over the past ten years, the popularity of the Ahuizotes Procession has produced a marked growth in mask making. In 1991, of four recognized mask makers in Masaya, only one, Norlan Méndez Briceño, specialized in ahuizotes masks.[25] He was both the youngest and the most innovative of the four. Torovenado festival masks were traditionally made of gourds, carved wood, or painted cardboard. Yet by the 1980s two Masaya Diablitos directors had already developed painted papier-mâché masks for their festival dancers. Briceño explained that he examined these masks and experimented with his own materials until he finally arrived at his present process. He works newspaper, water, and glue into a fine claylike consistency, which he then sculpts onto stone molds. After sanding the dried masks, he paints them with bright acrylic paint. In 2001, Briceño's son, Cristian, joined his father in the production of ahuizotes masks, and the daughter of another mask maker and a fourth man took up the trade. The Ahuizotes Procession provides an ambulatory gallery for this developing local mask-making industry.

Still, one might argue that the ghouls reflect a colonization of the local imagination by Hollywood slasher movies, but only if one can establish a direct identification; otherwise, the production of ghoulish masks or painted faces represents at most a transcultural adaptation and might in fact register the native tradition of supernatural imagery. I asked Briceño how he developed ideas for his masks, and he confided that he worked from personal experience with ahuizotes, from the stories other people had shared with him, from stories printed in the newspapers and popular magazines, and from his own imagination. Surely, internationally disseminated horror movie imagery may contribute to his aesthetic. Yet the similarity between many of the modern masks and nineteenth-century examples preserved in the nearby museum in Nindirí are also striking.

Cultural nationalists, who do not participate in the procession, would like Monimboseños to guard the national traditions by sticking to an antiquated and limiting conception of ahuizotes. Their major sources are books, with legends that are fixed for all time through writing. Their major paradigm is historical. For them, folk culture consists of traditions, of past practices and beliefs. Monimboseños, however, understand themselves as the nation's tradition bearers and therefore as the people most capable of describing what popular belief is. And so for their masquerades they draw on their own complex experiences with the supernatural.

Even though nationalists (and even some Monimboseños) decry the current scarcity of Ceguas and abundance of bloody ghouls, the Ahuizotes Procession has embraced from its inception an expansive vision of supernatural traditions. Estela Rodriguez, who organized a formal group of forty Ahuizotes Populares in the 1980s, described a typical skit:

> There's a legend about the bride who waited for her groom. When he didn't arrive, she killed herself. And so she remained in her bride's dress, with the skull mask. We presented this skit as well, dancing to the brass bands.
>
> We performed the skit of the burial. We had a coffin that we had sent out to be made. We used brass bands, and we mixed it with death marches. We had a tape of howls and screeches that we played as well—the howls of the wolf, of the dead—so as to instill fear. And so, we put this music on, and the procession entered slowly, slowly. With the coffin. And the people screamed and the little children crying. We had fun. And then we put the coffin down, the boys who were carrying it, all with white skulls, dressed in black. And a hand came out of the coffin. And the coffin opened with a great noise. And a girl, the dead person, rose out of the coffin. And the people screamed, eh? It was really impressive, fun. And then we started with the dancing music: "La gallina," "La bomba," "El guaro blanco."[26] In the street, we went out dancing, always with the coffin, but we didn't perform a skit. We went dancing along the street, the same characters but without the skit.

The organized Ahuizotes Populares thus imagine skits that are general depictions of scary phenomena—recognizable scenes, if not legends, from the neighborhood's store of supernatural imagery. Moreover, the grotesque delight of the presentations rests in alternately scaring audiences and amusing them with joyful, energetic festival dancing.[27] In the local understanding, Ahuizotes are neither limited to a particular set of historical characters nor stuck within a slavish imitation of a North American custom. Instead, Monimboseños draw on a broad range of images for their innovative torovenado.

Gang Violence

At the same time, rough play now threatens to transform the family-friendly nature of the Ahuizotes Procession. Ninoska Jarquín stopped participating in 2000 because another masquerader, whom she didn't know, began hitting her. When she told him to stop, he apologized, claiming that he thought she was someone else, but the experience bothered her enough to prevent her from masquerading the following year. More alarming, in 2001 a local gang arrived at the procession armed with real chains, clubs, and machetes that they wielded in a threatening manner. The procession's organizers quickly disarmed this band, but in a separate incident a drunken masquerader brandishing a yardstick embedded with six-inch nails cornered a group of adults and children and managed to drive one nail through a young man's skull. When a third masquerader tried to intervene, the attacker drove a nail through his arm. Given the setting, police were unable to identify the aggressor. Residents were concerned that the violence appeared completely unmotivated because the victims were not involved in gang activity.

Although youth gangs have traditionally formed part of the neighborhood, in the past they either functioned to protect the community's borders from outside intruders (Breso 1992; Gould 1998) or engaged in relatively contained fighting among themselves. Today, these groups are a visible sign of the rampant unemployment and general social malaise that has characterized the neoliberal period. In Monimbó, groups of young men congregate on identifiable corners to pass the long days and nights together, drinking, socializing, and sniffing glue. Neighbors observe them with dismay, cautioning visitors and one another to be wary because the gangs can be unpredictable. Unfortunately, the Ahuizotes masquerade provides an ideal cover for antisocial behavior. Unlike the Notting Hill Carnival in London, where gang violence is arguably an expression of political opposition to the police-protected establishment (Cohen 1993), gang violence during the Ahuizotes Procession appears to be a sign of community disintegration. How organizers and participants will deal with this threat over the long run remains to be seen.

Belief

Representing evil in festival can take two very different forms, depending on the degree to which communities believe in the masquerade. For example, indigenous Mexican and Central American carnivals traditionally exorcised evil by impersonating it through a variety of recognizable, traditional enemies, both real and supernatural. In Chiapas, such masqueraders were required to run barefoot over hot coals at the end of the festival (Bricker 1973). Currently, in the Pascoleras of the northern Mexican Mayo, wild spirits take over the community during Holy Week. At the end of the festival, however, the community banishes these spirits, ceremonially burning their masks (Crumrine 1983; see also Schechner 1993:94–130). In these festivals, masqueraders actually embody evil and require purification. This does not mean that every participant equates the masquerade actor with the evil character he plays, only that the community behaves as if this were so.[28] Such festivals display a ritual frame.

In contrast, a masking festival such as New York City's Greenwich Village Halloween Parade essentially adopts the play frame, implying no real encounter with evil. It showcases creative artistry, visual punning, social and political critique, and extravagant display. Although evil remains a theme for the Halloween Parade, preserving public safety in a practical rather than a cosmic sense now dictates the form of the event (Kugelmass 1991). Likewise, Masaya's Procession of the Ahuizotes sports ghoulish figures who dance through the night to the music of *chicheros* or local brass bands in playful celebration. Within the event itself, no identifiable ritual occurs. Even the ritual gesture of visiting the Saint Jerome Church was not introduced until 1998. And yet the festival asserts community, even if that community is now embattled by a new set of challenges to its integrity.

Local reaction to the nationalization or commercialization of community festivals has often been characterized as a return to religiosity—a matter of restoring the ritual or sacred dimension that has been lost in the celebratory show. For instance, García-Canclini notes a "tendency in capitalist modernization to secularize traditional events while rescuing their symbols if they can lead to higher profits" (1993:97). Yet he continues to recognize a kind of resistance to such commercialization among certain pre-Columbian rituals and Catholic processions (1993:102). Guss describes an annual tourist invasion of Venezuela's tiny Curiepe for a Festival of San Juan that had become for outsiders "an African bacchanal dedicated to drums, drugs, and free love" (2000:42). As the community reasserted control over the meaning of the public festival, they also created a parallel festival, an evening prayer, for residents only. This local reappropriation of the festival relocated it from the central square to the ruins of a church, recuperated the central cultural-religious figure, San Juan Congo, and reinserted religious reverence as a core festival activity, along with drinking, eating, and drumming.

Even the Greenwich Village Halloween Parade, Kugelmass reports, began as a sort of neoritual, but this core activity was quickly overwhelmed by ludic, carnivalesque celebration. Nevertheless, Kugelmass argues that "festival without ritual is hardly worth the effort" (1991:456), an attitude that leads him to identify a ritualizing tendency in costumes that mythologize rather than parody or satirize. One might argue that the Ahuizotes Procession also references the mythic dimension of the neighborhood, as opposed to the political and social targets of the torovenado masquerade, but such a view would distort the event's playful spontaneity. The move toward ritual, important as it is for restoring a community to itself, is but one of the available choices for communities under assault. The Ahuizotes Procession provides another model, where the community's understanding of itself as the source of cultural traditions continually generates new festival forms to mark that reputation. It is no less secular than Monimbó's torovenados, yet it has succeeded in integrating the community at least for the past two decades in a collective burlesque of the supernatural that both recovers a local aesthetic of grotesque masquerade and extends participation to all.

Part III November Dances

5 Constructing Hierarchies in Folk Dance

The Negras Reign Supreme

Monimboseños traditionally venerated Saint Jerome not only by taking out raggedly dressed groups of torovenados, but also by organizing elegant sets of marimba dancers: the Inditas discussed in chapter 2 and the all-male groups called Negras, in which half the members masquerade as women. If the carnivalesque torovenado expressed a desire to make the divinity laugh, the Negras, in contrast, addressed secular authorities, enacting a parody of Spanish court dancing by employing, despite the name, fine, whiteface, wire-mesh masks to conceal their identities. Parody, however, contains a conservative dimension because it implies homage as well as critique (Hutcheon 2000:15–16).

The humorous grotesqueries of the torovenados and ahuizotes have no place in the marimba performances that today continue to follow them in the festival calendar. Instead, marimba groups value refinement in movement as well as costume, enacting an ideal of restrained elegance and grace. These performances conform to a Mexican and Central American festival aesthetic that combines male cross-dressing with elegance, modernity, and whiteness, a constellation of characteristics that participants and anthropologists recognize as opposed to indigeneity (Bricker 1973; Esser 1988a, 1988b; Lechuga 1988; see also Mendoza 2000).[1] In Masaya, the Negras Dance is currently associated with better-off residents of the town center, who claim responsibility for elaborating its elegant artifice in contrast to the less interesting Inditas Dance of Monimbó, now no longer performed.

Scholars of Mexican and Central American community festivals, noting the unidirectional, male-to-female character of festival transvestism, have generally regarded it as a form of social control that male authorities exert over women (Brandes 1988; Bricker 1973; Esser 1983). According to this view, female impersonators in Michoacán, Mayan, and Tarascan carnival taught real Indian women how not to behave by masquerading as mestizas, a group that Indians regarded as immoral and other. Bricker observes that Zinacantan carnival performances of the 1960s worked to reinforce the ideal of womanhood by having cross-dressers perform women's work badly: "The Grandfathers often join in the humorous 'lesson' by picking out specific women to scold for being poor spinners and weavers. The women who have been chosen for such special comment pull back in real dismay and embarrassment, covering their mouths with their hands and pulling their shawls across their faces" (1973:20). Notwithstanding the validity of such instances of humorous didacticism, this overall explanation of festival transvestism appears reductive because the discussion of scripted social purposes eliminates any notion of play or serendipity.[2] Moreover, the assertion that such communication is unambiguously heterosexual ignores both the practice of homosexuality in these communities and the opportunities that festival performances provide for playing with categories of gender and sexual identity.

In contrast, scholars of sexuality view transvestism as a symbol of category confusion that may encompass much more than the gender order. Lancaster identifies the Nicaraguan (men and women's) delight with male cross-dressing in both festival and everyday performance contexts as rooted in its profoundly equivocal and multiply signifying character. The impersonator is "now a woman, now a cochón (male homosexual), now a low-class prostitute, now a refined and affected matron, now negra (black), now blanca (white), now just Guto, his own self in a dress, now something else entirely" (1997:563). Likewise, Garber notes that transvestism signals category distress, marking "displacement, substitution or slippage: from class to gender, gender to class; or equally plausibly, from gender to race or religion" (1992:37). Butler, in her analysis of simultaneously racialized and class-based drag performances, has pointed out that cross-dressing itself is neither inherently conservative, because it replicates hegemonic gender ideals, nor transgressive, because it signals the artificiality of gender, destabilizing its status as a natural identity. Instead, one must examine particular deployments of the practice or its representations. She adds that those who would challenge the existing system of social norms and controls must do it with the available symbols, ways of thinking, and ways of acting that are at hand (1993:121–40; see also Certeau 1988). Such observations complicate the reading of festival cross-dressing as always and only about the social control of women, a reading that privileges the dominant perspective of presumably heterosexual male community leaders. Indeed, modernizing transformations have exposed traditional community performances to multiple new significations, as Guss (2000) forcefully argues. These performance traditions offer tools for asserting distinctions among the myriad relations of domination and subordination within a community.

The Baile de Negras, an all-male marimba dance in which half the dancers impersonate women, rose to prominence in twentieth-century Masaya when it shifted from an indigenous to a mestizo practice, from a ritual to a cultural practice. Unlike similar dances throughout Mexico that gradually substituted women for male cross-dressers (Lechuga 1988:161), the Negras has retained its all-male character in order, I argue, to reinforce distinctions between an Indian and mestizo style and to assert the latter's prominence. During the Sandinista revolution, Masaya Negras groups claimed to preserve the marimba dance tradition in the face of innovations by the national folk ballets, but in the 1990s they themselves began a new period of innovation. The dance evolved into a statement of formal elegance, in which signs of gender are subordinated to those of wealth, professionalism, and artistry. Ultimately, I argue, the deployment of tradition in performance functions not only as the antithesis of innovation, its necessary constraint, but as the means by which innovation gains its legitimacy.

Marimba Festival Dancing

Negras performances exist within the larger context of marimba dancing in Masaya, which includes both *folklorized* staged performances and the traditional festival enactments that concern us here. Each year, a few months before the festival, marimba dance groups, consisting of four or five pairs of dancers, organize themselves to plan costumes, schedule rehearsals, and map out their performance route. Youth groups represent the largest number of the sixty or so marimba dance groups participating in the festival. They are followed by children's groups,

Negras groups, and adult mixed-sex groups, or Parejas. The dance itself is a duet that highlights romance and elegance. A festival presentation consists of separate performances by each pair of dancers, usually repeated for a total of eight to ten dances per set.

On any given Sunday morning between mid-October and the end of November, marimba groups perform outside the Church of Saint Jerome, each accompanied by its own marimbero, and each tightly circled by a crowd of onlookers. (The Negras have claimed the Sundays in November for their performances in part to increase anticipation and in part for practical reasons because they can thereby avoid the occasional torrential rains of October that might otherwise ruin their elegant costumes.)[3] The groups visit as many as forty homes in tours lasting about twelve hours, with dancers, musicians, and a band of supporters walking from one house to another. The dancer who offers the dance at a particular house dances first with his or her partner. Then, each additional duet performs, taking care not to repeat a piece that has already been performed at that house. The hosts offer performers, but not onlookers, light refreshments and snacks, alcohol for the adult groups.[4] At the final house of their tour, the footsore dancers enjoy a festive meal. The following day Negras groups hold a *parada del banco*, a festive luncheon with drinking to chase away the hangover of the previous day. Today, as in the past, marimba festival dances in Masaya include a ritual gesture followed by a marathon social and cultural performance. The unfolding of this performance in largely private and semiprivate spaces ensures that the primary audience is a local one.

In Masaya, town-center Negras groups predominate among the adult dance groups performing in the festival, and they lead the more numerous mixed-sex youth and children's groups in matters of style. Twelve of the fifteen adult marimba groups performing in the 2001 festival were Negras. Of the three mixed-sex adult groups, two were unmasked Parejas, organized among professional Masayans, and one was an Húngaras (Gypsy) group organized by street vendor Isabel Cano. Cano began dancing in 1945 when she was twelve to fulfill a vow her father had made, asking Saint Jerome to cure her of a physical disability. She continued year after year because she enjoyed the tradition. Masayans often identify Cano's Húngaras, who perform in pink wire-mesh masks and gypsy costumes, as the one remaining indigenous or

Inditas-style marimba group. At the same time, they generally disparage Cano's dancers, calling them old, graceless, and ugly.

All marimba groups dance to the same musical pieces, now numbering almost seventy, though only between twenty-eight and thirty-five are traditional (by an unknown author).[5] Dance aficionados consider the dance serious and stately in comparison to torovenados, which employ more lively and free-form body movements. Nicaraguans generally believe that the *sones de la marimba* (marimba tunes) evoke Indians' melancholy and sadness, whereas the brass band sones de toro of the torovenados are happy and boisterous. Scruggs (1994) points out that this association of Indian marimba with melancholy has no musical basis because the songs or pieces are all in major keys. Many traditional dancers complain that with the appropriation of the folk dance by national folk ballets in the 1980s, the pace of the dance has quickened. In fact, Scruggs has convincingly shown that the popularization of the marimba folk dance exerted considerable influence over the musical repertoire and playing style, thus codifying and in some cases radically altering the traditional tunes (1998:20–27). The stately pace of Masaya marimba dancing, then, must be continually defended against an alternate tendency to "liven things up."

A verbal description of the dance is always necessarily incomplete. For a videotape example of a Negras festival performance from the 1980s, interested readers should consult Scruggs' recording on the *Smithsonian Institution/Folkways Anthology of Music and Dance of the Americas*, volume 6. The dance consists of three basic steps: *paso corriente*, a walking step; *zapateado*, in which dancers glide across the floor by lightly kicking their lead foot and letting the body follow; and *cruzado*, a rocking step, combined with turns.[6] Although youth dance contests have standardized the step and turn sequences for most marimba pieces, older dancers turn according to their own hearing of the marimba. Local dance aficionados explain that the marimba aesthetic requires a judicious measuring of turns and steps. Despite this flexible dance aesthetic, it is possible to make a mistake. For instance, the oldest living Negras dancer in 1991, Rigoberto Guzmán, explained, "I can tell you, for example, there's a change in the marimba, a musical change from one step to another. And perhaps there was a change, and I didn't make the change immediately. And I continue on until I take note that

I am in the wrong step, and so, I change slowly."[7] Judgments of quality derive from the overall effect a dancer achieves.

The steps for the dancer in the female role differ stylistically from those for the dancer in the male role, although one Negras dance director, Alfredo Montalván, insists that there is no difference between the two. The dancer in the female role steps lightly, trying not to make any sound with his or her feet as he or she dances. This is particularly difficult with the zapateado, which requires one to close the gap between the back foot and the lead foot without shuffling or bobbing up and down. The dancer in the male role, in contrast, steps more forcefully, providing a *taconeo*, or audible heel clicking, to mark the rhythm. Body posture and arm position give the dance its elegant figure, and the aim, above all, is to remain erect but flexible, affecting a natural grace. Dancers in the female role lightly grasp a corner of their skirt with one hand, extending their arm in front of them in line with their shoulder, elbow bent to mark an angle of about 140 degrees. When they lead with the other hand, which holds a fan, the skirt hand rests on the waist, keeping the elbow parallel to the body and the shoulder relaxed. The dancer in the male role holds his elbow up to just below shoulder level and marks a right angle with his forearm in a line parallel to the chest. The other arm is crooked at the elbow with the hand resting on the waist. He will occasionally extend both hands out in front of him toward his female partner. Dancers periodically shift leading arms, following their own sense of when a change in the figure is needed. Too many changes of this kind make the dancers look jerky; too few make the performance repetitive and boring. Finally, displacement, or moving through the entire performance space, has become an important aspect of its overall aesthetic, though it is clearly an influence from folk dance presentations and contests outside the festival context.

The next level of aesthetics concerns the way in which partners dance together. Monimbó dancer, dance instructor, and Negras director Carlos Centeno commented, "When I teach, what I correct is the synchrony of the dancers, that they look elegant as a pair and that always, always the man maintains eye contact with the woman. The woman should bend, incline slightly toward the man without moving her torso because that would turn the marimba into *cumbia*, rumba, or salsa."[8] Indeed, in contrast to salsa, the dancer taking the female role leads the dancer in the male role in step changes, and the latter must watch and follow the former. Moreover, dance partners periodically move together and apart as they dance. There is, however, no rule for how dancers define and vary the space between them. In the best duets, dancers' subtly nuanced gestures vary the repetitive pattern of steps and turns. A slight change in arm posture, the fluttering of a fan, and the spatial tension between the dancers create the necessary tension for a superior performance. Thus, although the elementary movements in marimba dancing are easy enough to master, subtle inflections allow for the development of individual style.

Masayans consider the Baile de Negras to be the most elaborated of all marimba dances. This preeminence is in part owing to the fact that the Negras groups predominate among adult groups. Moreover, previous reputation shapes the public judgment. In other words, groups that have danced for many years tend to be recognized as good performers. This basis for judgment is so influential, in fact, that Bayardo González explained that even though he might make a mistake in the dance by accident, the public would be likely to interpret it approvingly as an innovation or variation rather than as an error. Perhaps most significant, however, are the special elaborations that Baile de Negras performers make in the dance in order to call attention to its more self-conscious style. These elaborations are constantly changing, as the younger, mixed-sex groups absorb the Negras innovations into their own practice. Yet at any given moment in the process one easily recognizes the Negras' special stylistic markers.[9] For instance, in 1991 an unmasked female marimba dancer would grasp the end of her skirt, holding it up and away from her body, palm facing in. The *negra*, the female role in the Baile de Negras, would do the same, but would occasionally vary the figure by pulling her hand in toward her chest, wrist bent backward and palm facing out, flirtatiously wrapping herself in her gown.

When performing a zapateado, a step in which the *viejo*, the male role in the dance, would move across the floor to a position directly behind the female dancer, the negra would playfully duck under the viejo's arm, circle behind him, and return to her position in front, thereby accentuating her role as the leader in the dance. Or, as the two dancers approached each other, each would make a quick turn, changing the direction of the zapateado. These variations—along with the fact that both dancers' identities were completely obscured by masks, wigs, hats, and gloves—heightened the abstract nature of the dance, calling attention to its artifice.

Elegance constitutes a common move toward distinguishing mestizo performances from indigenous ones. Mendoza (2000) notes that in the mestizo town of San Jerónimo, Peru, all-male Majeños dancers use an elegant body style (erect posture, gradual changes in position, smooth lines), along with a myriad of costuming symbols to assert their greater prestige in the social world, reinforcing in performance a socioeconomic distinction between themselves and other groups of ritual dancers and then using the performances to shore up their social prominence in the local arena. Another group, the Quollos, has attempted to carve out a space for itself in performance by asserting a contrasting style of Indian authenticity based on freer, more playful body movements. However, this choice compromises the group's ability to compete with the Majeños because continuing social prejudice against Indians brands group members' bodily enactments, like their social identities, as inferior. How did Masaya's Indian parody of Spaniards ultimately become a tradition dominated by mestizo dancers? The recent history of the dance reveals a familiar pattern of cultural revaluation, differentiation, and elitism in these festival performances.

Monimbó's Masked Dancers

Until the 1960s, marimba dancing remained largely an indigenous-identified performance form tied to the fulfillment of a vow to a saint. At that time, the costuming aesthetic emphasized elegance rather than national or regional identity. The Inditas wore a loose silk blouse adorned with sequins over a length of striped cloth wrapped tightly around the waist, a broad-brimmed hat adorned with a feather, a fan, and gold jewelry, and the Negras wore the tailored women's dress suits of wealthier mestizas. Pablo Centeno, who first danced with a group of Monimbó Negras in the 1920s, remembered going to Granada to search for imported fabrics and lace, an indication of an early emphasis on elegance. Centeno explained, however, that such materials were also cheaper then than they are today. Monimboseña Rosita Herrera remembered neighbors calling to borrow her gold jewelry for their dance performances as late as the 1960s. These dancers performed not only for their Monimbó neighbors, but also for better-off residents of the town center. For instance, another elderly Monimboseña named Amanda remembered having danced twice in the 1950s, visiting and performing at the homes where the Inditas worked as servants before winding back into Monimbó. She recalled that the dancers were always treated well. Felipita Cermeño recalled, however, that if some of Masaya's elite families patronized the dances, they did not recognize the dances as enactments of their own cultural heritage. From a wealthy Masaya family herself, Cermeño attested that before the 1960s, Indian, popular, and elite festival activities remained separate and distinct.

Adult dancers wore locally manufactured, white or pink wire-mesh masks with Caucasian features. The masks may have been of German-Austrian origin because similarly constructed and painted masks can be found throughout the Caribbean and Belize, having been exported to the New World in the late 1800s (Nunley and Bettelheim 1988:57–58). Local artisans connect the whiteface style of the wire-mesh masks to that of the carved wooden masks produced in nearby Diriamba for the colonial-era dance drama *El güegüense*. Older residents recall that the Húngaras emerged in imitation of a band of gypsies that had visited Monimbó in the 1930s. The Mexicanas were the innovation of Monimboseña Rosa Gaitán, who sponsored that group for more than twenty years in the 1940s and 1950s. The aesthetic appears to have been one emphasizing both finery and festive *othering*—the costumes, in fact, displaying incongruous layers, such as pink-faced gypsies. Thus, although the dances retained a potentially parodic quality, the costumes layered traditional with more contemporary materials. In contrast to the current expectation that each dancer pay a portion of the performance expenses, the pre-1960s Monimbó dance sponsor provided the marimba music, costumes, and food for the dancers he or she invited to perform in the group.

The religious motivation for Monimbó dance performances ensured their occasional nature. Instead of developing into fixed performing groups organized by a particular family or religious organization, marimba dancers formed only as necessity required among variously skilled dancers and then disbanded. The religious vow might also provide an excuse for refusing to perform outside one's social or cultural group. Pablo Centeno's 1920s Negras performance fulfilled a vow his mother had made to the Virgen del Candelario in the nearby town of

Diriomo, whom she had petitioned to cure another son of a poisonous insect bite. Some wealthy visitors from Granada saw the performance and offered to pay the group to dance at their home during a September festival. Pablo's mother refused, emphasizing that the dance had been formed only to fulfill her vow. Nevertheless, Pablo did dance three more times over the years at the request of neighbors who wished to pay a promise to the Virgin or to Saint Jerome.

Centeno's mother's resistance to selling her son's performance may also indicate a certain resistance to performing indigenous or popular culture for elite individuals with whom she had no prior connection. A boy of fifteen dressed as a woman might be vulnerable in unfamiliar contexts. Gould describes a "stark, fearful social and cultural distance between Ladino and Monimboseño" during the initial decades of the twentieth century (1998:153). Ladinos regarded the Indians as potentially violent, uncommunicative, and disinterested in progress, and the Indians regarded Ladinos as exploitative and untrustworthy, their progress inevitably involving the greater impoverishment of the Indian. Given elite prejudices against Indians, Centeno's mother could not have been sure that the Granadans would have treated the performers with respect.

The Negras of the Town Center

Although marimba dancing of the past was associated primarily with Indians, some town-center women also participated in the tradition, using children to fulfill their vows. Alonso Montalván (dance director Alfredo Montalván's father), who is credited with having brought the Negras to the town center, began dancing marimba in such a group organized by his maternal grandmother in the early 1900s. He first danced as a Negra in 1915, when he was between sixteen and twenty-one years old, when he was invited to perform for some Managua friends.[10] Whether this was the kind of paid performance that Pablo Centeno had refused, the fulfillment of a ritual obligation, or a social event is unclear. In 1917, Montalván organized his own dance group and began a long career of paying his respects to Saint Jerome.

Montalván was not a member of the town's high society. Instead, he was a prosperous mestizo furniture maker who successfully bridged the cultural divide between Spanish-identified elites and Indians. Dedicated to popular performances of all kinds, he was renowned for his acting skills and is said to have also played the marimba. Residing directly in front of the Church of Saint Jerome, Montalván delighted in watching the festival dances, according to his son, Alfredo. Dance chronicler and Negras director René Chavarría summed up the general impression Montalván the dancer left on his fellow Masayans: "Practically, he was a man dedicated to art. We call him, or at least I call him, the legendary dancer of the Baile de Negras because he went out year after year during quite difficult times in Nicaragua. He danced incessantly to Saint Jerome, and I think I'm right in saying that he stopped dancing in 1970 or 1972 because of a prostate illness and after that due to his old age and death. But by that time, there were several Negras groups."[11] Montalván distinguished himself by dancing repeatedly in the festival.

Furthermore, Masayans recognized Montalván's Negras as the most stylish and exclusive marimba dance group. In 1991, town-center resident and Diablitos dancer Donald Zepeda reported a story he heard from older dancers when he was a young man: "Don Alonso took out a dance of Marines, very elegant, mounted on horseback. They rode to Saint Jerome. And they say some Americans were there following the dance, enchanted. This was the year after the Marines were here, and they imitated their costume, but the manner of dancing was our own."[12] The U.S. Marines were sent to Nicaragua on and off from 1912 to 1928, yet Zepeda did not indicate whether Montalván intended to ridicule or honor the marines by adopting their costume.[13]

Many dancers even attribute the origin of the Negras tradition to Montalván, claiming that he was the first to create an all-male marimba group. Chavarría explained:

Before people believed that the Negras was eminently of the city center, and people believed that Don Alonso was the initiator of the Negras Dance. But that's not true. This is a cultural practice that comes from very remote times, from our Indians of Monimbó. The intrigue is whether don Alonso Montalván brought the dance to the city center. He wasn't really the person who brought the Monimbó culture here. Those who did were Felicito Franco, Adán Miranda, and Juan 'Chivo' Ortega, my grandfather's brother. Since they were

Figure 5.1 Alonso Montalván's Baile de Negras outside the Church of Saint Jerome in fall 1968. Dancers wear the tailored suits favored by the pre-1960s Negras groups. (Photo donated by Alfredo Montalván)

all from Monimbó, they brought the culture here. Don Alonso gave me this information. And in his first group, in 1917, he danced with these old, old dancers, who brought the dance to the city center.

In spite of the social origins of Montalván's early dancers, it was his name that became attached to and identified with the performing group. Moreover, his annual performances celebrated the dance as a cultural activity rather than as a ritual obligation.

Although Montalván initially danced with the old men of Monimbó, he quickly distinguished his practice from the Indian traditions. Alfredo does not remember his father ever using Monimbó dancers during his lifetime. He recalls his father having said that he only liked to dance in large, elegant rooms where he would cut a good figure. If he had accepted Monimbó dancers into his group, he would have had to perform in Monimbó, where accommodations were more rustic, because each dancer has the right to take the dance to four or five houses of his choice. Thus, Montalván's celebration of the Indian dance did not necessarily imply identification with the Indian community. Instead, he accentuated the elegance of the dance, marking out an elite space for performance in the salons of Masaya's great houses. At the same time, the brilliance and longevity of Montalván's group obscured the fact that other Negras groups continued to perform occasionally in the festival. Don Alonso's group came to be understood not just as the single most important group in the city, but as the only group that existed.

Rigoberto Guzmán, the adopted son of a wealthy landowner, was placed in festival dance groups as a child by his maternal grandmother and joined Montalván's Negras in 1939. By the 1950s, Francisco "Pichicha" Espinosa had organized a second Negras group in the town center. And in the 1960s, Dennis Bermudez formed a third group, which devolved to Horacio Palacios when Bermudez died in 1966. Throughout this period of growth, the Negras groups remained fluid and informal. As Guzmán explained, "Before, these groups didn't exist. But when the festivities drew near, friends who knew each other began to feel the desire and ask, 'How are things set, so we can go out to dance?'" In the town center, social and cultural motivations for dancing contrasted with the primarily religious purposes of the Indian dance groups. At the same time, new professional opportunities in marimba dancing began to emerge.

The Masaya Folklore Revival

During the 1950s and 1960s, staged folk dances and competitions provided a new context for marimba dancing. Although these events were not always sponsored by the state, they were conceived as displays of national distinctiveness. A new kind of performer developed who could "represent" the traditions of various localities to an unfamiliar audience.[14] In Masaya, these performers became the next generation of Ne-

Figure 5.2 Carlos Centeno's Negras group performs in 1991 wearing elegant costumes loosely based on folk costumes from around the world.

gras dancers. Regional composer Camilo Zapata formed a Masaya folk dance troupe in the 1950s that competed in various kinds of contests organized among the Central American countries. Bayardo González, a young dancer from the Masaya central neighborhood of San Miguel, won several prizes and was soon also performing with a Ministry of Tourism folk dance troupe organized by Managua cultural activist Chony Gutiérrez. The group performed largely for visiting diplomats and other elite audiences. At the same time, González enthusiastically promoted folk dance instruction at the normal school where he was training to be a teacher. Meanwhile, another Masayan educator, Horacio Palacios, convinced the minister of education to authorize the creation of the Masaya Folklore School in 1966, whose central purpose was to teach marimba dancing to all Masaya schoolchildren. By the 1970s, the directorship of the school had passed from Palacios to another young dancer from San Miguel, René Chavarría.

As the folk dance revival took hold in Masaya, however, the practice of marimba dancing shifted definitively from Monimbó to the more affluent town center. Now Masaya youth enthusiastically embraced marimba as a sign of their regional distinctiveness. But as revivalists revalued the marimba dance, they disparaged Monimbó dancers, whose traditional performances lacked the brilliance of a newly developing "folk" style. At the same time, town-center Negras groups began to establish fixed identities and to build their reputations as accomplished dancers. Just as López Pérez had privileged the active, masculine, Spanish element in his interpretation of the Inditas Dance in 1938, Masaya revivalists now privileged the stylish Negras over the rustic Inditas and claimed the former tradition as their own. At the same time, adult male dancers increasingly took over the role of preparing young people in the dance, a role initially played by the mothers and grandmothers who had once sponsored festival dances. The few Monimbó groups that continued to participate in the festival were either disparaged or ignored. Masaya marimba dancing, even as it was being popularized, took a decidedly elitist turn.

The young, semiprofessional dancers and dance instructors who formed the new generation of town-center Negras danced in shifting constellations with the older festival dancers through the 1970s. For instance, René Chavarría first danced as a Negra in a group organized by Horacio Palacios in 1969 that included Bayardo González.[15] Then, from 1973 to 1975, Chavarría danced with a group that included Rigoberto Guzmán and Alfredo Montalván, among others. In 1976, that group broke into two, one organized by Chavarría and the other by Alfredo Montalván. Chavarría's group included future Negras director Omar Calero, and Montalván's included Guzmán and González.[16] It was during this time as well that Negras groups discarded the older costume aesthetic and began to perform in fanciful imitations of folk costumes from around the world, a costuming aesthetic borrowed from children's marimba groups. One Monimbó Negras group organized by Carlos Centeno danced intermittently at the festival from the mid-1970s. In 1978, all festival activities were cancelled owing to the insurrection, but by 1979 Chavarría once more organized his group, combining members of his own and Montalván's earlier groups because, he explained, many of the established dancers had temporarily fled to Costa Rica.

The dance aesthetic that developed in the 1960s and 1970s, although grounded in the observable practice of older dancers, was achieved through rigorous training, practice, and continuous performance, a clear departure from the occasional nature of the earlier Monimbó (and town-center) dances. After all, González, Chavarría, Calero, and, later, Jairo Arista worked as marimba dance instructors and performed in the new projection groups of the Masaya folklore revival. Chavarría articulated the town-center perspective: "All the traditions of the city of Masaya are eminently indigenous, and this culture has come to us through the Indians. And over time, we have given it a certain gayer, more folkloric flavor. What happened is that we've made transformations in the city center; we've given the costumes brilliance; we've modified the dance quite a bit. And today the Negras Dance is of the city center." Such a perspective embraces the romantic nationalist view of popular culture as the raw material out of which middle-class revivers fashion art.

Moreover, class distinctions were reinforced by an underlying, unstated ethnic and racial understanding that is at the heart of Nicaragua's mestizo national identity. Omar Calero made this clear as he described how all Masaya dancers, men and women, now perform the *improved* town-center version of marimba dancing: "But I repeat, we are now dancing a Baile de Negras where the woman dances the same, they make the same arm movements as in the Baile de Negras. See? Because the dance has now undergone transformations, clearly. But we are referring to the time when the Indian woman goes out with her plain cotton *huipil* [blouse]. Now there is a more liberated woman than that of the Baile de Inditas, who is of the Conquest."[17] Significantly, Calero regards arm movements as the Spanish contribution to the dance, thus introducing a distinction between lower and upper body, Indian and European elements. Moreover, he relies on López Pérez's famous reading of the Inditas Dance—a reading, as noted previously, that owed more to the myth of mestizaje than to actual festival practice—to contrast that dance with the modern style developed by the Negras. He further posits a plain costume for the Indita, thus making elegance part of the Negras aesthetic. And, finally, he associates the Negras with liberation as opposed to Indian subjection. The elegantly dressed groups of Inditas and Negras that descended from Monimbó into the 1960s simply disappear in this historical reconstruction.

In 1991, Bayardo González insisted even more vigorously that Monimboseños' "authentic" dance style was neither accomplished nor beautiful. Thus, rather than breaking down class barriers, the 1960s revival effected a transfer of practices from one social group to another. To complete the appropriation, town-center Negras groups claimed for themselves the markers of mestizoness and elegance that had once characterized all marimba dances. Even if Monimbó groups demonstrated grace and refinement in the dance, they were understood to be imitating the tradition of the center.

The Negras in Revolution

As noted previously, with the revolution, new institutions for the promotion and celebration of popular culture developed. When the Masaya Folklore School was closed in 1980, formal dance instruction shifted to Managua, where the Association of Culture Workers supported the National Dance Academy and several folk ballets. The new hybrid form of marimba dancing that emerged among the rapidly professionalizing folk ballets appalled Masaya dance enthusiasts. Dismayed by what they viewed as Managua distortions of the tradition, Masaya dancers further resented the fact that the folk ballets were being filmed, broadcast, and exported as the popular traditions of the Nicaraguan people. In response, Masaya dancers embraced a traditional identity, preserving and defending their own dance style as the legitimate folk dance in contrast to the Managua distortions. Town-center groups had already appropriated the Monimbó Baile de Negras as a Masaya tradition, but now they performed the Negras in defense against the national appropriation of marimba dancing.

In the 1980 festival season, the core of town-center Negras dancers that had performed in shifting constellations during the previous decade split into four groups that became firmly identified with directors René Chavarría, Alfredo Montalván, and Bayardo González, and with the Arista Bolaños family.[18] Subsequently, these four groups claimed to be the most traditional, most accomplished dancers. Groups that formed or became known after 1980 were understood to be new, nontraditional groups that had emerged within the context of the Sandinista folklore revival.[19] The town-center Negras quickly elaborated additional markers that distinguished them as Masaya institutions. They published *recorridos del baile,* printed leaflets listing all the locations where the dancers would perform during the day as well as the names of contributing sponsors. Dancers passed out the leaflets in the weeks preceding their festival performance to recruit audiences to follow their dance. The size of the crowd a group commanded became an additional marker of its excellence.

Continuing social barriers marginalized the few remaining groups that descended from Monimbó. Omar Calero recalled:

> There also existed the group that Carlos [Centeno] directs, but it was never recognized during that period as—they didn't give it a place; there was a kind of isolation that occurred, they didn't take it into account, or they didn't take Carlos seriously. But Carlos is one of the dancers who had his group of Negras. He already had that group in which Bosco Canales went out, and I don't know who else. I think he had the group in the 1970s. It was a group that was very independent from us.

In addition to class, ethnic, and territorial differences, town-center dancers' insistence that the now nonexistent Inditas Dance belonged to Monimbó but the Negras was a tradition of the center obscured the existence of Indian Negras dancers performing in the contemporary style.

According to Carlos Centeno, the rising cost of festival participation made it impossible for Monimbó dancers to compete effectively in the spectacle aspect of the dance: "If we go to ask for aid from the commercial houses, they don't give us anything. But if the Negras dance groups from the center go, it's always the same: since they know each other, they're the same group of people, they help them. And you see the flyers there, the announcements and all. They're sponsored. While here we are wondering how we are going to take a dance out....We're pretty much stopped from developing in relation to other groups." Indeed, in the 1980s Bayardo González was rumored to have received $2,000 to buy his festival costumes, and Montalván, Guzmán, and Calero spoke of taking special shopping trips to Miami to purchase costume materials, an extravagance that working-class Monimboseños could not afford. A comparison between the price of a town-center dancer's costume in 1991 ($260) and a Monimboseña's costume ($50) demonstrates how much Monimbó and other working-class groups were disadvantaged in the spectacle aspect of the dance.

Nevertheless, the revolutionary-era folk dance revival in Masaya differed from that of the 1960s in two ways. First, Masaya dancers were more concerned with preserving a traditional style in contrast to the folksy artificiality of the Managua ballets than with improving on an indigenous model. Second, local cultural organizations, such as the city's Patron Saint Festival Committee and the Popular Culture Center, provided funding to support the artistic participation of the popular sectors. As a consequence, the number of organized dance groups participating in the festival grew. Some Negras directors viewed this growth as a healthy development; others complained that the new groups lacked quality.

By the mid-1980s, Masaya's "traditional" dancers were being invited to participate in occasional displays of national folklore along with the folk ballets. New performance opportunities, however, created a split locally between those Negras directors who asserted that traditional dancers should perform only within the context of the festival and those who favored staging cultural displays to respond to the folk ballet distortions. Bayardo González, Rigo Guzmán, and Alfredo Montalván flatly refused to participate in state-sponsored, popular venues, and René Chavarría claimed work obligations prevented him from doing so. This resistance to performing outside the festival was motivated in part by ideological antipathies to the Sandinista government and in part by established Negras directors' desire to carve out for themselves a performance context in which their preeminence remained undisputed. After all, Montalván, González, and Chavarría had earned their reputations by teaching and participating in staged folk dance presentations during the Somoza era. By subsequently limiting themselves to performing in the festival only, they reasserted the exclusive character of the Negras tradition. Youthful, unmasked, and mixed-sex marimba dancing might be performed as a sign of national identity, but the Negras belonged to Saint Jerome. If people from elsewhere wanted to see the dance, they had to come to Masaya during the festival, watch, and learn from the masters.

Bayardo González complained bitterly that during the Sandinista decade seventy-two groups were established in Managua. He considered such popularization an absurd substitution of quantity for quality. In the late 1980s, when he served briefly as the director of the Masaya Dance Union, he tried to institute a three-tiered ranking system among dance groups—superior, accomplished, and mediocre—an idea that other union members summarily rejected. González's elitism was directly at odds with the Sandinista movement to promote greater popular involvement in cultural production. Yet even in 1995, after a regime change, the town-center Negras groups refused to dance with other Masaya dancers on municipal stages because they felt that the attention and service they received was not adequate. Specifically, they objected to being given sandwiches instead of the delicacies they were accustomed to receiving in Masaya's most elegant private homes.[20]

The more Sandinista-identified directors—Calero, Centeno, and Arista—participated enthusiastically in national performances and in the revolutionary cultural revival. Arista, an English teacher working in Nindirí, organized dance groups, contests, and other activities through his high school. Calero worked for the Institute of Nicaraguan Culture, where he conducted historical research on lost traditions in order to revive them through performance. He also organized a projection group, which included Arista, that traveled to Europe to display traditional Nicaraguan dances in 1988. In 1990, Calero worked as director of Masaya's Dance Union, located in the Alejandro Vega Matus House of Culture (formerly the Masaya Popular Culture Center).

Centeno, the only Monimbó Negras director, worked through the Monimbó Sports and Recreation Committee, part of a larger community improvement initiative, to launch a neighborhood-level folk dance revival. Convinced that the marimba dance traditions constituted an authentic indigenous legacy, he fought an uphill battle to be recognized by his town-center peers. In 1987, he developed a neighborhood elimination contest for the city's India Bonita Contest, a festival queen and dance contest, in order both to promote marimba dancing among Monimbó youth and to prove to neighborhood detractors that Monimboseños also possessed mastery of the dance (Borland 1996). Centeno's persistence in organizing and funding this contest, in preparing neighborhood candidates, and in convincing his neighbors of the contest's importance eventually bore fruit. From the late 1980s, Monimbó dancers have consistently won the citywide title, and most Masayans now tacitly regard the India Bonita Contest as the property of Monimbó. The tactic of concentrating on the dance style for the female role did not challenge the established dichotomy between town-center Negras and Monimbó Inditas, yet Centeno succeeded in asserting Monimbó dancers' skills within Masaya's cultural sphere.[21]

During the 1980s, then, Masaya dancers became increasingly concerned with preserving the traditional style of the dance in opposition to the style being disseminated more widely by the Managua folk ballets. At the same time, Masayans recognized and applauded the effects of their own revival on the style and execution of the dance. They did this by positing a chronologically arranged sequence in which the indigenous Inditas style was improved, whitened, and made more elegant by the town-center Negras. Thus, what may have once been an indigenous parody of the mestiza now became a mestizo expression of the very best form of festival dance. As well-situated town-center dancers developed their reputations in performance, they added to their own social prestige as traditionalists. In this case, transvestism signaled a shift in performers' ethnic and class allegiances, rather than a challenge to the existing gender order. By virtue of its all-male character, the Negras preserved an aesthetic of festival othering that contrasted with the unmasked youth groups who performed a transparent or "natural" gender identity that was nevertheless based on the Negras model. In the 1990s, however, this construction became increasingly difficult to maintain as the homosexual social identity of many Negras dancers began to play a role in what the dance signified for its audiences.

6 Masking and Unmasking Sexuality in the Dance

Four Negras Rehearsals

By the 1960s, the town-center Negras groups had converted what earlier seems to have been an indigenous parody of mestizas into what they considered a superior or "improved" version of Indian dances. In so doing, these revivalists conformed to a more widespread pattern that values mestizo *style* more highly than indigenous *authenticity*. Such valuation demonstrates that judgments of quality in performance inevitably rest on the performers' perceived social status in a continual reproduction of social hierarchy (Bourdieu 1984; see also Mendoza 2000). If the free-form festival expression of the torovenado masquerades provided the Saint Jerome Festival with humor and social critique, the dignified grace of the Negras and other marimba dances enacted elegance and aesthetic accomplishment. In the face of a national movement to popularize the dance in the 1980s, the pre-revolutionary Negras groups asserted their superiority by claiming greater traditionality. And yet in the 1990s Masaya's Negras groups began once again to innovate. One of the most obvious transformations involved the relaxation of practices that once safeguarded dancers from public exposure. By 2000, some groups had even transformed once-private rehearsals into full-scale performance events. These backstage performances in which unmasked men dance with men draw new attention to the sexuality encoded in the dance.

Simultaneously, a transnational gay political and cultural movement now challenges Masaya residents' denial of gendered meanings in the dance. In a peculiar twist, dance directors who do not identify as homosexual worry about the dance becoming feminized. They accuse acknowledged gay directors of turning the dance into an expression of gay identity, but in so doing they project the gay directors' social identities onto their dancing style. Meanwhile, gay directors embrace the established ideal for Negras dance style even as they capitalize on the theatricality of unmasked rehearsals. Diana Taylor defines *theatricality* as "a noun with no verb and therefore no possibility of a subject position" (1998:162), a deliberate artifice that nevertheless has consequences for social life. In this case, the term *theatricality* is more apt than Butler's (1993) term *performativity*, which masks its constructedness as a natural or transparent expression of an internalized identity core. Even if dancers perform unmasked, local audiences understand the persona or role they perform as a culturally constructed, imaginary entity.

A close reading of four Negras rehearsals demonstrates how directors with different sexual-social identities deploy the Negras tradition to different ends. The shifting significance of Negras performances in the Masaya community once again shows that traditional festival transvestism cannot be ascribed a singular meaning. Nor can it be conflated with an individual's performance of a particular gendered identity in everyday life, for, as Marjorie Garber notes in her wide-ranging study of English and North American transvestism, "the question of cross-dressing as an intermittent or constant, public or private, historical or literary representation is neither equivalent to nor entirely separable from the question of sexual object choice, whether heterosexual, homosexual or bisexual" (1992:70). At the same time, the Masaya Negras tradition fulfills a conservative social agenda with respect to gender roles, reinforcing men's dominant, active position in the public performance arena.

Male Homosexuality in Nicaragua

As in other parts of Latin America and the Mediterranean world, male homosexuality has been defined in Nicaragua not as the choice of a same-sex partner, but rather as the assumption of a passive or receptive role in (anal) intercourse. Thus, sexual relations between men are conceived as involving a homosexual and a heterosexual partner, and the cochón or passive male has been historically stigmatized but not marginalized. Given this way of defining homosexuality, the cochón, Lancaster (1992b) argues, becomes a necessary object through which a machista male subject acquires honor and sexual prowess. During the Somoza era, male homosexuality was apparently tolerated as one of the minor sins (along with adultery and promiscuity), and male and female prostitution was controlled by a corrupt National Guard (Babb 2001).

The Sandinistas demonstrated an uneasy ambivalence toward open homosexuality. An early assertion of revolutionary morality in opposition to Somoza-era decadence led to a crackdown on brothels and visible homosexual nightlife in Managua (William Ramón Ramírez Méndez, personal interview, December 27, 1990). The revolutionary state itself celebrated heroic, defiant masculinity, equating cowardice both with treason and with the cochón. Moreover, Sandinista uneasiness with organizing outside of party structures provoked the arrest of gay and lesbian political activists in 1987. Those affected, however, report that Sandinista police were embarrassed by their own intervention, and the crisis was short-lived. Not long after, fifty gay and lesbian activists publicly marched in the celebration marking the tenth anniversary of the revolution. By 1990, homosexuals connected with an emerging transnational gay and lesbian political and cultural movement had an established presence in Managua near the Universidad Centroamericana (Babb 2001:231–32).

The neoliberal 1990s initiated both a conservative social backlash and support for individual expression. Violeta Chamorro represented and promoted an ideal of the nuclear family that few Nicaraguans could realize in their own lives. Formal marriages are uncommon among the poor and working classes, and female-headed households predominate. Serial monogamy for women and tacit polygamy for men remain the social norm. In the 1990s, even as economic necessity drove many women to seek work outside of the home, Chamorro urged them to return to the hearth (Babb 2001; Chávez-Metoyer 2000). However, new social movements and organizations proliferated as the Sandinista mass organizations faltered. These movements participated in the transnational critique of neoliberal democracy. They shifted their attention from a direct engagement with the state to diverse kinds of activism within civil society (Alvarez, Dagnino, and Escobar 1998). By 1992, the popular press recognized the Nicaraguan gay movement, attesting to its public presence. At the same time, President Chamorro reinstated an antisodomy law, known as Article 204, which criminalized same-sex activity. This law remains the most repressive in Latin America despite vehement protests from national and international human rights organizations (Babb 2001:234; Howe 2003).

In 1999, the opposition press ran an article in favor of accepting and understanding the homosexual transvestite as a natural category of person.[1] One year later the brutal slaying of a lesbian woman, Aura Rosa Pavón Pavón, in the small town of Niquinohomo created a public uproar. The incident and its aftermath demonstrated both continuing violence against homosexuals and a growing public recognition that sexual minorities deserved human rights protections (Howe 2003:225–50). State intolerance encoded in Article 204 thus coexisted with a non-judgmental, transnational view of gay life as well as with the more fluid, ambivalent conceptions inherited from the popular tradition. In this environment, gay rights activists in Managua publicly stressed their solidarity with heterosexual constituencies by calling for a sexuality free from prejudice (Howe 2003:178–94).

Nevertheless, gay activism in Managua focused most insistently on issues of self-esteem within the community. In discussion groups that were a cross between consciousness-raising and training sessions on transnational gay perspectives, facilitators encouraged participants to embrace their gay identities. Yet this identity work remained largely a private matter. Instead of "coming out" as gay people, participants worked to internalize a positive gay identity. In fact, some facilitators distinguished between identification and lifestyle choice: one might be gay without choosing to engage in same-sex relationships (Howe 2003:118–77). Therefore, even in the capital, an individual's gay identity was not something that he or she was likely to discuss openly with acquaintances (or with scholarly fieldworkers) who were presumed heterosexuals.

During my fieldwork in Masaya in 1990 and 1991 and again in 2001, I witnessed heterosexual Monimboseños express an amused tolerance for gay neighbors, who were often quite involved with religious and festival life, and who could be counted on as entertainment at social gatherings. At the same time, they regarded this group as unreliable, and people would admonish young boys not to be cochones or cowards, indicating continued social disapproval. Relatively few people seemed aware of the more political gay identity that was developing in the capital. I inferred that homosexuality constituted a *natural* gender category in the neighborhood, but one that predisposed an individual to ridicule and censure. Moreover, the neighborhood view strongly correlated effeminacy with homosexuality. People recognized effeminacy, flamboyance, and sometimes semitransvestism—wearing a woman's apron while working in the market, for example—as signs of gayness (see also Lancaster 1992b, 1997).

Hennen (2001) has pointed out that the association of effeminacy with same-sex desire is historically contingent in Euro-American culture. He adds, however, that except for a brief period after the Stonewall riots in 1969, the mainstream North American homosexual male community has preferred an erotics of masculinity to one of effeminacy. Thus, effeminacy, or "acting womanish," rather than homosexuality, currently produces stigma. This distinction appears applicable to the experience of homosexuality in Nicaragua, where only the passive sexual partner in the homosexual relationship is stigmatized as a cochón.

In Masaya, gay pageants, modeled after international women's beauty pageants, were being produced by the late 1980s. The gay rights initiatives of the 1990s transformed these semiprivate events into declarations of gay identity.[2] In October 1994, the Masaya Gay Association organized the first annual Miss Hispanidad event, a transvestite pageant held at restaurants and tourist attractions. According to its organizers, Miss Hispanidad is designed to increase respect for gays as the third sexual option. In 2000, however, the *Nuevo Diario* newspaper reported that a young contest winner faced expulsion from high school because he/she had named the school during the event. The Masaya Gay Association subsequently complained to the Ministry of Education, arguing that "it's not a crime to be a transvestite, and even less so to be gay, since they don't harm anyone."[3] The debate underlines a dramatic change in the way that gay identity is configured in Masaya. Amidst an atmosphere of discretion and secrecy surrounding gay identity, some sectors now openly demand acceptance and equal treatment. Of course, Masaya residents of all sexual orientations exhibit a range of attitudes toward homosexuality. Most remark, however, that although homosexuality is nothing new, homosexuals have become increasingly visible in both social and cultural spheres over the past quarter century. These social transformations necessarily affect the Baile de Negras, which, as an all-male dance, contains the potential for being reinscribed as a gay performance form.

Secret Rehearsals and Public Restraint

Marimba rehearsals always draw an audience in Monimbó. The loud music carries quickly, and crowds soon appear at open doors and windows, jostling each other to catch a glimpse of the dancers inside. In the town center, in contrast, sidewalk observers are more discreet, and the homes where rehearsals take place are more conducive to privacy. Although town-center Negras groups traditionally held two or three rehearsals before their festival performance, the elderly dancer Rigo Guzmán emphasized that these rehearsals were largely social events: "It's in order to get together, have a nice time, and pass two or three hours together happily." In the past, these rehearsals took place behind closed doors, with only a few family and close friends attending. Several Negras directors explained that before the 1980s, because men were dancing with men, it would have been unseemly for rehearsals to be open to public view. In the past, then, men danced as women in the festival, but they took precautions to safeguard their identities. In performance, of course, costumes covered the entire body and included wigs, hats, whiteface wire-mesh masks, and gloves. Ideally, the dancer performed the feminine role without placing his masculinity into question, even if he identified as homosexual.

The secrecy that pertained in rehearsals also increased the excitement surrounding the actual performance. Negras director Bayardo Cordoba recalled:

> So since everyone went with their mask and no one took it off, that always remained a secret. Some people knew, because the family went along, "No, he's my husband, he's . . . ," But the majority of the people who weren't connected, who weren't family, remained with the intrigue, the curiosity, "Who's that, who's that, who's that?" But since one went masked—I remember, because when I was a child, I would go along with my mother, following my father. It was that. It was the unknown. Who was that man dancing? And even after the dance had ended, the man would go masked until he arrived at his house to take it off.[4]

Cordoba constructed the pre-1980s Negras Dance as a mildly risqué, family-oriented tradition in which friends delighted in guessing the dancers' identities, while outsiders, who probably caught only a glimpse of the dances anyway, enjoyed the artifice.

Moreover, Cordoba and Carlos Centeno, both of whom dance as viejos, the male role in the dance, recalled that the Negras they observed in their youth danced in a very restrained style. Cordoba explained:

> The changes are in the steps. As I told you, I watched my father who was a man dance as a woman with a steady, calm step. That's what we call it—there wasn't much, how should I call it, tiptoe-ing, movement of the waist—it was a man dancing as a woman. A little rustic, but now it has been—now the one who dances as a woman wants to dance—some, not all—to make the dance almost feminine. That takes away a little of the sparkle for me because it's a man who is dancing.

The shift in dance style these dancers noted ultimately ascribes a ho-mosexual identity to contemporary Negras. Whereas the Negras were once representing an other—men dancing as women—now many ap-pear to perform transparently as the third sexual option. This change compromises the ambiguity on which the performance is ideally con-structed for established, heterosexually identified viejo dancers.

Yet if a male dancer does not wish to embody femininity, why would he dance as a negra? One reason is the dancers' semiprofessional ethos. Omar Calero explained that by the time he became a Negras dancer in the 1970s, it was a way to gain legitimacy in the dance world: "We all started out dancing in youth groups, but if one stopped there, there you stopped and there you died as a dancer. You died in the youth dances if no one came to invite you to accompany them." Moreover, once a person married, dancing in mixed-sex groups became problem-atic because the romantic overtones of the dance invited jealousies. This problem occurred for Calero:

> At that time, I had a formal married life, and so now I stopped going out in the youth dances, with the girls, my friends and all, because it doesn't look good for a married man to go out with an unmar-ried girl. So practically, I was outside the dance world. At that time, they arrived and asked me to accompany them to participate in the Baile de Negras that they'd organized in 1972. Well, I told them

yes, although my wife was not a lover of folklore, because we have to tell the truth. She said, well, it was alright if this was something I liked, well, I should go. And so, I began to go out from 1973 on, now as a dancer.

Calero acknowledged that even the all-male character of the Negras Dance might not assuage the resistance of an uninvolved spouse. At the same time, being invited to join a town-center Negras group meant that one was recognized both for one's skill and for one's social acceptability. Almost all the dancers at that time were well-off tradesmen or professionals, many of them teachers. They constituted part of Masaya's small middle class, connected in various ways with the city's elite families.[5]

In general, young recruits began dancing in a Negras group by taking the male role. Cordoba remembers his father dancing first as a man. One day a dancer's absence created an opportunity for him to perform as a woman, and he switched. Alfredo Montalván initially resisted the idea of dancing as a woman when his father urged him to switch from viejo to negra. He recalled that his father emphasized the aesthetic superiority of the negra role: "Look, he tells me. Well, first of all, dancing as a man and dancing as a negra is the same. 'But I want to go out as a man.' It's that nobody watches the man, he says. If you want to be somebody in this, you have to go out as a negra, and you're going to realize that, yes, from the moment you go out on the floor, people are all over you. The man is secondary. Don't even worry about the dancing, he says. The man is something secondary."[6] Thus, the Negras tradition as it developed in Masaya's town center inverted the gender hierarchy of the folklorized Baile de Inditas, where the woman's dance was less interesting than the man's. Indeed, dancing the negra role constituted the highest level of achievement for aspiring male dancers. The idea was not to impersonate women, something that several Negras directors indicated would have been impossible in any case. Instead, it was to bring the dance to the height of elegance. One might argue that the elevation of the female character in the dance and a resistance to feminizing the performance may have reinforced rigid gender categories by demonstrating the impossibility of gender crossing. However, the fact that three sexual identities existed—male, female, and cochón—complicates this view. Moreover, the performances *were* successful and did not devolve into humorous parody. Instead, they preserved an ambiguity in the transvestite enactment of elegance within a larger social context in which overt, effeminate, male homosexuality was stigmatized.

That the woman's role in the dance became aesthetically interesting only when it was performed by men underscores how women's social roles restricted them from attaining artistry. Before the town-center folk dance revival, Monimboseñas had performed in mixed-sex Inditas groups or singly as part of Las Promesantes,[7] but these performances were unpolished, motivated presumably by religious rather than cultural impulses. During the revival, young female marimba dancers artistically "died," to use Calero's description, once they married. Certainly, a few adult Parejas groups exist, but, notes Bayardo Cordoba, they are more difficult to organize and maintain because they require identifying married couples in which both partners enjoy dancing.[8] Greater opportunities for men to dance replicate men's greater freedom to choose sexual partners. At the same time, the relation between festival dancing and sexual activity remains a matter of conjecture. Some Negras dance partners might be lovers also; many more are certainly rumored to have been; but the relation between performed role and social identity, between transvestism and sexuality, remains attenuated and uncertain.

Director and dancer Bayardo González understands the Negras Dance as an exercise in elegant form. In contrast to the Inditas, it contains no narrative message. For González, the mixed-sex performance contains the possibility of a naturalized or transparent expression of romance. However, the all-male Negras denies that possibility, pushing the performance into the abstract realm of art. That the dance might depict homosexual attraction is unthinkable in this construction because that would simultaneously demote the Negras performance to the level of other kinds of marimba dancing and stigmatize it. Like González, most established directors resist assigning a homosexual meaning to the dance.

Nevertheless, René Chavarría argues that early dancers were, in fact, homosexuals. He insists, "From its birth, the Baile de las Negras was danced by homosexuals because those who participated in the old dances of Monimbó were homosexuals. So they saw the Inditas, and well, since they were homosexuals, they felt like women, and they put on all the women's things, and this is very clear." Chavarría places homosexuality at the root of the tradition. Like other dance directors, he also identifies homosexuality as a specifically Indian characteristic. Early accounts of pre-Columbian culture that register the Spanish observers' revulsion against publicly condoned homosexual behavior or symbols of homosexuality among the Indians support this view (Oviedo 1976). But the association of homosexuality with Monimbó also conveniently removes the stigmatized identity from the socially more powerful dancers of the town center.

As the dance tradition gained social status, the secrecy that once surrounded rehearsals was gradually relaxed. Cordoba explained, "Now people have assimilated the idea more that a Negras Dance is something professional, that those who dance in the Baile de Negras are professionals in the dance. And that the one who goes to see a Negras Dance is going because he's going to see a good dancer, a couple dancing the marimba well." Thus, although he believes that effeminate dancing by homosexuals in the negra role detracts from the tradition, he claims that Masayans today understand that the dance is really about form and quality, not about sexual identity. For this reason, watching unmasked men dance together has become a socially acceptable practice.

In fact, some Negras groups now use their rehearsals as occasions for unmasked backstage presentations that function as full-scale dance events. The modern transformation of rehearsals into performances responds to several phenomena. First, such elaborations emphasize the local character of the Negras tradition, for the rehearsals form part of Masaya's shared private life. Second, they assert or display social prestige, a continuation of the elitist turn of the 1960s and 1970s. Third, they constitute an arena for the creation of additional stylistic distinctions between and among the groups that embrace this new performance space. A comparison of four different Negras group rehearsals in 2001 demonstrates a range of approaches to negotiating tradition, homosexuality, elitism, and inclusion in the dance.

Alfredo Montalván and Heterosexual Exclusivity

Alfredo Montalván claims the oldest continuous Negras dance group and represents himself as an absolute traditionalist. He continues to use a very fine, expressive plaster mask that he inherited from his father, a costume element that distinguishes his festival performances from those that use the more common, uniformly painted, wire-mesh masks. Montalván holds three private rehearsals at the homes of influential friends, which he describes as social gatherings for the other dancers. "We all know how to dance," he quipped, "the dance doesn't change." The rehearsal I attended was at the home of María Adela Correra, whose daughter dances marimba in a mixed-sex group. It was a very large, spacious, two-story house. The entrance opened out into an L-shaped tiled room, with clean white walls, and a patio that let in light to the right. Behind this front area was an enclosed dining room and a hallway. The marimberos were positioned outside and sideways to the dance area, which was lined with white wicker rocking chairs and a few potted plants. Correra's daughter offered light refreshments from a tray to the handful of invited guests. The dancers occasionally withdrew to the back room where rum and finger food had been set out for them. Thus, the house offered a "stage" and a "backroom" for the dancers, with the marimberos situated in the space between these two areas. Although Montalván himself is not wealthy, he solicits elegant rehearsal spaces among his friends and connections, a continuation of his father's tradition of dancing only in large salons.

Montalván was careful to point out that the group itself does not solicit funding; rather, members take financial responsibility for their festival performances. Yet the group does have a *madrina*, or godmother, who collects donations from her friends and associates to help defray performance costs. The madrina explained that she loved the Negras tradition, but was not an accomplished marimba dancer herself. At the rehearsal's midpoint, however, she danced briefly with each member of the group to the lively tune "El viejo y la vieja." This is one of the few comic dances in the marimba repertoire, in which dancers imitate a salacious elderly couple. The effect is light and clownish, quite distinct from other marimba pieces. Dancing with the madrina, however, was a means of paying homage to her.

As in all the rehearsals, the negras held a fan in their right hand. Montalván was dressed in pink pants and a salmon pink shirt, and the other dancers wore casual clothes in muted tones—pressed pants, button-down shirts, leather shoes. Midway through the rehearsal, Montalván tied a piece of skirt to his belt as a sign for his absent costume. All the other members of his group save one were mature men; one negra had brought his teenage son to perform as his viejo. The young man was not yet proficient, and his father commented several times that he would have to work with him at home to develop his style. No coaching took place at the rehearsal itself. The madrina commented that Montalván's two brothers usually returned from the United States and Costa Rica to participate in the dance, but were unable to do so this year, so Montalván was short a few viejos.

Montalván was the only director I spoke with who claimed to prohibit overt homosexual behavior in his group. He frequently emphasized the importance of maintaining a restrained style of dancing, commenting, "And that's, well, as I tell them, if you are what you are, please stay in your place. I don't care. But if we're going to go out as a group, you'll have to behave yourself. Make the greatest effort that you can. After we finish, do what you want, it's your life. I don't care what a person is, but we can't let out what we are! I tell my dancers that. Bayardo González, well, he's my friend, but—he's Bayardo González!" Montalván explained that if the Negras dancers mix with open homosexuals, they begin to acquire a reputation and have problems with their wives. Homosexuality in the dance represents a relaxation of the elegant form and should be avoided.

A dancer that I had seen at other rehearsals was among the handful of guests. He appeared to be shopping for an invitation to join a Negras group. Toward the end of the evening, Montalván invited this man to dance as his partner. The guest declined, insisting that he didn't know how to dance as a viejo. Alfredo dismissed his concerns, saying that the male and female parts were exactly the same. They danced a *jarabe*, which employs the gender-neutral cruzado step. Nevertheless, body posture and arm movements for the negra and viejo differ. The invited dancer looked awkward and uncomfortable. Another visiting dancer from Chavarría's group danced several times as well, once as a negra, a few times as a viejo. When he danced the male part, however, he continued to employ a light, gliding step for the paso corriente rather than the forceful taconeo that distinguishes the male and female roles. Montalván seemed to be challenging these negra dancers to show that they could cross roles and perform as viejos, even as he insisted there was no difference between the male and female roles in the dance. However, this challenge is inflected with another deriving from the performance hierarchy within the dance. A new recruit in the Negras is typically a younger, less-accomplished dancer, and that person begins with the less important viejo role. Ultimately, Montalván's rehearsal highlighted the Negras' exclusive character not only in terms of class and dancing competence, but also in terms of a heterosexual erotics of transvestism, for, although denying any difference in the dance style of viejo and negra, he underscored the two visiting dancers' incompetence by insisting they dance as viejos.

Bayardo González Makes Art

Montalván's greatest rival, Bayardo González, has earned the reputation for being perhaps the most elitist of all Negras dance directors. He is also renowned as the most innovative director, a characteristic that several other directors regard as either dangerous or farcical. Montalván commented, "Bayardo González has completely destroyed folklore with some pieces that he's taken out, that he says, 'do this for me, do that for me,' and some dances that are so strange that people here, to use the word broadly, are infuriated [se ponen arrecho] by watching him dance.[9] Why does this craziness exist? There are people who love it, and they applaud him. And when they applaud him, they add to his illness, so he thinks he's doing some great thing." González's elitism, his flexible reading of the tradition, and his presumed homosexuality combine to alienate him from some other Negras directors.

Nevertheless, González is well connected in Masaya society and has an established reputation as a first-rate Negras dancer. Consequently, many individuals request that he hold a rehearsal at their home. Like Montalván, he requires a suitably large or elegant space for dancing. He also requires great attentiveness, which means that the best-quality food and drink must be served.[10] In 2001, González held seven rehearsals before his festival performance, more than double the number of any other group. The two I attended were held in elegant settings that emphasized the group's quality and connection to Masaya society. Moreover, both rehearsals were framed as semipublic performances in a number of significant ways.

The first rehearsal took place in a large, private hall that was entirely lined with seated guests. The second was held in a much smaller but infinitely more elegant living room. Here, the front door and window were opened so that the dance might be viewed from the street. González's dancers arrived in uniform dress: brown dress pants, white satin dress shirts, and black leather shoes. All were mature men who demonstrated a synchronization in their steps that bespoke earlier preparation for the rehearsal. All kept their skirt hand in their pocket and employed only the traditional fan as a prop. At the first rehearsal, González gave a speech, thanking his hosts for their loyalty to the dance and, after a drum roll, presenting a gold pin to the head of the family. He also announced the locations and sponsors for his upcoming rehearsals, one of which would be in Monimbó at the home of a retired Negras dancer, Carlos Arévalo.[11] Thus, González established connections not only with the town elites, but also with the Indian roots of the tradition. Finally, he recognized and formally welcomed guests from other dance groups but did not invite them to dance.

The most notable characteristic of these dance events, however, were the innovations in the dance itself. González's dancers executed several tightly choreographed new sequences of steps to the marimba pieces. Ignoring the traditional aesthetic of performing a judicious combination of steps and turns, one pair performed an entire marimba piece without any turns at all. They introduced variation by changing the direction of their steps when the marimba music indicated a turn. Another pair ignored the custom of partners mirroring each other's movements. Instead, the dancers occasionally performed completely different steps to the same musical pattern. In one instance, for example, when the music called for a turn, one partner turned, while the other danced around him, accentuating the turner. In another, when the music played the zapateado (the coupled step) pattern, the negra performed a simple zapateado, while the viejo followed behind with a zapateado doble.[12] In a subsequent zapateado in the same piece, they introduced yet another variation. Facing each other, both leaned to the same side, and while the negra performed a simple zapateado, the viejo moved in the same direction, but performed an inverted zapateado (kicking backward instead of forward), a step I had never seen before. The effect of using two dancers to create one novel and unconventional figure, coupling them in a way that could not be read as romance, underscored González's preference for formal experiments.[13]

In spite of these stylistic innovations, however, González's dancers neither minced nor tip-toed as they danced, and their overall performance style achieved the refinement that traditional directors prize. In fact, Gonzalez's mature, synchronized dancers exhibited a kind of tight professionalism that dancers at other rehearsals lacked. Their abstract, graceful style betrayed little slippage into a stigmatized effeminate performance. Thus, although the dancers' and the director's presumed homosexuality may have provoked censure among some local dance enthusiasts, their dance style accomplished the Negras ideal of ambiguity—form drained of any gendered content, the dance as a flexible art form.

Nevertheless, this achievement provokes constant criticism from other Negras directors, who see Gonzalez's experiments as destructive to the tradition rather than as an extension and elaboration of its underlying principals. González, who is eager to take credit for his innovations, frequently claims certain steps or pieces as his own invention. Thus, rival directors complain, he claims exclusive ownership over a tradition that is in fact a shared cultural inheritance.

Jairo Arista Promotes Folklore

The youngest of the established town-center Negras directors, Jairo Arista, held his first rehearsal in 2001 at the Alejandro Vega Matus House of Culture, formerly Masaya's Popular Culture Center. Like González, Arista's rehearsal functioned as a full-scale dance event, but the style and tone emphasized civic inclusiveness. A large, open, tiled room with a stage at the far end provided ample space for both dancers and audience. Chairs lining three sides of the dance floor were three deep, filled with Masayans of all backgrounds and even some international visitors. In addition to the marimbero, who occupied a centrally prominent position on the elevated stage, a brass band played rousing numbers at interludes, increasing the festive ambience. The hall was decorated with palm leaves, the stage with woven straw hats and bags, and the recently elected India Bonita, a festival queen who is also recognized as the city's best female marimba dancer, sat in her huipil, with her sash and a flower crown, presiding over the dance floor as a kind of living folklore icon. A long table on one side of the room was brimming with food and drink, yet this hospitality departed somewhat from the delicacies offered at other group rehearsals. Here, the food was typical fare, a demonstration of the regional cuisine of corn-based dishes, pork, and rice and beans. Both dancers and guests were invited to help themselves. Thus, Arista marshaled signs of civic-mindedness, placing the Negras squarely among the city's public (as opposed to elite) traditions. His gestures were inclusive rather than exclusive.

Like González's group, Arista's dancers wore a rehearsal uniform. The viejos wore bright green embroidered *cotonas*, and the negras wore bright orange ones. These cuffless, collarless shirts once formed the garb of the Nicaraguan peasant farmer and now constitute the folkloric garb of the male Inditas dancer and of Masaya's various religious and cultural cofradías. Thus, the cotonas emphasized both that the rehearsal should be regarded as a performance and that it should be understood within the category of the popular. At the same time, the dancers wore their cotonas uncharacteristically tucked into their pants rather than loose as is customary—a gesture, perhaps, toward elegance or difference.

During intermission, Arista formally welcomed the audience, repeatedly framing his rehearsal as a Masaya folkloric event. Emphasizing the youth of his dancers, who ranged between seventeen and thirty-nine, he then introduced each one, with blasts of band music and fraternal hugs. He also took a moment to remember a dancer who had died recently. Next he acknowledged special friends of the group, for, like González and (to a lesser degree) Montalván, he relies on sponsors to defray the costs of his festival performance. Each sponsor was invited to the stage to receive an amulet, a small *jícaro* gourd on a leather string. Then each was invited to ceremoniously drink "Indian" style from a larger gourd. Finally, Arista publicly thanked a foreign visitor who had given money to the House of Culture. This benefactor was invited to dance marimba with the India Bonita in a performance reminiscent of the Montalván group's homage to their madrina. In this case, the gender roles were reversed as the best female marimba dancer danced opposite a foreigner who lacked mastery.

Arista's dancers appeared to take a moderate stance toward formality and technical expertise. One dancer, for instance, performed in street clothes, and all the negras employed a length of plain black cloth tucked into their belts to indicate the absent skirt. All the dancers were polished in their execution, but one was noticeably disabled, giving his style an uncharacteristic jerkiness. Indeed, individual stylistic variations were more evident in this group than in González's because the dancers were not deliberately playing with the conventions of established musical pieces, steps, and sequences of steps. Arista employed a great deal of spring in his walking step (paso corriente), which heightened the gaiety of his performance without diminishing its elegance. One negra danced a diminutive cruzado with an erect body posture but a pronounced leaning from side to side, producing a more artificial, abstract effect reminiscent of the González dancers. Yet another demonstrated more fluid movements, accentuated by a tendency to drop his skirt hand behind his body. Of course, the musical pieces influence certain variations in the dance, but overall the group's technical proficiency did not obscure individual stylistic variations, nor did these variations depart from the established aesthetic of abstract elegance.

Carlos Centeno and Indigeneity

For many years, Carlos Centeno has been the only Negras director in Monimbó. His working-class background, Indian ethnic identity, and viejo role in the dance serve to marginalize him in Masaya cultural life. Thus, Centeno has struggled to be recognized and respected by his peers. In 2000, the city finally honored him for his contributions to the city's cultural life, an honor that he shared with Bayardo González. At a special ceremony sponsored jointly by the Masaya Office of Culture and the House of Culture, the two directors received gold medallions.

Nevertheless, Centeno continues to fight an uphill battle to achieve recognition for his Negras group. Although he identifies strongly as a traditionalist in matters of style, he would welcome the sponsorship that town-center dance directors enjoy. Unfortunately, he lacks the social connections that make such sponsorship possible. His dancers must divide the costs of performance among themselves. For this reason, Centeno held his first rehearsal in 2001 at his own, moderately spacious home in Monimbó. The room was lined with wooden rockers typically manufactured in Monimbó, inexpensive metal chairs, and a plain wooden bench. The cement walls were dark and scuffed, the tile floor had been covered with sawdust to prevent the dancers from slipping on wet patches of floor resulting from a leaky roof. Owing to the family's straightened economic circumstances, no refreshments were served to dancers or guests. Because Centeno's group did not have the reputation or the financial backing that the town-center groups do, no guests arrived to shop for a position in the group.

The dancers, with the exception of Centeno and the dancer who partnered with him as the negra, were young men in their teens and early twenties. All arrived in street clothes: T-shirts and jeans mostly. The audience included four gay men from the neighborhood, a few women whose children train with Centeno in mixed-sex marimba groups, and a multitude of barefoot children in worn clothes. What the setting lacked in elegance was made up for in warmth and informality. Like Montalván's and Arista's dancers, these dancers performed to the marimba pieces by fitting the conventional steps to particular musical patterns and varying figures by varying arm position and the space between dancers. Centeno had drafted one viejo from a mixed-sex youth group that he also coached. When this dancer made a mistake, the audience and dancers responded with amusement. Otherwise, the dancers were proficient but had clearly not practiced together previously.

However, the very complaint that Centeno and Cordoba had earlier raised about the use of an effeminate style for the negras role among established town-center groups seemed applicable to the younger members of Centeno's group. The subtly nuanced body language of these relatively new negras dancers—a slightly swayed back, a weak wrist, a slightly elevated chin—could be read as signs of effeminacy. One negra arrived with a wallet strapped around his waist that accentuated his groin area. He had tied a small towel to his belt loop, which he held taut with his skirt hand during his first dance. He subsequently abandoned this strategy, placing the towel across the wallet instead, where it flopped in a curious way as he danced. Clearly, these dancers were not trying to feminize the dance. All strove for and partially achieved the graceful, elegant figure that marks the Negras style. It appeared to me, however, that they hadn't sufficiently learned to mask stigmatized signs of effeminacy, which are equally performed, but which interfere with the elevation of elegance over effeminacy that a Negras dance ideally effects. Nevertheless, these dancers were neither teased nor challenged for their shortcomings, for they were already fully integrated members of the group.

Like Arista's group, but from a different position in the social field, this group articulated an inclusive rather than an exclusive ideal, for Centeno positions himself outside the center and in opposition to its sometimes intentional, sometimes unintentional elitism. He maintains his group in Monimbó because he believes passionately that the dance tradition is indigenous, not mestizo, and should be preserved by neighborhood dancers. Nevertheless, the dance style he projects and that he would like to see in his young dancers is one that is clearly influenced by the innovations of the 1960s folklore revivers. Like Montalván, Centeno has not transformed his rehearsals into dance events. They remain semiprivate social occasions for dancers and their friends. The group's Sunday festival performances remain relatively unknown and marginal because the group as a whole is neither fully proficient in the tradition (although Centeno and his negra partner certainly are), nor radically innovative.

Centeno's desire to claim the dance as indigenous heritage threatens to contain its contestatory power within a rubric of folklorization, as the naturalized performance of a particular identity, of heritage. He continues to organize a Monimbó group in order to contest the binary construction of the tradition elaborated by town-center revivalists that assigns the inferior Inditas Dance to Monimbó and reserves the elegant Negras Dance as its own. By dancing year after year, he disproves this construction. Yet as he clings to the notion that folk dance transparently represents ethnicity and should therefore be preserved in its pure and most authentic form, he becomes complicit in the continuing devaluation of his own group, for indigeneity continues to be equated with inferior style and recently with homosexuality.

Conclusion

Although Montalván claims the tradition as a family heritage, González makes it art, Arista celebrates it as a civic accomplishment, and Centeno asserts its Indian authenticity, all remain committed to the elegant formality of the Negras style, a style that continues to lead in local innovations in the dance. Clearly, a more open homosexuality in contemporary Masaya has impacted the dance, yet directors who do not identify as homosexual appear to have confused the dancers' sexual orientation with the kinds of performances they enact. It is true that Arista and González have transformed their rehearsals into unmasked performances, but they continue to project an image of abstract elegance in the dance itself. It is among less-accomplished members of their own groups that some heterosexually identified directors encounter the expression of homosexuality that they find unsettling.

Nevertheless, each of the directors redefines sexuality, movement, maleness, and femaleness through the practice of the dance, even if he does not publicly articulate this redefinition as his goal. In essence, all of them resist effeminacy and, consequently, the correlation between effeminacy and homosexuality, which is a historically contingent correlation. These directors may define the tradition differently and deploy it to different ends, but they continue to mark out a socially acceptable space in practice where unmasked men dance with men. They have, through their practice, instructed the community to understand such performances as normative. That some directors have moved this space from the semiprivate to the public sphere indicates once again how invoking tradition enables profoundly innovative performances.

If the previous chapter demonstrated how the Negras Dance was deployed to support the dominance of one class and ethnic group over another in the performance arena, this chapter has shown how that deployment is inflected by questions of sexuality. Both focus on people constructing and making use of a traditional aesthetic system. But this approach, as Garber notes, looks through rather than at the transvestite dance, eliding the erotics inherent in the dance itself, an erotics in which viewers participate. Garber challenges us to see the transvestite as a "spectral other who exists only as a representation—not a representation of male or female, but of, precisely itself: its own phantom or ghost" (1992:373). Having domesticated the transvestite performance as tradition, might not the Masaya community also construct the Negras as the quintessential representation of artifice? The legendary history of the dance certainly revolves around an absence, for, contemporary Masayans reason, the conquering Spaniards had left their womenfolk at home. Therefore, when they danced, they were forced to substitute either a male companion or an Indian woman for the absent lady. Then, Indian men, donning whiteface masks but calling themselves blacks, parodied either the dominating Spaniards or treacherous Indians. "It was a form of resistance," Omar Calero explained in 1991.[14] Or perhaps it was imitation, as Indian men joined a growing list of impersonators. That centuries later mestizo men identified the form as their own, investing in the once parodic elegance as a sign of distinction, attests to the double-edged nature of parody, a simultaneous critique and homage, resistance and appropriation (Hutcheon 2000).

Negras today uniformly adopt folk costumes from around the world for their festival performances, and almost all other festival dance groups have followed suit. Although some Masaya cultural activists see this innovation as a sign of self-hatred—a denigration of the local in the slavish imitation of the foreign—might we not understand this gesture as a parodic explosion of the naturalized connection between folk costume and national identity, and between national identity and festival performances? Might the celebratory adoption of other people's national costumes (or Masayans' imaginative reconstructions of other people's national costumes) represent a resistance to the folklorization process itself? Might it suggest that Masayan identity does not conform to a nationally marketable image of the Nicaragua folk but is instead whatever Masayans want to be?

The tradition, for all its competition and exclusions, remains a form of play, a dream world of bright costumes and stately dancers that departs from the everyday realities of this impoverished, provincial, Central American city. The erotics of these performances hinges on the tension of two dancers gracefully circling, approaching, retreating, turning in synchrony, coupling, and uncoupling without ever touching. That both dancers are men provides an additional layer of unreality, even as it forces the audience to examine the surface more closely than we might otherwise do, searching for nuance, detail, and fissures. Having established itself as a cherished town tradition, one of Masaya's many marks of distinction, the Negras Dance now discards its masks and secrecy in rehearsals. But what is revealed presents only another surface, as stylistic elegance replaces costume props. "This emphasis on *reading* and *being read*," says Garber, "and on the deconstructive nature of the transvestite performance, always undoing itself as part of its process of self-enactment, is what makes transvestism theoretically as well as politically and erotically interesting" (1992:149–50, emphasis in original). That the audience for these performances is made up of women as well as men provides yet another dimension to reading and being read.

I have suggested that the anthropological view of male festival transvestism as a means to control women's behavior by negative example is perhaps too reductive. Yet the transvestite performance tradition in Masaya festival enactments, even as it admits homosexual performances, remains a masculine tradition. Skillful female marimba dancers occasionally take the viejo role to accompany other young women in rehearsals. In fact, I was often accompanied by a female viejo in rehearsal, when I was learning the dance. I also witnessed a preadolescent girl dance as a viejo opposite her younger sister for play and family entertainment. But in Masaya these female to male crossover performances occur within the confines of the home, among close friends in rehearsals or training sessions for mixed-sex public performances. No female equivalent of the Negras performance tradition exists. Thus, although the Negras performance does not constitute a misogynistic put-down of women, it effectively excludes women's active participation, reproducing and perhaps even supporting the notion that men dominate the public performance arena. Many young women dance marimba in mixed-sex groups, but marriage brings most of them early retirement from the dance world. In the marimba dance tradition, then, the Negras remain supreme.

Part IV Leaving San Jerónimo

7 The Neoliberal Religious Turn
Monimbó's Wagon Pilgrimage to Popoyuapa

Since at least the 1960s, Masaya's Saint Jerome Festival has provided the wellspring for national heritage even as Masaya performers have enacted popular identities that resist the constructions of nationalist intellectuals. Modern festival performers and organizers understand their work as cultural and folkloric. They deemphasize the festival's religious motivation, which once provided the generative core around which masquerades and dances revolved. Has the attention to heritage replaced religious meanings altogether? Returning to Saint Jerome's three religious processions, we do find grateful supplicants performing a subdued hopping dance among rowdy cofradía members, merrymakers, and politicians. Most are adult women wearing ordinary street clothes. Moreover, in individual homes throughout Masaya, fervent believers petition many saints: the Purísima Concepción de María, patron of both Nicaragua and Monimbó; San Pascual Bailón, the finder of lost things; the Virgen del Fátima, guardian of the poor; El Señor de los Milagros, the Lord of Miracles; El Señor del Rescate, the Lord of Rescue or Redemption; as well as Tata Chombo. Thus, although the cultural performances may overshadow religious fervor in the Festival of Saint Jerome, many Masayans continue to express a strong and compelling belief in the miraculous powers of the saints.

The veneration of the saints constitutes a "foundational religious experience" in Latin American popular Catholicism (Marzal 1992:77). The saints actively intervene in one's fate, and believers can petition images of them—statues, prints, or other representations—for favors. In addition, however, the saints require placating, for they may punish the unfaithful. Supplicants at minimum light a candle and dance in front of the saint's image, or they may host a party on the saint's day with group prayer, music, and a festive meal. Alternately, they may perform a service for the cofradía or mayordomía responsible for the saint's festival or, if the saint resides elsewhere, make a pilgrimage to visit the shrine. Within the Masaya community, of course, are nonbelievers, believing nonchurchgoers, church-going Catholics, Protestants, members of the progressively oriented Christian Base Communities, and members of the conservative Charismatic and Catacombs lay religious organizations. No affiliation, except perhaps atheism and Protestantism, precludes the private veneration of the saints or participation in the mayordomía system.

Mayordomías, like the cofradías, sponsor religious festivals. They are smaller than the cofradías, and they may venerate church-owned images in the mayordomo's home in addition to organizing religious processions. Unlike the cofradías, whose members are predominantly male, mayordomías attract substantial participation by women, who often assume leadership roles. Although the mayordomo/a is nominally responsible for hosting the festival, he or she recruits a *cuadro* or team of usually seven assistants who share the duties and financial burdens involved. For more elaborate festivals, such as that dedicated to the Baby Jesus,[1] a *padrino* (godfather) and madrina may organize a second cuadro to assist the mayordomo's group. Minimally, the mayordoma and her cuadro meet monthly to wash and dress or decorate the image and hold a small house prayer. Participation is strictly voluntary, usually lasts for two years, and is most often motivated by the mayordoma's passionate attachment to a particular saint.

Monimbó is home to a number of mayordomías that venerate images from several Masaya city churches. These mayordomías are notorious for excessive ritual drinking and social schism, particularly during tension-filled transfers of leadership. Indeed, mayordomos may have trouble relinquishing their leadership of a particular festival because the beloved image has adorned their homes, occasioning visits from neighbors, periodic festive luncheons for the cuadro, and the festival preparations and activities themselves. Many Monimboseños view the mayordomía as an important form of mutual assistance that residents provide one another. This mutual assistance creates a heightened sense of community that, in the absence of a separate language or communally held property, makes their indigenous-identified community qualitatively different from other neighborhoods in Masaya.

Masaya priests oversee the activities of the mayordomías, tolerating but not fully approving of them. A priest who is also a Monimbo-seño explained to me that the mayordomías are a form of paganism. They encourage the worship of and attribute supernatural powers to the religious images themselves. Moreover, he commented that official church leaders frown on the drinking, dancing, and fighting that occur during mayordomía-sponsored events as well as the jealousies the system inspires among neighbors. Grassroots community organizers complain that the mayordomías waste energy and resources that would be better used in community-improvement projects. Despite these criticisms, despite the growing membership in new lay religious organizations of all kinds, and despite the Torovenado del Pueblo organizers' modernizing innovations in festival sponsorship, the Monimbó mayordomías remain vigorous.

The mayordomías' resilience contrasts markedly with the deterioration of Mesoamerican civil-religious hierarchies or cargo systems after the introduction of Protestantism (Annis 1987) and of new religious movements such as Catholic Action (Warren 1978). Scholars have argued that the civil-religious hierarchies constituted defensive reactions to late-nineteenth-century state attempts to incorporate Indian communities. In the twentieth century, however, the cargos became forms of economic vassalage that prevented Indians from advancing in the larger national economy (Chance [1990] 1998; Nash 1970; W. Smith 1977). Others argue that the cargos represented forms of separatism that did not directly confront the larger order of inequality (Annis 1987; Warren 1978). In contrast, voluntary festival sponsorship in Mexico and Central America involves the circulation of goods and services among families who rotate the official sponsorship role (Monaghan 1990). Alternately, it mobilizes a dense network of small and large gift exchanges among those involved in the system, exchanges that are often, though not always, motivated by smaller or larger vows to a saint (Nájera-Ramírez 1997:105–16).

In Monimbó, festival sponsorship is not related to political advancement; it is not required of prominent community members; and mayordomos are not punished or jailed for their failure to fulfill ritual obligations, as was true of communities that retained a civil-religious hierarchy. Instead, Monimbó's mayordomías rely on extensive networks of relationships. Members of the festival team request material assistance from their friends and relatives to help meet their own sponsoring obligations. In short, the mayordomía structure constitutes a traditional resource for festival production. The veneration of a particular saint may wax or wane, but the mayordomía system continues to exist as a familiar way to organize both long-established and novel religious practices.

The 1980s heralded a growth in the national uses of Masayan folklore and a corresponding growth in the cultural enactments associated with the Saint Jerome Festival. They also witnessed the creation of a number of new mayordomías, particularly in the neighborhood of Monimbó. Perhaps the most interesting and multilayered instance of this deployment of tradition was the creation of the Monimbó Wagon Pilgrimage, a nostalgic reenactment of pilgrimage to the shrine of the Lord of Rescue (Redemption) at Popoyuapa, Rivas. The Monimbó Wagon Pilgrimage emerged during the insurrectionary period as one woman's response to a personal miracle. Organized as a mayordomía, it quickly became another traditional enactment of Monimbó's indigenous difference, a festivalized display of popular devotion motivated by both cultural and religious sensibilities. The pilgrims' nostalgic desire converged with Rivas parish priests' successful marketing of Jesus the Redeemer to create a renewal that far exceeded anything either group could have imagined. During the 1990s, religious and political leaders in Rivas appropriated the wagon pilgrimage, harnessing it to their vision of harmonious hierarchical order. This development is comparable to Sandinista leaders' celebration of the torovenados a decade earlier. Yet, for participating women, the wagon pilgrimage remains an expression of divinely sanctioned popular agency, equality among believers, and Masayan authority in matters of tradition. Therefore, the convergence of popular and official religious practice appears to be a case of "mutual misunderstanding" (Sallnow 1991), even as it reflects the current strength of the Catholic Church in postrevolutionary Nicaragua.

Origins

A little more than forty miles south of Masaya on the Pan-American Highway, the tiny village of Popoyuapa forms part of the municipality of San Jorge, which hugs the shores of Lake Nicaragua, providing

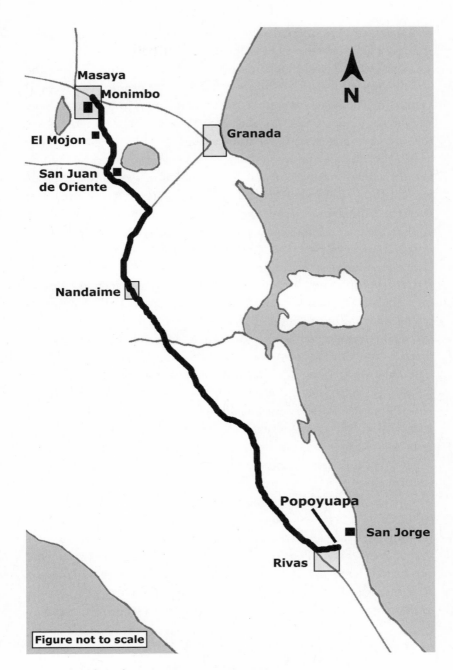

Figure 7.1 The pilgrimage route to Popoyuapa.

an impressive view of the double-peaked Island of Ometepe. San Jorge is home to about eight thousand people, mostly banana workers. The adjacent city of Rivas, population twenty-seven thousand, is about the size of Monimbó. Each year during the hot, dry, penultimate week of Lent, tiny Popoyuapa welcomes more than thirty thousand visitors who arrive by bus, truck, car, and wagon to visit the miraculous Jesus the Redeemer and swim in the nearby lake.

In the absence of documentary or archeological evidence, the origin of the pilgrimage to Popoyuapa is a matter of speculation. Nicaraguan historian Alejandro Dávila Bolaños associates Jesus the Redeemer with the Nahua wind god Hecat, who is responsible for both illness and misfortune. Dávila Bolaños states that Hecat had a large sanctuary in Popoyuapa (1977:17). Gonzalo Fernández de Oviedo and Francisco Bobadillo, who visited the area in 1528, identified Hecat as one of three major divinities, but they did not mention his sanctuary specifically (Bobadillo [1527–29] 1998; Oviedo 1976:344). Their informants related that during religious festivals they refrained from work and sexual intercourse and became drunk. According to local legend, the image of Jesus the Redeemer was found floating on the waves of Lake Nicaragua—hence, the *Rescued* Christ. Living memory attests that the pilgrimage has existed for at least the past 150 years, but it is likely older.[2] A pamphlet distributed at the site claims that a small image of Jesus the Redeemer was broken in the earthquake that hit Rivas in 1844, but was restored sometime later by faithful Popoyuapans. Some believe that this small image is the original image. It is stored at a Rivas city church and brought out only on the first Thursday of Lent, when residents of Popoyuapa hold a candlelight vigil in the little Chapel of Sangregrado. Two contemporary accounts for why this image is not publicly displayed indicate a history of tension between Rivas's Catholic leaders and Popoyuapans concerning appropriate practices of veneration. A sanctuary employee explained that the original image is stored because the authorities fear theft. But an eighty-four-year-old resident of the village alludes to a conflict with an Italian priest during an earlier period who refused to let the Popoyuapans have the image, keeping it locked in the church instead.[3]

Some historical evidence supports the possibility of this second claim. In a move to Christianize indigenous and peasant Catholics during the 1940s and 1950s, priests seized images formerly controlled by communities in many areas of Nicaragua. Gould (1998) mentions that during the 1940s a priest prevented an image from circulating within a rural community in Matagalpa. Adams ([1957] 1976) mentions similar incidents in the 1950s in the Nicaraguan highlands. We can infer, then, that the removal of the original image of Jesus the Redeemer from Popoyuapa may have been a former priest's attempt to stamp out popular religious practices because he objected to them. However, in 2002, Father Leonel Navas, the parochial priest at Rivas since 1992, denied that the Catholic authorities were ever antagonistic to popular religious practices. He insisted that the large Christ figure housed in the sanctuary at Popoyuapa, whose festival occurs the week before Holy Week, is the only one that has ever been venerated. He explained that Rivas owns six smaller images that the priests lend out to communities in order to solicit donations to underwrite sanctuary and festival costs. Several months before the festival, community members carry the smaller images from door to door to solicit funds. Father Navas refrained from commenting on the Thursday night vigil at the Chapel of Sangregrado.[4] It appears, then, that two parallel venerations occur in Popoyuapa, one promoted by the parochial priests and another, popular one that they tolerate but do not endorse. Of course, some believers participate in both, but the vigil for the small Christ image at Sangregrado remains a local affair, attracting mostly Popoyuapans. The festival at the end of Lent, however, attracts visitors from other areas of Nicaragua. Masayans who recall visiting the Popoyuapa festival in the 1940s and 1950s described it to me as a small, merry fiesta with lots of dancing and drinking.

Catholic Marketing of Jesus the Redeemer

In 1972, when Father Edgardo Santamaría arrived at the Rivas parish, the Popoyuapa sanctuary was much smaller than it is today. Pilgrims arrived in buses, trucks, and cars. Only a very few still traveled in oxen-drawn wagons. These wagon pilgrims spent their three-day journey to the sanctuary drinking and arrived at Popoyuapa inebriated. They brought marimbas inside the church and danced. Thus, they followed the general pattern of popular worship that combined gaiety with devotion. Yet Father Santamaría viewed these practices as serious errors.

In the "official" view, because the festival occurs at the end of Lent, it should be somber not merry. More egregious were the erection of houses of ill-repute, dance halls, and liquor stalls in the square immediately in front of the church. The atmosphere was more like that at a fair than at a sanctuary. With the assistance of the Rivas city government and police, Father Santamaría cleared the square, removing the festive marketplace to the highway.

At the same time, he initiated an extensive building project from 1973 to 1983 to enlarge the sanctuary and enclose it with stone walls topped by iron gates. Beside the site, he erected a convent where four missionary nuns from the Order of Christ the King now reside. The nuns run a religious concession next to the sanctuary in addition to ministering to the community of Jesus the Redeemer devotees. Father Santamaría also constructed a corridor along the back of the sanctuary, where the life-size Christ is now housed. Now the crowd of pilgrims visiting Jesus the Redeemer are organized in a single line running the length of the corridor. Inside the church, a glass window behind the altar allows a view of the image, but the line of pilgrims remains hidden from view. These physical transformations allowed those responsible for the sanctuary, the Rivas priests and missionary nuns, to control access to and behavior within the sacred space more effectively.

Thus, the 1970s saw both the enlargement of the sanctuary to accommodate greater numbers of visitors and the removal from the immediate church environs of certain popular practices that religious authorities considered inappropriate. Father Santamaría recalled that Popoyuapans at first resisted his efforts to clear the plaza (Hatton 2000); however, visitor attendance at the festival and the sanctuary increased as a consequence of his innovations. Indeed, Fathers Navas and Alfonso Alvarado Lugo, who assumed responsibility for the sanctuary in 1992, described their work as marketing the site and its tradition. Navas commented that the nuns at the sanctuary not only sell statues and prints of various popular saints, but also have developed a brisk market in Jesus the Redeemer bumper stickers and ornaments to hang in one's car—all of which, he explained, inserts the image into the everyday environment of contemporary Nicaraguans. In addition, Cardenal Obando y Bravo regularly attends the festival, bringing national exposure to their work.

This aggressive marketing has been accompanied by what Father Navas described to me as a move to restore the festival to it original Christian meaning and form. Obviously, *original* does not refer to a prior historical reality, but rather to an ideal of Catholic practice that these religious leaders endorse. Indeed, published restrictions indicate that many Popoyuapans continue to view the festival primarily as an economic opportunity, even though the priests have monopolized trade at the site itself. For instance, regulations published in 2001 allow Popoyuapans to sell and serve food inside their homes and patios to festival guests, but not to use sidewalks or streets for this purpose as they had in previous years. Moreover, though the celebratory aspects of the Jesus the Redeemer Festival have been removed from the immediate site, they have not been eliminated. Pilgrims have only to return to the highway for merrymaking or head down to the restaurants and bars that line the shores of Lake Nicaragua. Thus, despite increasing church control of the festival, unsettling incidents continue to occur. In the 2001 festival, one youth suffered a fractured skull and another drowned in Lake Nicaragua, where he had been drinking heavily with friends.[5]

Journalistic discourse, however, supports and even advances the priests' Christianizing effort by erasing the history of merrymaking in the central plaza. For instance, in February 2001 reporter Lourdes Vanegas López wrote, "Parochial priests Alfonso Alvarado Lugo and Leonel Navas, since they arrived to take charge of the Rivas Parish seven [sic] years ago, have fought to conserve the religious tradition of the fiestas of Popoyuapa because they are losing those values with the establishment of public dance halls on the outskirts, which made the place inviting for evildoers and antisocial types."[6] Thus, Vanegas describes festive practices rooted in tradition as recent deviations from an ideal past model.

The Vow

While Padre Santamaría was actively cultivating religious observance at the Popoyuapa sanctuary, Masayan pilgrims were developing their own set of traditions. Socorro Ortíz de Vívas and her husband, Juan Vívas López, both in their forties, were living in the rural settlement of El Mojón on the southern outskirts of Masaya. Their farm faced the Catarina road that leads to the Pan-American Highway. In the spring, they would occasionally witness a wagon pilgrim traveling to the Popoyuapa festival. Socorro describes herself as a poor, illiterate campesina, a farmer's wife. Nevertheless, she was quite active in community improvement projects in El Mojón[7] and in the mayordomía system of nearby Monimbó. She and her husband had served as mayordomos for the prestigious Lord of Miracles veneration in Monimbó. During the 1980s, Socorro became mayordoma of the Baby Jesus of the People and later served on Bosco Canales's festival cuadro when he became mayordomo of that festival. The Vívas family also hosted a Charismatics meeting until the group disbanded in 1990 owing to political differences among the membership. Yet no one in the Vívas family participated in the Saint Jerome festivities, which Socorro regarded as a lot of fuss and confusion.

The couple also made material donations of firewood and corn to other mayordomías they supported. In fact, Socorro refused to join the Sandinista-era cooperative in El Mojón because it would have prevented her from freely donating to the mayordomías. This may not have been her only complaint about revolutionary forms of production, but it shows that religious reasons are persuasive. Mayordomía obligations, though they are voluntary, are emotionally compelling.

Colburn (1986), Dore (1990), and Saldana-Portillo (1997) have cogently analyzed campesino resistance to Sandinista economic programs. They point out that the production goals of the revolutionary state continued to privilege urban over rural groups and production for export over food self-sufficiency. A commitment to subsistence farming and low prices for farm produce (set by the state) led small farmers to work less rather than produce more when the government offered easy credit. Such responses marked a continuation of the oppositional practices campesinos had employed during the Somoza era. Not surprisingly, one Somoza-era complaint about the mayordomía-sponsored festivals was that they provided excuses for Monimboseños to absent themselves from work (Peña Hernández [1968] 1986:38). In this sense, these festivals and their proliferation in Monimbó might be seen as "weapons of the weak" against both state and private employers (Scott 1985).

In 1980,[8] Socorro made a promise that ultimately resulted in the creation of the Monimbó Wagon Pilgrimage. Her narrative of that miracle, which I recorded in the spring of 1991, reveals a notion of pilgrimage rooted in popular social and religious conceptions that, if not resistant to Father Navas's Christianizing mission, provide an alternative basis for practice. Socorro recalled that Juan had initially invited her to go to the Popoyuapa festival in a fit of nostalgia:

> He said, "Look," he says, "Coco, let's go some day. It's fun to go to Popoyuapa," he says, "in a wagon."
> "Yes," I say. "It is fun, because I went," I tell him, "when I was nine years old, seven, eight. My old people took me for about fourteen years."
> "Let's go in a wagon," he says, "some day."
> "All right," I tell him.
> "We've got oxen," he says.
> "Yes," I say, "let's go with all the kids. Let's camp out with them."[9]

As Socorro remembers, both she and her husband focused on the pilgrimage as a recreational family activity. Going in a wagon, rather than by bus or car as more and more pilgrims were doing, would allow them to re-create their childhood experience with their children, for in the 1940s, when they had previously attended the festival, the Pan-American Highway was not yet completed. In fact, up to the mid-1960s, most rural Nicaraguans traveled by foot, horseback, wagon, or train. Being independent farmers, the Vívas family had the necessary oxen and wagon, so the pilgrimage did not represent an excessive expenditure. Nevertheless, when Socorro tried to take her husband up on his invitation the following year, he refused, claiming that his oxen were not good enough to display in such an event. Socorro's desire to participate in the pilgrimage was not sufficient to overcome Juan's concerns about the family's available resources because, essentially, such a pilgrimage represents an optional life activity, a peasant's vacation of sorts.

But a promise had been made. In Masaya, the proverb "Jugar con el santo, menos con la limosna" (It is better to fool with the saint than the offering) is commonly employed to emphasize the importance of following through with an intended act of veneration. If, after having said that one will go to the festival of Jesus the Redeemer, one doesn't follow through, bad luck is sure to follow:

> But look. Who's going to believe it! But things happen so that one believes and has faith. Well! It happened. I think that was Monday or Tuesday, but about two days after I had said that, look, that ox went lame. And the ox with his two shins stiff. He stretched himself to straighten up and it made it worse. And plun! he falls down again.
>
> He [Juan] comes back frightened about two in the afternoon. He says, "Look," he says, "the ox is lame," he says, "like stiff shins, like a paralysis," he says, "like I don't know."
>
> "Oh my," I say, "massage it," I say, "with gas, with this [rag] I clean with, massage his legs."
>
> So, that was Tuesday. Wednesday, look, he goes to Masaya. He had recently recovered from an illness they call "the breaker." Well! He went, he was walking well, just as he is now. He came back about six. He had a strong pain here in his throat.
>
> "That's the air, because you went and you're so troublesome!" [He became ill because he went out before he was fully recovered and was therefore susceptible to the folk illness of bad airs.] But I started like that, to buy him medicine.
>
> "Yes, but it's that you are very troublesome. Remember that the doctor told you that you are forbidden to do that."
>
> Look, the man was dying on Thursday. He was really ill. Pa! His mouth, his throat was completely closed. By then he couldn't talk. Because he's, he didn't say it, with gestures he said he was dying. He told me to sell the animals, that they should be left alone. Well.
>
> I go to my daughter and say, "Your father is very ill." The little one was around, the one who is married now, see. I say, "Look, go," I tell her, "find some injections. Maybe you'll find injections in the Milagrosa Pharmacy because it's the only one I haven't been to. And maybe they have it. God first."

Confronted with her husband's sudden and serious illness, Socorro resorted first to modern medicine, but in Nicaragua, where medicine is often in short supply, an element of chance remains and has to be dealt with. Suddenly Socorro made the connection between her earlier discussion with her husband and the onset of illness:

> But it was as if someone told me, remember what he said. And that's why he's this way. But wham! I remember. I go to my daughter. Lila, that one.
>
> I say, "Lila, but I think your father, he's ill because your father said that he couldn't go to Rivas because he didn't have good oxen and because I don't know. And this is that Jesús de Rescate is punishing him," I say, "because of what he said."
>
> Ay, Jesús de Rescate, my beauty, fix my ox and cure my husband. Fix my husband, Lord. Take pity on me because I have a number of daughters to feed. Don't do that, Lord, forgive him for his, for his humility. Because he is poor, Lord, I don't say it to offend you—and I begin, look, to beg: Ay, Jesusito, let there be injections to cure this man.

Socorro's "breakthrough" into prayer and supplication was provoked not by the normative view of saints as sources of supernatural assistance. Instead, the prayer was intended to counteract the Lord of Popoyuapa's perceived punishment of his noncompliant devotee, Juan. Miraculously, her supplication was answered quickly and dramatically: "Immediately at eleven o'clock, my little daughter came flying back with the injections, and they give him the first one. When it was about one in the afternoon, he was already talking, and he began to take liquids. When it was five in the evening, he was talking. And the ox stretched his calf and stood up." The fates of Juan and his ox are effectively linked in this narrative. One sees that their parallel illnesses and cures stem from Juan's initial insistence that his oxen were not good enough to use on the pilgrimage. Now Socorro could add the force of devotion to her desire to attend the fiesta at Popoyuapa, and, because of the role that the ox played, pilgrimage in a wagon became a necessity. Socorro concluded, "So, look, I come and say, 'Look, that's where you screwed yourself. I'm going to Popoyuapa. As long as that ox lives.' Then when that ox dies, then you [Jesus the Redeemer] can forgive me that promise I made you. I'm not bringing you money, I'm not bringing anything. I'm just coming to visit you, which is what I promised the Lord, and if the ox gets better and my husband gets bet-

Figure 7.2 The Monimbó Wagon Pilgrimage in 1991.

ter, I will travel to Popoyuapa." Socorro's discourse contains the power to make things happen, at least within her own sphere of influence. By the end of the tale, decision-making authority in the Vívas household has moved from the husband to the wife, for she transformed a simple invitation of husband to wife into a much more serious vow of a supplicant to Christ. In the process, she enabled the family to do what they desired all along, which was to go to the fiesta and camp out along the way, reliving a fondly remembered childhood experience.

And yet, though Socorro challenged her husband's authority and relied on the discourse of miracles to sanction her desire, we must be careful not inflate her autonomy. Rather, we might see her as temporarily gaining advantage by recognizing an opportunity to thwart the larger systems of domination that constrain her. In de Certeau's terminology, she has exercised a *tactic*, but she has not ultimately transformed her reality (1988:xix). At the same time, negotiations with the divinity are flexible. For instance, Socorro limited her act of supplication temporally, indicating that although the saint cannot be denied his devotion, the faithful can and do negotiate the terms. For the Vívas family, at least in 1991, when Socorro recalled her vow, the pilgrimage would continue as long as the ox lived—that is, ideally for several years.[10]

In her 1991 narrative of a previous momentous event, Socorro's initial journey in a wagon was clearly motivated by devotion *and* nostalgia. And during the 1980s, the event appears to have fulfilled both devotional and recreational purposes. She explained that she and her family decided to travel with a few other people from Masaya and nearby San Juan de Oriente. After a few years, this nucleus of pilgrims decided to establish themselves formally as a group. The act of veneration took on additional form when the group availed itself of an existing traditional resource, the mayordomía, in order to organize and elaborate their journey. This move represented a self-conscious self-fashioning, as Masaya-area pilgrims turned a visit to another town's festival into a Monimbó tradition.

Before this time, individuals who chose to travel by wagon would simply start out for Rivas in the days preceding the festival. Once the mayordomía was established, however, the wagon pilgrims visited one another in their respective homes to plan their trip. They collected resources for redistribution in the festive context and marked their departure from Masaya by forming a procession with jubilant brass band music and sponsoring a feast and an all-night vigil. Organizing the event thus implied increasing social interaction and festive elaboration. The mayordomía intensified the sense of community among wagon pilgrims. In 1989, however, the Masaya mayordomía was temporarily weakened by internal conflicts. The first-named mayordomo, Concepción Torres of San Juan de Oriente, separated from his wife,[11] and the group disbanded for that year. In 1990 and 1991, however, Socorro and Juan accepted the office of mayordomo, and the wagon pilgrims gathered at the Vívas farm in El Mojón. According to Socorro, from year to year numbers varied from four wagons in 1986 to nine in 1987 to eleven in 1988 to nineteen in 1990 and seventeen in 1991, but, overall, the effect of creating the mayordomía was to increase participation. None of this growth, however, registers in journalistic accounts that identify the "revival" as a phenomenon of the neoliberal 1990s.

The 1991 Monimbó Wagon Pilgrimage consisted of a number of patterned festival practices centered by a devotional core. The mayordoma hosted a meal the night that the pilgrims set off, which attracted nonpilgrim well-wishers who arrived to celebrate with the pilgrims. The first night's departure provided a time of heightened religious intensity, as pilgrims set off in the dark chanting and praying. This religious fervor would be repeated the following Thursday evening, when a much larger group of pilgrims at Popoyuapa participated in a candlelight vigil at the Lord of Redemption Sanctuary, and on Friday, the day of Jesus the Redeemer's procession.

In between these devotional moments, the event was characterized by relaxation, recreation, and humor. Pilgrims broke their three-day walk to Popoyuapa by camping at rivers that offered shade and refreshing bathing. Relatives and friends of the pilgrims trickled down by bus or truck to these campsites. If the journey represented a break from everyday routine, however, social distinctions, particularly those between friends and strangers continued in force. Turner's (1974) notion that pilgrimage constitutes *antistructure*, or a situation in which roles and hierarchies operating in the secular realm become unimportant, has been repeatedly demonstrated not to pertain in actual reports of pilgrimages from around the world (Eade and Sallnow 1991:4–5). Kendall's (1991) survey of pilgrims at Esquipulas, Guatemala, for example, confirms that participants' distinctive routes, interactions, and activities are all strongly determined by overlapping social categories of class, ethnicity, rural/urban, and national/foreign origin.

In 1991, Monimbó pilgrims remained with their family groups during the journey itself. One inebriated marimba player attracted a small crowd, and some pilgrims engaged in mild drinking or joked about drinking. Yet there were no communal gatherings. Nor did pilgrims mingle with local residents. Perhaps owing to the intense political polarization of that year, they remained wary of people they didn't know. Moreover, although the pilgrims as a group were involved in a religious enactment, individual reasons for attending varied. Some cited a religious promise, others went out of custom, and many others explained that they participated to support another traveler, usually an elderly female relative. The mayordomía structured the event—planning the route and trying to keep the pilgrims orderly and safe—just as Rivas organizers attempted to control a larger, rowdier crowd later in the week.

The complementary purposes of the two sets of organizers also displayed significant differences, however. The evening before the wagon pilgrims entered Popoyuapa, they camped at Gil Gonzalez Bridge. Father Santamaría drove out in his jeep with two nuns to welcome the pilgrims formally and to enjoin them to arrive at the church by eight, as he would be saying a mass for them. The next morning, however, the pilgrims were more concerned with creating a festive entrance than in hearing mass. They adorned their oxen with flowers and, as they neared the settlement, set off fireworks at short intervals to announce their arrival. A marimba musician and young costumed dancers headed the procession. They stopped periodically to dance energetically in the streets. Someone blew merrily on a kazoo, while Socorro fretted that they should be blowing a conch. By the time the wagon pilgrims reached the church, it was well past eight. The priest gave another short welcome from the church steps and invited the pilgrims to share *mondongo*, or tripe soup. The weary pilgrims, who had broken camp at four that morning, set off to park their wagons and rest.

Harnessing the Wagon Pilgrims

During the 1970s and 1980s, as noted, Father Santamaría had enlarged the church and set limits on fiesta activities in the plaza. The Masaya wagon pilgrims had organized themselves and elaborated additional festival activities both to celebrate their departure in their home community and to mark their entrance into Popoyuapa. Fathers Navas and Lugo subsequently harnessed the wagon pilgrimage to their own project to christianize the festivities. Father Navas recalled that when he first arrived at the sanctuary in 1992, very few wagons arrived in Popoyuapa, and Masaya had the only organized group. He and Father Lugo therefore visited the towns of individual wagon pilgrims to help them organize pilgrimage committees. In addition, they named Juan Vívas president of the entire group of wagon pilgrims. Soon six communities participated in an organized wagon pilgrimage: Masaya, Granada, San Juan del Oriente, Nandaime, Santa Teresa–Los Encuentros, and San José de Gracía. The priests also required that wagon pilgrims take a vow of sobriety for the duration of the pilgrimage.

Civic leaders in Rivas approved of the wagon pilgrimage. In the early 1990s, they began to organize welcoming activities to encourage participation. Dr. Ramón Valdéz Jiménez had begun to act as a padrino for the pilgrims, providing them with light refreshments at the Gil Gonzalez Bridge and food at the church when they arrived the next day. With the priests' blessing, Dr. Valdéz recruited individual padrinos for each wagon and thus began a custom of providing a food basket to each pilgrim as a stimulus for their participation. By 2001, the Rivas padrinos had become quite generous. In addition to the food basket, one padrino prepared three thousand nacatamales (steamed corn and pork dish), another provided pasturage for the animals, while a third offered silo packs for the oxen. The mayor and his council, the police and fire departments, and bus drivers were recruited to welcome, honor, and provide for the wagon pilgrims. *Nuevo Diario* reporter Flor de María Palma described 160 oxen-drawn wagons carrying perhaps two thousand pilgrims being greeted by an equal number of Rivas padrinos. She asserted, "In this way is commemorated the renewal of that tradition which began more than 150 years ago and that twelve years ago was at the point of being lost when only four pilgrim wagons arrived to venerate the famous and miraculous image of Jesus the Redeemer in his sanctuary at Popoyuapa."[12] The wagon pilgrimage had indeed grown in the 1990s as a consequence of church and civic leaders' efforts. Yet what Palma identified as the low point in the tradition corresponds to the year the Masaya mayordomía temporarily disbanded. Moreover, she associated the renewal with the postrevolutionary neoliberal period by dating it from 1990, but at the same time projected the tradition back 150 years by conflating general attendance at the Popoyuapa festival with traveling in a wagon. Of course, general attendance had been rising ever since Father Santamaría's innovations of the 1970s.

The Rivas padrinos' generous welcoming activities singled out the wagon pilgrims for special treatment. At the same time, however, they introduced a hierarchical model of class relations into the performance of pilgrimage because all wagon pilgrims are poor (Socorro is emphatic on this point), whereas many of the Rivas padrinos are people of means. Establishing a padrino group to assist a mayordomía represents a traditional option in popular Catholicism, but a padrino is both a festival sponsor and a godfather. In either case, the word implies a relationship that grants the padrino respect and authority, while it requires his generosity. The padrino participates in the festival, but his role remains distinct from that of the pilgrim. Although wagon pilgrims are not forced in any way to turn themselves into nostalgic symbols for the Rivas town fathers, one can see in the display of festive cooperation between host and visiting group an assertion of social hierarchy. Indeed, newspaper coverage of the wagon pilgrimage depicted the padrinos as the party responsible for increasing participation from 4 wagons in 1989 to 160 wagons in 2001. It is their largess that has renewed the religious tradition,[13] even while the pilgrims remain the singular performers of the symbolically intensified cultural-religious act of traveling to the festival in wagons.

In addition, the priests and Dr. Valdéz elaborated new activities specifically for the wagon pilgrims. They created flags for each locale, and on Tuesday the wagon pilgrims parade with these flags when they enter Rivas. On Wednesday, they congregate at the church to visit Christ the Redeemer and pin their *milagros* (small replicas of body parts, jails, and other symbols) to the image's robes. This is the only day that pilgrims actually handle the saint because the image is usually placed high up out of reach. Thus, the priests allow the wagon pilgrims a privileged intimacy with the miraculous Christ figure. Dr. Valdéz has also organized a Wednesday event outside of the church itself, at which wagon pilgrims provide personal testimony of the saint's miraculous power.

Father Navas connects the belief in miracles to the biblical story of Christ curing a woman who touched the hem of his robe with faith. He instructs visitors to the sanctuary with this story, explaining that it is their faith in God that produces healing, not any power residing in the Lord of Redemption image. In this way, Father Navas reconciles popular discourse with the authoritative textual tradition and Christianizes popular practice. He accommodates but does not promote the miracle-story session organized by Dr. Valdéz.

On Thursday, the wagon pilgrims travel in procession to nearby San Jorge for a swim. A candlelight vigil at the sanctuary that evening and hourly masses mark the central religious event of the festival. Hatton (2000) attended the vigil in 1999 and described it as a happy fiesta. People filled the grounds and the plaza with hammocks and cooking fires. Inside the church passageway, the atmosphere was subdued and serious, but outside people were relaxed and having fun. By the time the sun set, the area was so packed it was hard to move.

On Friday, the plaza clears, and the faithful accompany the Christ figure in procession. Although excursion buses continue to arrive with pilgrims throughout the day, these latecomers stay only a short time. Zulema Romero Mercado recalled attending the festival by excursion bus:

> And I saw, well, that it was a lot of people, that—but when I entered [the church]—my handkerchief (gesturing to her mouth)—I left almost suffocating, almost strangled. So, I said, no. Next year, if he [Jesus the Redeemer] gives me the means, and I am able, I'm coming a day earlier, because this is not going to happen again. To come in excursion—you don't see the saint well, or ma—you don't hear mass, because now, when you get out, the bus says, "At this time we're on our way." And so, in those excursions, they spend more time in San Jorge or in San Juan del Sur, bathing, and they don't spend time in the church.[14]

As she pointed out, the way one travels to the festival affects the quality of one's experience. And although it would not be fair to categorize the wagon pilgrims as more religious than those who travel by excursion bus, a distinction has emerged between the two kinds of visitors to the festival. The wagon pilgrims arrive early in the week and are welcomed with a variety of special events, whereas those who arrive by excursion bus hardly stop at the church. In fact, after a fatal traffic accident in the late 1990s, the Rivas priests instructed wagon pilgrims to leave Friday morning at dawn for safety reasons. Now, Juan Vívas laments, the wagon pilgrims do not accompany Jesus the Redeemer on his procession around the village. Now they overlap with other visitors to the Popoyuapa festival only for the Thursday night vigil.

As nostalgic and modern pilgrimage practices collide at Popoyuapa, the older form of travel takes on heightened religious significance. For Zulema Romero, though, becoming a part of the wagon pilgrimage has been liberating as well. In this religious setting, a woman alone can travel, socialize, and enjoy herself. She explained, "So I said, 'This isn't happening to me again. I'm going to go spend the night there in Popoyuapa.' And so. I would go by myself. By myself. And there with somebody, somebody I knew, I would approach them. I would put my little suitcase there. I'd spend the night there, because the night is fun there at the church, well, the music, and so I went. I'd spend the night.

Then where I felt sleepy, I'd go sleep where my friend was." Such a perspective again demonstrates how religious devotion may sanction poor women's desires, in this case for independence and freedom of movement. Several older women remarked that their children worry about their attending the wagon pilgrimage, but help them financially because they understand the activity as a mother's treat or pleasure.

Using popular devotional practice to assert an independent agenda appears to be nothing new. American student Dana Munro stumbled upon a women's house prayer around 1916 during his travels through Central America.[15] His description demonstrates that women ignored the normal demands of husbands, children, and guests to pursue their devotions:

> One woman, standing in front of a table on which stood a little statue of the Virgin, was leading the group in prayers and hymns. In a row facing her, on wooden boxes and other improvised seats, were eight or ten other women who joined in the prayers and hymns with loud shrill voices. At times there was a pause, and a bottle of guaro passed from hand to hand, followed by a gourd full of water. Each lady took a swig from the bottle and then a mouthful of the water, which she spat out on the dirt floor behind her. All were clearly having a wonderful time, but the *rezo* had already gone on beyond the usual supper hour, and from time to time a husband would look in the open door and withdraw with an audible groan. Sometimes a small child, probably encouraged by the men, would enter and gently pull his mother's skirt, only to retire in tears when his mother cuffed him. Finally, the other ladies left, looking rather pleased with themselves, and the mistress of the house graciously listened to my request for supper and for permission to hang my hammock on the front porch. Her husband, as soon as she turned her back to get out the beans, sadly examined the almost empty guaro bottle. (1983:59)

Today such devotions may or may not involve drinking alcohol, but the fervor and pleasure in participating remain identified particularly though not exclusively with mature women.

In 1998, the sanctuary erected two monuments to the wagon pilgrims, which formally recognize their important contribution to the festival. These statues, one a male pilgrim in midstride and the other an oxen-drawn wagon, stand on five-foot pedestals in front of the church but within the gated area. Thus, the wagon pilgrims have been transformed into model or "good pilgrims" who behave properly and are organized under the auspices of the church. They are contrasted with the drunken merrymakers from elsewhere who threaten the "traditional" character of the festival. Of course, not all wagon pilgrims behave perfectly, and not all of those who arrive by bus for Thursday's and Friday's celebrations are without faith. The oxen-drawn wagon has become more than just an antiquated form of travel; it now symbolizes controlled religious devotion and, with the addition of the padrinos' activities, a hierarchical social structure that benefits the poor.

In 2001, the Liberal Party presidential candidate Enrique Bolaños made a "pilgrimage" to petition Jesus the Redeemer during his electoral campaign, further linking the Popoyuapa festival with the political establishment.[16] That year, participation in the Monimbó Wagon Pilgrimage dropped precipitously for the first time, from thirty-nine to twenty-three wagons.[17] Pilgrims belong to all political parties despite the anti-Sandinista bias of Catholic Church leaders, and the 2001 decline may have resulted from Sandinista pilgrims' electing not to attend an event that had obviously been appropriated by the Liberal Party. The decline illustrates the delicate nature of the convergence of popular with official religious interests in the pilgrimage and reminds us that hegemonic appropriations of the popular are never complete.

The response of Masaya wagon organizers to the changes of the 1990s, however, has been positive overall. Juan and Socorro have achieved a status they never dreamed they would have. Although heading a mayordomía brings honor within one's home community, now important people from outside their community also visit them. Juan told me that he is the most looked for president of all the wagon pilgrims and that it is a *don*, a great honor, to receive such recognition from the church. Socorro reiterated this attitude, saying that she never imagined that she would be working so closely with the nuns or be so involved with the veneration of the saint and all the activities that go with it. Like the Toribio family, who were honored to receive Daniel Ortega as mayordomo of their Torovenado de Malinche, the Vívas family proudly acknowledges their association with Rivas civic and religious leaders.

Moreover, their current understanding of the pilgrimage reflects the more religious focus the priests have created for the festival. In 2001, Juan emphasized the sacrifice that the wagon pilgrimage entails compared to traveling to the festival by bus:

They go now in the morning; they come back in the afternoon. We are different in that we go Saturday and come back Saturday, eight days later. We come, as the saying goes, paying what we promised. Well, what we asked from the image. And we come back safe and sound from the trip. But those who come by—go by bus, it seems to me it's a pleasure trip, well, like any other trip they [might make], we can say. Because they come to the church, they decorate it with flowers, they put their flowers there, and they go to the beach. It isn't the same. While from the time we get there, we're visiting him in the afternoon, in the morning.[18]

The wagon pilgrims spend more time at Popoyuapa, Juan pointed out, specifically visiting with the image of Jesus the Redeemer.

Moreover, Juan noted that the walk would not be a sacrifice if pilgrims had a broad pathway to travel on, but because they must go on the highway, they risk their own physical safety. Quite reasonably, he wants the government to build such an alternate route.[19] This observation provides an interesting perspective on how recreation has been transformed into sacrifice in the contemporary context. Another form of sacrifice, of course, is financial. Few participants own their own oxen, and drivers charge from seven hundred to one thousand cordobas (about fifty to seventy-five U.S. dollars) plus meals to take a group on the pilgrimage. Indeed, a common miracle attributed to the saint by Masaya pilgrims is his sending money their way (usually through generous family members or neighbors) so that they can make the journey.

A few pilgrims even object to the padrinos because they see the padrinos' generosity as interfering with this notion of sacrifice. Socorro emphasizes that the important aspect of festival largess is not the material gift, but the attitude of brotherhood[20] (not patronage) that the giver expresses. Thus, she rejects any view of the Monimbó Wagon Pilgrimage as an enactment of subordination. There are wagon pilgrims, Socorro admitted in 2001, who may be attracted by the padrinos' gifts, "but I see that most of us go with faith. With faith in the saint. There are some

Figure 7.3 In 2001, Juan Vívas (left) carried the small image of Jesús del Rescate that Masayans now circulate for several months each year.

who don't come to the church much, and having come a few times, they don't participate anymore. It seems that they go—they don't go with that great faith. Like—I don't go out to the—to those parties they make, I don't go to the beach, I don't go—[I go] from my wagon to the church and from the church to my wagon."²¹ Socorro clearly prioritizes the religious motivation for the pilgrimage over its recreational aspect. She also articulates a notion that the good pilgrim is a constant participant, traveling year after year. Indeed, by 2001, she asserted that she had promised the saint to attend his festival until her death, even though the ox whose lifetime had provided the initial period for her devotion has been dead for many years. For his part, Juan remembered the original vow having been for *his* lifetime. Thus, the Vívas family Christianized their own practice. They now see themselves as better pilgrims than some others who attend the festival.

In the mid-1990s, at the pilgrims' request, the Rivas priests began to lend out a smaller image of Jesus the Redeemer to the communities that sponsored wagon pilgrimages. Now, each year on April 20 a group from Granada arrives in Popoyuapa to receive the image. On August 5, about five hundred Masayans travel to Granada to take the image back to their community, where they pass it from house to house, holding daily prayers in his honor. Juan takes the image in procession from one household to the next, accompanied by fireworks. He explains that these processions call attention to their attraction, which is the Monimbó Wagon Pilgrimage. On December 2, six busloads of Masayans escort the image back to Popoyuapa, where they celebrate a mass at the sanctuary, go for a swim, and then return, saddened because they no longer have Jesus the Redeemer in their possession. Although these new activities have increased religious practice and contributed to the church's coffers, they paradoxically represent increased community control over the image and the full establishment of a mayordomía. If the mayordomía was originally established to organize the wagon pilgrims on their journey, now it also involves venerating the image of Jesus the Redeemer in their homes.

In spite of their closer association with Rivas church and civic leaders, Juan and Socorro Vívas continue to articulate a view of the wagon pilgrimage that is firmly rooted in popular belief and practices. Juan explained to me, "I can prove and I testify that my trip is a sacrifice because I asked him—my wife asked him to perform that, this miracle, and it's where she did it, with what she asked him, well, he saved my life. And it's there where we believe that, that there's the belief that there's that Jesus who rescues one's life for one." Although Juan begins with the notion that Socorro's faith is what cured him, he ultimately returns to the popular belief in the miraculous powers of Jesus the Redeemer.

Moreover, despite his more religious focus, Juan and other Masaya wagon pilgrims frequently refer to the wagon pilgrimage as an *attraction*, indicating that he continues to see his activity as a display or show. Most pilgrims I spoke with in 2001 stated that they first participated in the event not because of a religious promise, but out of curiosity or because a friend had invited them. Moreover, an avowedly agnostic family from Monimbó expressed a desire to rent a pair of oxen and join the pilgrimage because it represented a colorful neighborhood tradition. Although Socorro's faith provided the initial impetus for the wagon pilgrimage, she also understands the event as a performance of local identity. She pointed out that Masayans are the only organized mayordomía and that they provided the model that Father Navas replicated elsewhere: "There is no mayordomía in the other caravans. Nor is there the organization that they have here, where they come with music, they come in procession, they come in a parade. There isn't any of that. In none of the, of the, of the, eh, committees do they have that. It's only in the Masaya group that this exists. The Masaya group grew that, and the Masaya group was the one that started that, it's that example from here, from the Masayans." This emphasis on the proper form of organizing as a group, of displaying oneself to one's own community and to other communities, allows Socorro to retain a sense of her own activities as centrally important. The wagon pilgrims are not only good Catholics, but are also Masayans, who are recognized as authorities on popular traditions or folklore. Moreover, Socorro explained, although there are always a few newcomers, most of the wagon pilgrims are old friends, people who know her and whom she knows very well because they have participated year after year. Thus, the mayordomía and the pilgrimage promote, facilitate, and cement social relations within the Masaya community, reproducing that quality that distinguishes this indigenous-identified area from other surrounding communities.

By 2001, the wagon pilgrims had even been incorporated into the Saint Jerome Festival, if not in person then as another symbol of traditional indigenous identity. At the annual India Bonita Contest, young female marimba dancers compete for the honor of embodying the indigenous cultural ideal. Judges select a winner based on racial features; proficiency in the dance; authenticity of costume, jewelry, and hair; and knowledge of the city's cultural traditions. The young contestants arrive at the contest accompanied by marimba or brass bands, if they can afford them, and traditional neighborhood leaders or figureheads, if they can entice them (Borland 1996). As I waited with four young candidates to enter the contest arena in 2001, a burst of brass band music from the east alerted us to another arrival. Seated high up in a covered wagon pulled by two massive, flower-garlanded, dancing oxen, this candidate made an impressively boisterous entrance. A printed sign announced that she represented the Monimbó Wagon Pilgrimage to Popoyuapa.

Thus, in the nation's folklore capital, the Christianized pilgrimage was reinscribed as a lively cultural performance of indigeneity.

Convergent Motives, Distinctive Identities

The growth of the Monimbó Wagon Pilgrimage to Popoyuapa reflects a "convergence of interests" between Rivas festival organizers and Masaya-area pilgrims (Eade and Sallnow 1991). Clearly, civic and religious authorities successfully harnessed a popular impulse. Rivas festival organizers use the wagon pilgrimage to distinguish (however slippery the distinction may be in practice) between "good" pilgrims and the rabble, while simultaneously asserting the greater traditionality of the former. Welcoming activities and public monuments honoring the wagon pilgrims demonstrate a clear preference for this pilgrim group. At the same time, the neoliberal restoration of religious purpose to the festival must be understood within the context of the Sandinista-era celebration of Masaya festival as a heritage of indigenous resistance to domination. Despite journalistic claims to the contrary, the pilgrimage to Popoyuapa represents an improvement on an indigenous model in the same way the Torovenado del Pueblo organizers improved on the Catholic model they believed had been imposed on the community.

Masaya wagon pilgrims are pleased to assume the role of model participants, yet they continue to find in their performance a powerful assertion of cultural difference based on the popular religious organization of the mayordomía and the festivalizing practices it generates, practices that embody their distinctive identity. This indigenous difference does not directly challenge the constructions of Catholic religious authorities or Rivas civic leaders. In fact, each group works to incorporate other parties' understandings within its own framing, in what Sallnow has labeled an act of "mutual misunderstanding" (1991:149–50).

De Certeau identifies the discourse of miracles as a form of consumer poaching on established Catholic religion. Believers are able to use a system not of their own making to escape the fatalism imposed on them by a hierarchical social order, where poverty, rural origin, illiteracy, and indigenous identity conspire to limit their aspirations (1988:17). Yet they are not the creators of this discourse. Nor does their temporary escape transform their social reality in any lasting way. I would argue that miracle discourse in contemporary Nicaragua reflects a popular rather than an established Catholic doctrine, although, certainly, Rivas priests attempt to educate their congregation to understand the concept from a Christian rather than a popular perspective.

More important, the belief in miracles remains the foundation for devotional practice. It provides a flexible sanction for desire that is capable of mobilizing large numbers of people, both believers *and* their supporters, who may or may not venerate the saints. Women who ordinarily subordinate their own desires to those of husband and family find in the popular fiesta a culturally sanctioned space for pleasurable religious and social experience. Therefore, although Rivas's religious and civic leaders have harnessed, enlarged, encouraged, and celebrated the Masaya pilgrims' attraction, the wagon pilgrims retain their own form, leadership, and meaning.

The wagon pilgrimage is meaningful to participants precisely because it combines religious devotion with a display of distinctive identity. Its very form, which multiplies social interaction and requires an extended stay, reinforces community integration. And yet the wagon pilgrimage is simultaneously a show, in which Masaya pilgrims folklorize themselves, performing their identity for Masaya, for Rivas, and for the nation. Even as newspaper reporters, padrinos, and priests redefine the wagon pilgrims' actions, locating agency for the event in Rivas, the Masaya pilgrims continue to value the enactment as an expression of their own difference. Their reaction is not counterhegemonic, yet they continue to generate alternative meanings as they mark out a space for popular expression, creativity, and action in the festival context.

Pilgrimages thus contain an important performative dimension, in addition to their religious, recreational, and market functions, for the way in which one travels counts as much as what one does when one arrives. In Masaya, this performative dimension of pilgrimage folds back into the Festival of Saint Jerome, as the Monimbó Wagon Pilgrimage becomes a celebrated neighborhood tradition that can be humorously represented in the torovenados or drawn on for heritage displays such as the India Bonita Contest. National journalists represent the wagon pilgrimage as a continuation of something very old, but the mayordomos and their neighbors understand the attraction as something novel and unique, an improvement on what they remember from the past.

Once again, Monimboseños and Masayans have made themselves the guardians of tradition not because they preserve it, but because they create it through performance. For Masayans, the tradition becomes their own lived experience, which embraces both progress and nostalgia. It expresses, differentially perhaps, the religious, artistic, and playful sensibilities of a multifaceted community.

8 Conclusion

Folklore revival is a phenomenon connected both to nationalism and to international capitalism that necessarily affects the forms of local culture. When privileged members of a society revalue, refashion, and perform the cultural arts of a marginalized group, they inevitably mark the forms with new kinds of distinction and employ them for new purposes (Thompson 1979). These new forms, attached as they are to the socially powerful, become the models to which other performers aspire (Bourdieu 1984). In Nicaragua, the myth of mestizaje (Field 1998; Gould 1998) posited the absorption of Indians into the national collective both as racialized, sexualized bodies and as political communities. This myth facilitated the folklore revival, enabling both a popularization and a transfer of leadership in the festival arts primarily from Indian Monimboseños to mestizo professionals and secondarily from women to men.

During the Somoza era, the revival produced two opposing aesthetics: the raucous, oppositional Torovenado del Pueblo, sponsored by an indigenous-identified professional class, and the elegant Baile de Negras, sponsored by mestizo-identified Masayans reaching toward elitism. The Negras groups were temporarily associated with the revolution because their whiteface masks were linked to a güegüense-like ridiculing of foreign authorities. Yet they played only a minor role in the nationalization of folk dance that followed, in part as a consequence of Masaya dancers' resistance and in part because this kind of marimba dancing did not, in fact, express values of revolutionary populism. The carnivalesque torovenados were much more amenable to revolutionary refashioning. During the 1980s, creative critiques flourished, but the emphasis on protest, in particular protest aligned with government policy and against its enemies, alienated local residents, who preserved a notion of parody as an homage to the subject being represented. The older torovenados had provided indigenous-identified Masayans with humorous self-representations that both relied on and reinforced neighborhood integration. If the two great torovenados of the 1980s reflected the politicized cultural reality of that time, they failed to maintain and assert residents' difference from national and international communities adequately. Furthermore, the great torovenados introduced an aesthetic of finery and lascivious display that seemed inappropriate to a torovenado. The grotesque aesthetic of earlier torovenados had highlighted poverty, not wealth.

The creative surge of the revolutionary period also gave rise to new forms that were quickly accepted as traditions in Monimbó because they reasserted a local sense of appropriate celebration. The Procession of the Ahuizotes avoided divisive issues and opened up participation to women, thus providing the kind of neighborhood integration the great torovenados lacked. As a playful invocation of one aspect of the neighborhood's supernatural past, this enactment remained firmly secular, yet it avoided the fixity of folklorized forms because the past it indexed constituted part of living memory for many Monimboseños.

Neither the torovenados, with their strong revolutionary associations, nor the Negras, with its emerging identity as a homosexual form, provided the opportunity for neoliberal refashioning. The pilgrimage to Popoyuapa, however, restored religious belief as the underlying motivation for cultural display. As such, it was amenable to Catholic appropriation. The Masaya pilgrims turned away from Saint Jerome toward the Lord of Redemption in part because the focus of the Saint Jerome Festival had become primarily cultural. And yet cultural display remains a central aspect of Monimbó pilgrims' experience. How they organize and present themselves continues to be a sign of their difference from other kinds of pilgrims, even other wagon pilgrims.

Folklorization, or the transformation of expressive behavior into heritage, continually reinvents community identity through performance. In a pulselike movement, cultural forms are enacted, appropriated, refashioned, invented anew, appropriated, and refashioned once again. Scholars often equate revivalists' creative refashioning of traditions with a growing secularization of culture, or they may view it as a capitalist incursion into a more communitarian ideal (García-Canclini 1993; Guss 2000:24–59; Lombardi-Satriani 1978). The restoration of local authority, then, involves a reinsertion of religious ritual as the reason for cultural performance. Yet the latest convergence of interests between and among Rivas priests, city promoters, the Catholic-identified Liberal Party, and Monimbó wagon pilgrims demonstrates that the tendency for national or urban or political groups to draw on a traditional community's inventiveness is not restricted to the secular aspects of their tradition. Different extracommunity forces—some with a secular, others with a religious focus—draw on popular culture, reshaping it to fit their own agendas (Magliocco 1993).

In his penetrating study of the Notting Hill Carnival of London, Abner Cohen (1993) suggests that carnival represents a joking relationship between the state and its citizenry, characterized by both alliance and enmity. Yet this formulation fails to take into account the gendered nature of a citizenry that engages in rowdy excesses and violence. Recognizing the masculinity of traditional festival performances encourages us to rethink arguments that carnival remains a privileged site for the articulation of popular resistance to domination (Scott 1990). The growth in Masaya's festival activities in the 1990s, for instance, entails assertions of identity that intersect with and even challenge hegemonic aspects of the local community. As women and gay men who self-identify as the third sexual option increasingly intervene in both the production and performance of festival, they reveal that the festival expressions of the "people" have been largely circumscribed by gender. Neither group attempts to impersonate men, yet their visible presence in a festival context that constructs masquerading as an expression of male shamelessness provides a new set of possibilities for performance.

Judith Bettelheim (1998) suggests that Woman is a construct as much for female-identified as for male-identified female impersonators. Thus, she argues, unmasked Caribbean women masquerading as Sexy Women in carnival processions engage in festival othering just as much as the masked, cross-dressed men do. Masaya's Negras directors, in contrast, attempt to strip their performances of signs of gender in order to achieve an ideal of abstract elegance and romance that opposes carnivalesque licentiousness. That this form now also provides a vehicle for gay identity attests to an erosion of heterosexual male dominance in both the festival and larger social arenas. If the challenge to local control over the aesthetic system could be identified as external to the community in the 1980s, that challenge now arises from within the community itself.

And yet if gay men have capitalized on the liberatory possibilities of traditional festival forms to develop powerful, innovative expressions of artistry, women's limited entry into the performance sphere remains circumscribed by the gendered nature of the performance tradition itself. In masquerade, women exhibit more controlled movements than men, and women's participation increases largely in forms that conceal rather than reveal their bodies. In marimba dancing, however, when young women incorporate the stylistic innovations of mature Negras dancers, directors quickly correct these distortions of the women's performance form. Even though women have stepped assertively into the performance sphere, their challenge to the established gender order appears muted at best.

In revisiting Bauman's (1977) central text for performance theory, Sawin (2002) has pointed out that in addition to the two benefits the theory confers on performers—approbation for a display of competence and the power to persuade or direct an audience—we might see performance as inducing certain emotional states or pleasures. Thus, a performer may enjoy a temporary loss of self-consciousness in the flow state induced by aesthetic accomplishment. Alternately, the performer may become an object of his or her audience's desire. Sawin argues:

> A patriarchal system survives by keeping women under control, requiring them to subordinate their will and their desires to goals set by and for the advantage of men. Ideally this is achieved hegemonically, by persuading women they are inferior and do require male guidance and by requiring women to internalize their own surveillance. So it makes sense that women can be granted only limited access to the satisfactions and the persuasive powers of performance provided that this experience reinforces their awareness of being watched by men and of needing to comply with standards for behavior and appearance set by men. . . . A woman who slips into the flow state and transcends self-consciousness, forgetting that she is being evaluated both for the skill and effectiveness of her display of esthetic competence and for her performance of self, is supremely dangerous. She potentially wields the power of per-

suasion and erotic allure and receives reinforcing approbation, uncontrolled by hegemonic forces that insist she employ these capacities to reinstantiate her own subordination. (2002:46–47)

In such situations, women cannot play as men do. However, if we recognize desire in the audience as well as in the performer, and if we recognize that women form a significant if not predominant audience for Negras performances, then we might imagine why the assertive, seductive negra role fascinates female as well as male audiences. Women watch the Negras dance and imagine what a "shameless" performance of female elegance might look or even feel like.

Why is folklorization a spur to greater creativity in Masaya, whereas in other places it leads to a deadening of tradition, all vitality sucked from it? Cultural activists in the Sandinista folklore revival may have uncritically accepted the myth of mestizaje, yet the heroic role Monimboseños played in the insurrection and the new government's celebration of that heroism provided neighborhood residents with a sense of themselves as popular leaders. Traditionality gives people a sense of authority. Marginality gives them a critical perspective. Cultural authority, as we now know, begins with self-definition. As long as subaltern groups allow themselves to be defined by others, they remain passive and voiceless. When, however, they respond to the representations fashioned by others by creating their own alternate representations, they resist limiting definitions. Masayans are not the guardians of national culture because they faithfully maintain a set of cultural forms, but because they continually generate new forms to promote local integration, a potential social basis for resistance to larger systems of power. If tradition is a creation of the past that serves present needs, it also remains a powerful, enabling construct for communities as well as for nations.

Notes

Note: Many of the newspaper articles cited in the notes can be accessed online at the newspapers' Web sites.

Chapter 1. Living Festival

1. The Feast of Saint Michael is September 29; thus, his procession has been incorporated into the larger Saint Jerome procession on September 30. During the colonial period, Masaya was divided into four sectors; Saint Michael and Saint Jerome were patrons of two of these sectors. Several towns in Nicaragua organize traditional events called *topes,* in which two or more towns process their saints to a central location, where they ritually greet one another. The events symbolize the interdependence of the small communities. Such symbolism may also apply in the Masayan festival.

2. The presence of two sets of traditional leaders is a symptom of the current disorganization of the indigenous movement in Monimbó. When the traditional indigenous representative, *alcalde de vara* Vicente Jiménez, died in 1992, Humberto Salinas, who had worked with Jiménez, retained the symbols of office. However, neighborhood organizers became concerned that another man, Lorenzo López, was soliciting international aid in the name of the indigenous mayor, but that the aid was not going to the community. These organizers, who were mostly Sandinista, collaborated with representatives from city government, then controlled by the Liberal Party, to hold an election in 1995, but it was not well attended. Jesús López won with 175 votes. Vicente's son, Ramon Jiménez, retained control of the council of elders, a group of elderly men who assisted the alcalde de vara. He held an alternate election in the Isabel Gaitán Dance Hall, attended by about two hundred people. There, another man, Miguel Téllez, was declared alcalde de vara. Both groups have established themselves as nonprofit organizations and are therefore legally recognized. Nevertheless, residents generally regard the indigenous mayor as a symbolic figure only and are disinclined to participate in the infighting of this small group.

3. This figure is originally from León, where she once danced with Cabezones, or Big-Heads, which were dwarflike figures with oversized heads who recited vulgar couplets to the Giant Lady as they danced (Lancaster 1988:49–50). Today, the mute Giant Lady dances in many Nicaraguan festivals without her male companions.

4. The group's director, Haydée Palacios, had recently been named Masaya

cultural liaison for the Institute of Nicaraguan Culture, the national government's cultural arm. No Masayan festival performers or politicians were consulted about this appointment. Although Palacios is a native of Masaya, she has a national reputation as a Managua folk ballet director. At the festival, her dancers performed a choreographed version of Las Promesantes, a marimba dance once performed by believing adult women to whom the saint had granted a favor. This particular form of marimba dancing lost popularity in the 1960s. Current performances of Las Promesantes are thus imaginative re-creations of a former ritual practice. A version of this dance is still performed in the Guanacaste region of Costa Rica for religious processions, probably brought there by earlier migrants from Masaya (Carlos Fernández, personal communication, 2000).

5. This deference departs from the pattern of the previous four years, when President Arnoldo Alemán, also a Liberal, received a "cold shoulder" from the saint. Masaya's Liberal Party mayor, Carlos Iván Hüeck, head of the Saint Jerome Festival organizing committee, had appointed Bolaños *mayordomo*, or chairman, of the festival. Bolaños, originally a Masaya cotton grower, was head of COSEP, the business group that supported the revolution and then opposed Sandinista economic policy in the 1980s. He became vice president under Arnoldo Alemán in 1996. Alemán soon earned a reputation for being more corrupt even than the Somozas. In 2001, Bolaños succeeded to the presidency, and in 2002 he stripped Alemán of his immunity from prosecution and began proceedings against him for his extravagant personal use of government funds. This move responded to popular demands as well as to those of foreign aid agencies, who refused to provide additional support to the Nicaraguan government, citing corruption. For a brief English-language summary and analysis of these events, see Kinser 2003.

6. In Nicaraguan elections, each party receives a number that indicates its position on the ballot and by which it is subsequently identified. In 2001, the Liberal Party was first, the Sandinista coalition was second, and the Conservative Party was fourth on the ballot. Thus, one finger signals support for the Liberals, two for the Sandinistas, and four for the Conservatives.

7. Hüeck, son of a Somocista-era mayor, had been elected the previous year and proved intransigent in dealing with non-Liberal members of his city council. After only a year, he was considered a do-nothing mayor, and his threat to resign if the Sandinistas won the national elections did nothing to improve his popularity.

8. The study of popular enactments as theater remains undeveloped in Nicaragua. In his examination of postsocialist Nicaraguan theater, Randy Martin (1994) focuses primarily on the productions of educated intellectuals, both historically and in the contemporary moment. From national intellectuals' perspective, popular festival enactments are "inauthentic, inaccurate and fragmentary" versions of a (written) national heritage and identity, and, Martin adds, serve mainly as a means of displacing productive capacity to a nonproductive realm, translating the "mobilization of labor," a profoundly political act, "into the labor of mobilization" (76). At the same time, Martin allows that festival enactments make processes of social

identity visible (51). Given that festival enactments and their description provide only a counterpoint for Martin's analysis of other kinds of theater (so much so that he mistakenly identifies the patron saint of Jinotepe as Saint Jerome), the latter point remains undeveloped.

9. For a highly readable account of how politically motivated testimonial music, in particular that of Carlos Mejía Godoy, fostered revolutionary consciousness among the popular classes, see Scruggs 2002.

10. For more on the ideological construction of the "new man" during the 1970s and 1980s, see Hodges 1986:256–91.

11. For an explanation of the cultural goals of popular education programs, see Tünnerman Bernheim 1983. White 1986 provides a selection of interviews and commentary from cultural policymakers. See also Beverly and Zimmerman 1990 for a provocative discussion of how alienated sectors of third-world elites make common cause with an oppressed majority, using literature as a means to produce an oppositional consciousness. Whisnant 1995, 189–270, provides a cogent overview of Sandinista cultural policy and its detractors.

12. For an excellent discussion of the conflict between the two cultural planners and the deficiencies of both institutions from the perspective of popular artisans, see Field 1987 and 1999:77–124. For a comprehensive review of cultural theories, policies, and debates during the Sandinista period, see Wellinga 1994.

13. For more on Monimbó's culture wars with Masaya, see my ethnography of the neighborhood, Borland 1994, especially chapter 6; for a discussion of the neighborhood political polarization as it relates to the India Bonita Contest, see Borland 1996; for a summary of the local opposition to the national folk dance revival under the Sandinistas, see Scruggs 1994 and 1998, Borland 2002.

14. The Institute of Nicaraguan Culture, which replaced the Ministry of Culture after it was closed in 1988, attempted to safeguard the artistic, historic, and cultural patrimony of the nation in the 1990s. However, a glance at its preservation projects, listed in its 1997 publication *Nuestro patrimonimo cultural* 1, no. 2, demonstrates a marked emphasis on projects in Nicaragua's two Spanish colonial cities. Of fourteen projects completed or in progress, seven are located in León, six in Granada, and one in Río San Juan (the restoration of a Spanish fort and castle). Of the four projects now in the planning stages, two are located in Masaya, one in León, and one in Managua. None, however, involves archeological or ethnological explorations of indigenous cultures, even though the first article in this publication calls for the protection of precolonial petroglyphs, statuary, and pottery, which are currently threatened with destruction.

15. Rist (1997) makes a strong case that the post–World War II development project has done little to advance real living conditions of popular groups in the "developing" world. Although the development paradigm has constructed international institutions dedicated to relieving poverty and has created a professional class of aid workers and consultants, the difference between rich and poor nations grows exponentially, as has the difference between rich and poor within

the "developing" nations themselves. For an account of the effects of Nicaragua's neoliberal policies in the past decade, particularly on working-class women, see Babb 2001.

16. The desire to be recognized and treated as artists is not limited to Masaya festival performers. In the nearby town of Niquinohomo, a traditional theater group that was recognized both by Somoza-era and Sandinista culture workers wondered why, if it constituted the seat of traditional theater in Nicaragua, the government wouldn't build a theater and theater-training program in Niquinohomo. See also Clifford 1988 for a broader discussion of this issue.

17. Of course, extinction, cultural or biological, is also a possibility for communities that stand in the way of powerful global interests. However, as Guss points out, the more common outcome is that communities negotiate change and participate in the transformation of their cultural landscapes (2000:2–3).

18. Vogt's (1955) early discussion of the racial divisions evident in the Laguna Festival, where Indians, Spaniards, and Anglos exhibited discreet orbits of activity, suggests that even before the global transformations of the past few decades, community festivals expressed multiple, rather than unitary, meanings. Kendall (1991) identifies similar distinctions based on class and ethnic origin in participants' trajectories and activities at the pilgrimage to Esquipulas, Guatemala. See also Abrahams 1981 for a discussion of festival as an arena for expressing conflict, and Bauman and Abrahams's (1978) argument for carnivalesque performers' distinctive social identities in small communities.

19. For an examination of the relation between social class, taste, and aesthetic discrimination, see Bourdieu 1984; for a good corrective to Bourdieu's deterministic view, see Thompson 1979. Whereas Bourdieu associates an interest in folklore with the intermediate class of schoolteachers and therefore as a marker of a particular class, Thompson explores how the cultural property of one class can be appropriated by another more powerful class by first emptying it of its lower-class associations. See also Kirshenblatt-Gimblett's discussion of good and bad taste as social constructions that "deny the *possibility* of cultural production of any significant value anywhere but at the top" of the social and taste hierarchy (1998:281, emphasis in original).

Chapter 2. The Capital of Nicaraguan Folklore

1. Pedro Guiterrez, artistic director of Masaya's Old Market, explained that he uses upwards of eighty nonprofessional festival dance groups on a rotating basis for his stage shows in order to assist all groups with their festival expenses in an equitable manner. The monetary payment that groups receive, however, is minimal, about twenty dollars per appearance for eight to ten dancers and a director. Personal interview, September 17, 2001.

2. Each time the Masaya Office of Culture changes hands, outgoing employees remove the archives, making even the most recent cultural developments difficult to

document effectively. None of Masaya's churches contains historical records. Local scholars and church workers explain that priests and private individuals—nationals as well as foreigners—have carried away what records the churches once had. The absence of local archives in Nicaragua is a commonly lamented phenomenon. Elizabeth Dore (1996), who is working with the materials in a municipal archive in Diriomo, remarks on the rarity of encountering such a complete record.

3. Mendoza (2001) reports that Saint Jerome in his persona as Doctor of the Church is the patron of the mestizo community of San Jerónimo outside Cuzco, Peru. Residents are particularly proud of his participation in Cuzco city's Corpus Cristi Pageant. This community also owns an image of the saint as hermit, but does not venerate it. Thomas Gage noted that Indians he visited in Chiapas in the 1620s venerated Saint Jerome accompanied by his *nagual* or animal spirit, the lion, and that they were much given to dancing ([1648] 1958:234, 245–46). Today, a handful of small communities in Mexico also celebrate Saint Jerome as their patron, either in his aspect as scholar or hermit. His name also graces many streets and boulevards in Spain and Latin America.

4. Early-colonial Nicaragua was the scene of violent struggles for the spoils of conquest among different groups of conquistadors—Gil González de Ávila, Pedrarías Dávila, Diego López de Salcedo, and, briefly, the followers of Cortéz. Valdivieso was killed by the sons of then governor Contreras (the son-in-law of Pedrarías Dávila), whose abuses he had denounced to the Spanish authorities.

5. For a list of Nicaraguan bishops, see Lévy [1873] 1976:50–54. Arellano 1990:15–48 provides a summary of the Catholic Church in early-colonial Nicaragua.

6. Chorotega is the Nahua name for the Mangue Indians.

7. León-Portilla (1972) made a careful comparison of the early information on the Nicaraguan Nahua and on the Nahua of Mexico's central highlands. He found many striking parallels in their beliefs, practices, and social organization, as well as some differences that he relates to the influences of geographically proximate culture groups. He indicates that ritual drunkenness was frowned upon by Aztec elites of central Mexico. Nicaraguan accounts of Nahua practices, based on Oviedo's observations and interviews in 1528 and 1529, predate those collected for central Mexico. See also Chapman 1974 and Arellano 1990.

8. This dance is now performed only in central Mexico. Oviedo was describing a performance he witnessed in El Viejo, Nicaragua (1976:428–30); for a discussion of the mythological subtext of the modern version of this dance, see Gipson 1971.

9. In this passage, Oviedo reveals the marked influence the Spaniards' arrival had on Indian belief. He relates that the prophetess told the Indians "that the Christians were bad and that until they left and were thrown out of the land, she didn't want to treat with the indian as she used to." He believed this story was proof that the Indians had indeed been conferring with the devil (1976:392–93). (Unless otherwise cited, translations from the Spanish are mine.)

10. Mace points out that the preservation of the Patzcá in Rabinal, Guatemala,

was in part a consequence of the Dominican presence in that area. Unlike other religious orders that simply outlawed the native forms of worship, the Dominicans adapted native practices by providing a Christian overlay to the images, songs, and prayers used in rituals (1970:30). We know that Dominican friar Blas de Castillo entered the Masaya volcano in 1539 to disabuse the indigenous people of the beliefs that they must sacrifice children to the god within. (See the *relación* of Friar Tomás de Berlanga in Incer 1990:229). We do not know whether he or another religious figure substituted Saint Jerome for the Vieja del Volcán.

11. Both Flavio Gamboa from Monimbó and Justo Pastor Ramos from Nindirí insist that the veneration of Saint Jerome began as an elite practice during the late 1700s and was not popularized until the mid-1800s. They are representatives to a national indigenous organization formed in the 1990s in anticipation of the Columbus Quincentennial. Gamboa is self-taught and has published several articles on local history and customs in *La Barricada,* the newspaper of the Sandinista Party. He has also collaborated extensively with North American anthropologist Les Field and historian Jeffrey Gould. Pastor is the national coordinator for indigenous communities in natural medicine and director of the Nindirí House of Culture and is in the process of publishing a book on folklore. Masayan Bayardo Ortíz places the origins of popular devotion to Saint Jerome even later. He claims that a print of Saint Jerome was passed among the elite Caldera and Hüeck families during the nineteenth century, and popular devotions did not begin until the early twentieth century. None of these local authorities effectively documents his claims.

12. Stanislawski estimated that each Spanish settler or encomendero would have required about forty tributary Indians to support a family. But he found that, in fact, most encomenderos relied on many fewer Indians and therefore supported themselves through the trades (1983:102).

13. Cofradías organized to venerate a local saint formed part of popular religion in sixteenth-century Spain as well as in the New World. The degree to which residents were obligated to participate in cofradías activities varied from town to town (Christian 1989:50–52).

14. The notion that cofradías taxed rather than supported indigenous communities derives from an extensive body of anthropological literature on the nineteenth- and twentieth-century civil-religious hierarchies in closed corporate communities in the highlands of Mexico and Guatemala. Chance provides an excellent review and comparison of individual community studies that allow him to plot change through time and space. He concludes that during the colonial period the civil-religious hierarchies "facilitated colonial economic exploitation from the outside . . . at the same time they helped maintain the indigenous social strata of nobles and commoners that were recognized by the Spanish colonial legal system" ([1990] 1998:223). Different communities in different regions, however, developed different mechanisms for festival sponsorship, so the civil-religious hierarchy should not be viewed as a structural model for all of Central America.

15. See Sallnow 1991 for a discussion of this phenomenon among indigenous descendants of the Inca.

16. A manuscript version of *El güegüense* was recovered in Masaya and published by North American scholar Daniel G. Brinton in 1883. Brinton got the manuscript from ethnologist Dr. C. H. Berendt, who got it from Juan Eligio de la Rocha, a Granada lawyer, who had hand-copied two originals from Masaya in the 1840s. Brinton dates the play or plays to the seventeenth century based on linguistic evidence. Later Nicaraguan scholars, concerned with promoting mestizo national identity, placed the original in the sixteenth century at the birth of Nicaragua's post-Conquest society. Field provides a perceptive overview of how Nicaraguan intellectuals have used the play either to anchor the nation's mestizo identity or, less commonly, to support a view of regional indigenous cultural resistance to Hispanicization. Whereas Brinton and other foreign nineteenth-century scholars regarded the comedy as rustic and low humor, Cuban poet and nationalist José Martí celebrated it as an act of rebellion. Somoza-era scholars, following Pablo Antonio Cuadra, generally interpreted the play's main character as Nicaragua's first mestizo, providing a literary origin for national character. In contrast, the revolutionary intellectual Dávila Bolaños interpreted this central figure as an indigenous leader bent on resisting Spanish colonial domination (Field 1999:40–76).

17. By the twentieth century, only a danced, mimed version was being performed in towns in the Masaya-Carazo region. During the Somoza period, this dance without dialogue was performed only in Diriamba for that town's Saint Sebastian festivities. Although the elimination of the dialogue may be viewed as an instance of the devolutionary principal in folklore, the heavy, whiteface, wooden masks that dancers employ in these kinds of dramas muffle the dialogues, making them incomprehensible to an ambulatory audience anyway (Mace 1970:23 n. 4).

18. Harris (2000) makes a similar argument for the Moor and Christian plays performed throughout Mexico and Guatemala (as well as in Boaco, Nicaragua) that Trexler (1984) regards as humiliating dramas of defeat.

19. León became the largest population center after the Spanish Conquest, both in real numbers and in terms of its ladino and mestizo presence. In the mid–twentieth century, Managua eclipsed León and now houses one-third of the nation's entire population of 4 million. Masaya is now the fourth-largest city in Nicaragua. With a population of 114,000, however, it is significantly smaller than Managua, León, and Chinandega.

20. Nineteenth-century census material is unreliable. Lévy reports alternative figures of 153,000 and 258,000 people. Nevertheless, even the higher figure would signify that almost one-fifth of the country attended the Saint Jerome Festival ([1873] 1976:196–99)

21. Lévy also mentions what he considered rather peculiar Indian recitations that occurred at intermissions in Spanish Zarzuela shows, an indication that Indians performed in popular culture arenas as well.

22. Gould (1998) reports that Indian communities of Nicaragua were legally abolished sixteen times between 1885 and 1916.

23. See, for example, Lévy's discussion of race in Nicaragua ([1873] 1976:173–216), which lauds the benefits of racial purity over race mixing.

24. This difference within the community explains Gould's puzzle of Monimboseños both "selling" their daughters to white ladinos in order to whiten their race and patrolling their borders to keep ladino men out and away from their Indian women (1998:163–65). As DeValle points out, ethnicity may unify a group at one moment of political struggle, but it cannot be conflated with any particular ideology or position (1989:67).

25. In his more sustained opposition to the U.S. occupation from 1927 to 1933, Augusto Cesar Sandino, a mestizo from Niquinohomo, remained silent about the substantial indigenous element in his movement. A nationalist, Sandino believed in the myth of mestizaje and the extension of full citizenship to all Nicaraguans. He did not recognize that a uniform national program implied losses in land, political authority, and social identity for indigenous minority populations in the Pacific Coast urban centers, the rural highlands, and the Atlantic Coast (Gould 1998; Whisnant 1995).

26. Mulattos constituted part of the tiny non-Indian presence in Masaya during the colonial period. They worked as the municipal police force (Romero Vargas 1987). Up to the 1920s, Monimboseños referred to other Masayans disparagingly as mulattos, denying them Indian blood (Gould 1998:164–65). African Creole and Garifuna groups located on the Atlantic Coast remain distinctive cultural minorities in Nicaragua and in the 1980s achieved a measure of political autonomy from the central government in Managua. In contrast to the Nicaraguan case, the African influences on Indian festival forms in Mexico and Guatemala are quite evident. See, for instance, Esser's (1988b) work on Mexican Blackman dances of Michoacán as well as Blaffler's (1972) and Bricker's (1973, 1983) work on the festival Blackmen of the Chiapas region.

27. In 1968, Peña Hernández glossed López Pérez's description of the dance with a detail about the typically employed festival masks, apparently unconcerned about the challenge this detail offered to López Pérez's interpretation.

28. Republished in *Nicaragua Indígena; Revista Farmaceútica;* Peña Hernández [1968] 1986; and *La Barricada* in 1980.

29. The January 1963 *Revista Conservadora* 5, no. 28, is dedicated in large part to Masaya. This national magazine notes that Masaya is a factor in the national economy because it constitutes a reserve of agricultural laborers and craftsmen. It further notes the excessive division of lands immediately outside the city, ironically suggesting a return to cooperative farming as a solution to this problem. The numerous photographs of Monimbó reveal a rural ambience, lack of infrastructure (water, paved roads, light, toilets), and home-based crafts production.

30. See, for example, Peña Hernández's sympathetic yet patronizing descrip-

tion of neighborhood residents ([1968] 1986:28–38) in the only widely available ethnography of Monimbó before 1992.

31. Taussig (1987) traces the relationship between European American myths of Indian savagery and the appropriation of Indian labor in the early-twentieth-century Amazon. In this case, capitalist intruders deployed the myth of savagery to keep out competitors and to justify their own reign of terror over the region's indigenous inhabitants. At the same time, the *savage* thus constructed resisted forms of incorporation by manipulating this image to his own advantage. Numerous oral narratives exist in Monimbó that recall how fearful National Guardsmen were of savage Monimboseños. Many of these stories focus particularly on the attitudes of foreign mercenaries who worked for the Somoza government.

32. Indeed, Nicaragua has had a remarkably long history of U.S. intervention in local affairs, starting with the establishment of the Nicaragua Interoceanic Transit Company in the 1830s, which brought thousands of northern adventurers through the country on their way to the California goldmines. North American filibusterer William Walker was briefly president in 1860, and the country was occupied twice by the U.S. Marines, from 1909 to 1925 and from 1926 to 1933 (Walker 2003). But the revolution briefly enlarged the country's importance on the international scene. See Babb's discussion of the shift in world attention away from Nicaragua during the neoliberal 1990s, so that the revolution now appeared "a tempest in a teapot" (2001:24).

33. The institute did, however, pass a law to promote national artistic expressions and to protect Nicaraguan artists in 1996 (*La Gaceta* 134 [17 July 1996]). This law establishes a protected space for the works of Nicaraguan professional artists in various media and cultural venues, but it has had virtually no effect on popular enactments.

34. The transition from a revolutionary to a neoliberal government in 1990 and 1991 was marked by a forceful attack on revolutionary cultural projects, most notably Managua mayor Arnoldo Alemán's erasing of the many murals that had adorned that city. See Kunzle's (1995) book-length study of the Nicaraguan murals. Scruggs (1999) notes a decline in recording opportunities for Nicaraguan musicians after a period in which regional music formed a strong basis for a multiethnic national consciousness. See also Babb's (2001) discussion of the new monuments to Catholicism erected in Managua during the 1990s.

35. Unlike other popular enactments in Masaya, the Diablitos is regarded as a traditional dance of the city center and therefore of mestizo rather than indigenous origin. The music appears to be in the style of the late nineteenth century. Omar Calero, a Masaya cultural worker, asserts that it began as an elite practice, danced in the salons of Masaya's great houses and was subsequently adopted by the popular classes and performed in the streets (personal interview, July 19, 1991). Donald Zepeda, a long-time member of the Diablitos dance group, remembers that before the 1960s elite Masayans scoffed at the popular dancers, calling them Indians. Personal interviews, July 4 and August 19, 1991.

36. Bendix (1989) points out that the plays performed by small communities in Interlocken, Switzerland, and billed as tourist attractions demonstrate very little concern for whether foreign visitors will find them palatable.

Chapter 3. When a Little Tradition Modernizes

1. Bakhtin carefully distinguishes between modern satire, which does not identify with the object being satirized, and inclusive carnival laughter of the premodern era (1984:12).

2. Schechner identifies even the license of modern festivals as a form of social control. See particularly his discussion of Florida spring break as a corporate-sponsored, hedonistic training ground for young consumers (1993:78–82).

3. Technically, *carnival* refers to festivals of license and inversion that occur immediately prior to Lent in the Catholic calendar. However, in pre-Christian and Christian Europe the whole winter season from Christmas to Lent was marked by carnival-like celebrations of renewal (Santino 1995). Because the torovenado occurs in October, it is technically not a carnival, but it shares many features with Middle American rural carnivals. Flavio Gamboa, autodidact and Monimbó historian, suggests that the Monimbó torovenado may have migrated to the Saint Jerome Festival in the nineteenth century from Monimbó's Feast of Saint Sebastian, which falls on January 19. However, as mentioned in the previous chapter, the carnivalesque performances associated with pre-Columbian mountain festivals provide another possible model for the torovenado.

4. Brinton was most interested in indigenous theater, and he viewed the festival dances as deteriorated versions of dance dramas that once had plots and scripts. He remarks that the Mangue people of Masaya were well known in the nineteenth century for their interest in theater and recitations of various kinds.

5. Eskorcia has written a few pamphlets on Masaya history and folklore. His views on popular culture coincide roughly with the Granada Vanguardia, a group of poets and intellectuals who began collecting folklore texts in the 1930s and 1940s in an effort to construct a national culture. Eskorcia founded the tiny Nicaraguan Socialist Party in 1944. His political activities resulted in a two-year imprisonment on Corn Island during the Somoza period. In 1991, he disapproved of the Sandinista leadership, claiming that they were autocratic, not socialist.

6. For a description of Middle American indigenous carnival symbolism focused on Chiapas, but also surveying the southern United States, central Mexico, and the Maya Yucatán and Guatemala, see Bricker 1973; for carnival dances of the Mexican highlands, see Esser 1988a.

7. I heard of only two cases, both recent, of torovenados originating in city neighborhoods other than Monimbó. One was the torovenadito of Juan Castro, a shoemaker, who lived at the Seven Corners, close to Saint Jerome Church. This children's torovenado was created in the mid-1980s through the city government's Patron Saint Festival Committee under Sandinista mayor Ernesto Orte-

ga. In the 1990s, Castro moved to the neighborhood of Santa Rosa and continued to sponsor his children's torovenado from there. The Torovenado de Ramos, revived in 1993 by Eduardo Cortez Delgadillo, appears to have emerged from a similar effort during the neoliberal period of Mayor Sebastián Putoy. Delgadillo, who lives in San Miguel neighborhood, also served on the Patron Saint Festival Committee in the early 1990s. He claims the Torovenado de Ramos is a revival of an earlier torovenado from the rural El Pochote community that began in the mid-1800s and was sponsored by one Chica Pavón up to 1963. Several city residents emphasized the important participation of rural communities in torovenado processions.

8. This and all subsequent quotations from José del Carmen Suazo are from a tape-recorded interview, Masaya, April 2, 1991.

9. This and all subsequent quotations from Anita Vívas López are from a tape-recorded interview, Masaya, November 19, 1991.

10. Prayer leaders are members of the community who have learned a number of standard Catholic prayers either from older prayer leaders or from small pamphlets now available at stationary stores. A house prayer usually constitutes a group recitation of the rosary.

11. Typical festival foods include chicha, nacatamales, and rosquillas—all corn-based foods—and *guaro*, an inexpensive cane liquor.

12. Mutual assistance has been observed in many different kinds of festival sponsorship in Central America and Mexico. This kind of cooperation challenges the view that festival sponsorship is a form of economic leveling and suggests instead that sponsorship works to circulate goods and services among community members, while at the same time reinforcing social ties. See Monaghan 1990 on rural Mexico and Nájera Ramírez 1997 on the Prenda system in urban Juchitan for two examples of mutual assistance.

13. Quotation from José Cornelio from a tape-recorded interview, Quebrada Honda, October 6, 1991.

14. With the revolution, García's house was burned, and the family went to live by a sanctuary in the countryside outside Monimbó. In the late 1980s, García's children began to host a small torovenado from their new location.

15. A parallel example in North America would be the subversive use of blackface by African Americans in the New Orleans Mardi Gras. See de Caro and Ireland 1988; Roach 1996, 20–24; Shechner 1993, 74–77.

16. The Salesian High School has an ambivalent relationship with Monimbó. Constructed in the 1920s, it remains the largest building complex in the neighborhood. Even though Monimboseños voluntarily participated in its construction, few attended the school thereafter. Instead, it served primarily to educate the children of local elites (Mora Castillo 1991). Moreover, after the Salesians took possession of the San Sebastian Church, which stands adjacent to the school, they discouraged Monimbó's Saint Sebastian Festival. The cofradía now celebrates the feast of January 19 on a small scale at the nearby Magdalena Church. For more on this aspect of

neighborhood history and festival practice, see Breso 1992. In the 1950s, the Salesians constructed an annex, the Don Bosco School, to serve the neighborhood children's educational needs. Today, many Monimboseños do attend the Salesian High School, even though it remains private. Some Monimboseños also object to a mural inside the church that shows Saint Sebastian being martyred with arrows shot by Indians.

17. This and all subsequent quotations from Manuel Villagras are from a tape-recorded interview, Masaya, May 11, 1991.

18. Even after the democratizing influence of the revolution, Nicaraguans, although avowedly mestizo and antiracist, display a preference for whiteness. Lancaster (1992a) has documented subtle and not-so-subtle preferential treatment of "whiter" children in Managua families that leads to greater family investment in these children's success. Gould has gathered historical evidence that shows some Monimboseños attempted to "whiten" and therefore improve their community through race mixing (1998:165–68).

19. This and all subsequent quotations from Donald Ortega are from a tape-recorded interview, Masaya, July 9, 1991.

20. The Monimbó mayordomías are also notorious for social dysfunction and conflicts, particularly when leadership is passed from one mayordomo to another and often related to excessive ritual drinking. The tendency for festival excess to destroy rather than to cement community relations is one of the peculiar paradoxes of living festival. See Bricker 1973:126 for a discussion of a similar dynamic in Chiapas carnival.

21. Honoring martyrs in this way was a common practice at the time. Moreover, Elías had served as mayordomo of the torovenado. The Sandinista Party also instituted several national holidays to commemorate the revolution and its heroes. Locally, these holidays included remembering historic combatants of Monimbó on the anniversary of Camilo Ortega's death (February 26, 1979), honoring mothers of heroes and martyrs on April 20, reenacting the arrival of Managua forces in Masaya on July 17, and celebrating the revolutionary victory in Managua on July 19. See Beezley, Martin, and French 1994 for a discussion of how festivals have been used in different historic moments to instill faith in an infant state.

22. This and subsequent quotations from Flavio Gamboa are from a tape-recorded interview, Masaya, March 4, 1991.

23. The social network supporting these activities appears remarkably stable. In 2001, the same families from the rural settlement of Quebrada Honda who had helped initiate the festival still provided the *palo lucio* or greased pole for the alborada.

24. The revolutionary government also prompted the torovenados (as well as the religious cofradías of Saint Jerome and Saint Michael) to institutionalize themselves. It was not until 1982, Miguel Bolaños noted, that the Torovenado del Pueblo established itself legally, with a governing board, records, and auditing procedures: "So, what we did," he said, "was make that cofradía have a historical memory through their book of acts, their statutes, their accords and their constitution." In a country and a community where institutions for the preservation of popular

culture hardly existed, this move provided a first step toward building a popular memory. It also recognized the important cultural work of voluntary, popular organizations. Of course, the records are only as good as the recorders make them. When I visited the mayordomo of the Saint Michael cofradía, the book of acts he showed me was a torn, ragged notebook with very few entries. Illiterate himself, he depends on his granddaughter to record the proceedings of their meetings. Because most of the twenty-five members understand the general procedures for participating in the cofradía, the group rarely consults the written record. These festival organizers are also unaware of their organization's colonial past, when the cofradía owned lands and cattle, made loans, and presented annual reports of its transactions to the church (Peña 1998).

25. See, for example, the paraphrase in Carlos Alemán Ocampo, "El torovenado y la resistencia cultural," *Ventana* (cultural supplement of *El Nuevo Diario*), October 31, 1981, 2–3. The absence of newspaper coverage of torovenados and other festival enactments in the years prior to the revolution is a striking indication of how little attention popular cultural enactments received before the 1980s.

26. The Plumed Serpent is an Aztec god who entered the pantheons of many Middle American groups before the Spanish Conquest. Precolonial carvings adorn the canyons that run down to the Laguna de Masaya, and some appear to depict a plumed serpent. Many Masayans believe that a huge, prehistoric serpent still inhabits the lagoon. Serpent sightings are even occasionally reported in the news. Thus, the presentation of the Plumed Serpent both recalls an indigenous cultural past and references a contemporary neighborhood belief.

27. This and all subsequent quotations from Oscar Marenco are from a tape-recorded interview, Masaya, July 14, 1991.

28. Eugene Hutchinson was an American pilot whose plane was shot down in 1986. His presence in Nicaragua provided concrete proof of U.S. military support of the counterrevolution.

29. Lancaster reports a similar turn away from direct political commentary in Managua's Santo Domingo Festival. The Big-Heads traditionally accompanied La Gigantona, dancing with her and reciting vulgar verses. Immediately after the revolution, they spontaneously inserted anti-imperialist messages in their poetry. Lancaster argues that once the Big-Heads exchanged an indirect, popular style of verbal transgression for a conscious voice of critique, however, they became irrelevant to the festival context, and by 1983 they no longer participated in the festival at all (1988:49–50).

30. The Empresa Nicaragüense de Abastecimiento Básico (ENABAS) was the food-distribution program during the Sandinista period that was responsible for rationing.

31. This and subsequent quotations from Evelyn Montoya are from a tape-recorded interview, Masaya, July 25, 1991.

32. For a discussion of a similar bacchanalian invasion of a local festival form, see Guss's description of transformations in the San Juan Festival of Curieppe, Venezuela (2000:24–59).

33. Roman soldiers are a prominent feature of the *Tradicional Judea de Monimbó*, a play based on the last days of Christ performed by amateur actors during Holy Week. One might argue that Roman soldiers *do* represent a local theme, if one understands the masquerade as a caricature of the actors in this play. Of course, for Villagras, the *Judea* is itself a Spanish imposition.

34. Quotation from Norlan Briceño from a tape-recorded interview, Masaya, August 26, 2001.

35. A pejorative nickname, or *malapodo*, referring to the victim's roundness.

36. A malapodo meaning cutter ant.

37. Quotation from Roberto Augustín Marenco from a tape-recorded interview, Masaya, July 14, 2001.

38. Information provided by Dolores Ortega, mayordoma of the Torovenado del Pueblo in 2001.

39. The festival planning committee moved the torovenado up three weeks to accommodate the November elections. Some observers felt this change accounted for the poor showing that year because masqueraders were unused to performing so early in the calendar and had been caught unprepared. Rogelio Toribio explained that hosting the festival on its traditional date, the second week of November, meant risking a complete loss of community enthusiasm if the Sandinistas lost the elections.

40. Compare these behaviors, for example, with carnivalesque activities that celebrate violence and filth: Managua's Santo Domingo Festival, where young men smear black and red grease on unwary victims; the Hindu Holi Festival, where neighbors douse each other with colored flour and water; and the medieval Portuguese *entrudo*, where participants assaulted each other with filth and violent blows. Pérez notes that the Holy Week celebrations in Masaya of the 1830s involved entrudo-like activities. Rowdy young men stole old furniture and other worthless objects from poor people, then left them in the main square (1977:778–82).

41. See Miguel Bolaños Garay on the opinion page of *El Nuevo Diario*, November 6, 2001: "Truly, the quality of the costumes and above all, the good humor have been absent in the torovenados."

42. The *canasta básica* or basic food basket was a development of the Sandinista period, when it was distributed to supplement people's earnings. It included staple foods such as beans, rice, oil, salt, and sugar.

43. Most Masayans argue that the revolutionary property redistribution most benefited those Sandinista leaders who confiscated and continue to occupy luxurious estates. For an excellent discussion of the public discourse surrounding Zoilamerica Narvaéz, see Howe 2003:225ff.

44. This and subsequent quotations from Miguel Bolaños are from a tape-recorded interview, Masaya, November 4, 2001.

45. It would be a mistake to view this group as a nondrinkers' torovenado, however. Suazo remains the only nondrinker in the group. The Monimbó Association of Traditional Artists, organized by Sandinista neighborhood activist Carlos Centeno, have

tried to adopt this torovenado as part of their effort to attract nongovernmental organization support for local cultural initiatives, but the Thirtieth of September Traditional Torovenado has vehemently resisted these attempts at incorporation.

Chapter 4. Spooks, Nostalgia, and Festival Innovation

1. Mask maker Norlan Briceño identified seventeen traditional spooks when I asked him to represent them in masks. In addition to the figures mentioned in the text, he provided La Chancha Bruja (the Bewitched Pig), El Viejo y La Vieja del Monte (the Old Man and Woman of the Mountain or Wilds), El Duende (a child-size figure dressed in red with pointy ears, reminiscent of Celtic fairies), La Mocuana (the ghost of an Indian princess), and a European witch/hag. La Llorona, a pitiful abandoned woman who either drowned her children or allowed a father or lover to drown them, is a legendary figure that exists throughout Middle America but is not prominent in this part of Nicaragua. Residents know of La Llorona but do not relate stories about her or regard her as a local presence.

2. Palma (1984) records several Nicaraguan accounts of this procedure; see Blaffler 1972 for comparable descriptions of the corpse-eating Zinacantan (Mexico) skeleton woman.

3. This story was taken down as notes during an informal conversation with María Bernabéla García on October 19, 2001.

4. Latin America in general has experienced rapid urbanization, a consequence of both the dangers of living in the countryside during periods of conflict and the attraction that cities provide—schools, water, jobs, transportation.

5. Figures taken from the *World Gazetteer*, at http://www.world-gazetteer.com; accessed February 26, 2005. The Christmas earthquake of 1972 displaced thousands from Managua to Masaya and represented the first great influx of outsiders to Monimbó.

6. Degh (2001) points out that global communications networks, far from eliminating unscientifically verifiable beliefs in our times, act as the newest conduit for such beliefs. In 2001, for example, Liberal Party opponents of the Sandinista presidential candidate hosted an influential televised talk show called *Fuego Cruzado* (Cross-Fire). For several days, the anchors delighted in fading Daniel Ortega's photograph into a painting of the Christian devil, thereby revealing his secret affinity with evil. The anchors for this clearly reactionary news program also argued that the Sandinista Party was diabolical because its new color, pink, was a sign of the devil. They identified Ortega's partner, Rosario Murillo, as a witch because she customarily wore multiple sets of bangle bracelets. Journalists for the national newspapers subsequently reported on the television program. To what degree such arguments convinced the already polarized popular classes remains unclear; what is important to recognize is that mass communication contributes to the wider, more rapid transmission of rumor, legend, and unscientifically verifiable beliefs (Degh 2001).

7. Orso (1990) interprets similar Costa Rican stories told by a man as the

means by which women attempt to exert control over men's behavior. Palma (1984), however, collected accounts of the Cegua's transformation process from elderly female narrators in northern Nicaragua who appear to believe in her existence. These accounts were told as legends rather than as memories, and men were always the victims.

8. The Carreta Nahua is said to have square wheels that produce a distinctive sound. Monimboseños alternately report that it disappears when it comes to a crossroads or that one can see it only as it turns a corner. There is no driver, only the cargo of skulls and bones.

9. This and all subsequent quotations from Luis Méndez are from a tape-recorded interview, Masaya, November 3, 2001.

10. A person typically encounters a Cadejo when he is out alone at night. When the Black Cadejo threatens the traveler, the White Cadejo appears to fight his counterpart, allowing the traveler to pass. The White Cadejo may then accompany the traveler along his journey.

11. Quotation from Roger Muños from a tape-recorded interview, Masaya, January 1, 1991.

12. The vela del vestido is a Monimbó custom of displaying one's First Communion dress to neighbors the evening before the ceremony. It was adopted by festival marimba groups as well; however, town-center groups keep their costumes secret and regard the Monimbó custom as quaint or in bad taste.

13. The Torovenado del Pueblo also holds a scary masquerade social dance called the Festival of the Mocuana prior to the October festivities to raise money for events. La Mocuana is a legendary figure related to La Llorona and to the medieval Spanish tale of a Moorish commander who walled up his only daughter after she helped the Spanish invade Cáceres (Paredes 1971:103; Robe 1971:117). One Nicaraguan version relates that the Mocuana was the daughter of a cacique who fell in love with a Spanish soldier. The soldier convinced her to tell him where her father kept his gold, and when she did, he stole it and abandoned her. After ruining her father and losing her lover, the Mocuana subsequently went mad. When I commissioned local mask maker Raúl Zepeda to produce a mask of this legendary figure, he created a split-faced mask, one side depicting a white-skinned, black-haired, rosy-cheeked beauty, the other a skull.

14. Many individuals, in particular youth, don ahuizotes costumes for the Sunday torovenados that follow. In those contexts, the ahuizotes may receive prizes, although the prizes are usually less substantial than those given to adult masqueraders who organize skits.

15. This and all subsequent quotations from Estela Rodriguez are from a personal interview, Masaya, July 22, 1991.

16. This and all subsequent quotations from Dolores Ortega are from a personal interview, Masaya, October 12, 2001.

17. This and all subsequent quotations from Carlos Centeno are from tape-recorded interviews in Masaya on various dates in 1991, 2000, 2001.

18. Jarquín explained that a married woman might continue dancing marimba if she formed a new group made up only of married couples. Because her husband is not a marimba dancer, she will probably not form such a group.

19. This and all subsequent quotations from Ninoska Jarquín are from a personal interview, Masaya, November 8, 2001.

20. Edwin Sanchez, "Máscaras de Halloween? No problem!" *El Nuevo Diario*, October 29, 1998.

21. In the absence of museums, the Central Bank has been a major cultural institution since the Somoza period. It houses a fine library and has underwritten numerous cultural projects related to preserving the national patrimony. For more on the role of the Central Bank in Nicaraguan culture, see Field 1999:82–88 and Whisnant 1995:14–47.

22. Edwin Sanchez, "Halloween o nuestros espantos?" *El Nuevo Diario*, October 31, 2000.

23. "Halloween, ignorancia y subcultura," *El Nuevo Diario*, November 2, 2000.

24. These calendar festivals are not highly marked in Masaya, perhaps owing to abundant activity surrounding the patron saint festival, which lasts from early September to November 30.

25. José del Carmen Suazo was both a sculptor and a mask maker. He specialized in the wire-mesh masks used in marimba dancing. Augustín Marenco and Raúl Zepeda, both directors of Diablitos dance groups, made *diablo* as well as torovenado masks. All these mask makers claim to have learned their art by trial and error and indicated to me that an earlier generation of mask makers had refused to teach their craft.

26. These tunes are all lively *sones de toro* traditionally played to accompany masqueraders in their torovenado dances.

27. This group was organized in 1987 through the Popular Culture Center within the context of Sandinista efforts to popularize local traditions. The group traveled to towns throughout Nicaragua to perform at their festivals and participated in some national variety shows at the Rubén Darío Theatre. In the 1990s, such fledgling theater groups disintegrated as state support for popular culture evaporated. Norlan Briceño, originally a member of Rodriguez's group, continued to organize his own youth group, now through the Monimbó Association of Traditional Artists, an informal nonprofit organization, but with no financial resources, his group was unable to progress.

28. For a discussion of the problems of inferring individual belief from ritual practice, see Halpin 1983:219–20.

Chapter 5. Constructing Hierarchies in Folk Dance

1. Esser (1988b) points out that in Michoacán, elegant male dancers use black masks in an interesting twist in the tradition.

2. Elsewhere, Bricker (1973) remarks that in many ways carnival unravels the social fabric, leading to fights and schism between and among women and men, observations that qualify her reading of festival as an assertion of social control.

3. Similar elegant whiteface dances in Mexico have retained an association with ancient practices of invoking rain by carrying umbrellas. These dances also include one or more transvestite dancers (Lechuga 1988). None of the Masaya Negras dancers makes any association between their dance and such rituals.

4. Although most dancers say they do not drink heavily during the day, some dancers and musicians do become intoxicated and lose control over the dance as the afternoon wears on. This eventuality may cause either delight or dismay among onlookers.

5. The corpus of tunes continues to grow. In 1991, dancers identified about fifty danceable marimba pieces. By 2001, a young dancer preparing for a contest counted seventy. Some dancers refuse to dance to the newer pieces, however, indicating a range of opinion about what constitutes authentic marimba dancing. For more on marimba music and musicians, see Scruggs 1994.

6. Certain pieces require additional steps. The *saludo* is a bow or curtsey. In *paso pa'atras*, dancers step backward. *Zapateado doble*, until recently, was performed only in one piece, "El mate amargo." Negras director Bayardo Gonzalez claims to have invented the step during a performance in the 1960s. It entails alternately stepping forward and back with the lead foot while gliding sideways.

7. This and all subsequent quotations from Rigoberto Guzmán are from a tape-recorded interview, Masaya, October 21, 1991.

8. Although the marimba was once a social as well as a ritual dance, it has been replaced at parties and social dances by contemporary Latin dances, such as cumbia and merengue. Maintaining the marimba's stylistic distinctiveness has become increasingly important as a consequence.

9. Several dance directors mentioned to me that they try to keep mixed-sex youth groups from adopting the Negras innovations in order to preserve that autochthonous dance. Carlos Centeno remarked that one can't control the Negras because they are all adults, but the youth can be coached and corrected.

10. Dates, especially people's dates of birth, are difficult to determine in Masaya. For instance, don Alonso's daughter Miriam Montalván prepared a résumé for her father in which she recorded that he was born in 1894, danced first in 1914 at the age of fourteen, and died in 1973 at the age of eighty-three. Here, I have followed the dates given by René Chavarría, which, if equally unverifiable, are at least consistent.

11. This and subsequent quotations from René Chavarría are from a personal interview, Masaya, November 8, 1991. Chavarría was director of the Masaya Folklore School in the 1970s. When it was closed in 1980, he became a taxi driver but continued his interest in chronicling the local marimba tradition. For several years, he meticulously recorded the dancers he saw at the Saint Jerome Festival each year

and conducted his own inquiries about notable musicians and dancers of the previous generation. In 1988, he published a twenty-three-page pamphlet, *The Marimberos of Masaya*, at his own expense. In the mid-1990s, he suffered a paralyzing stroke that ended his active participation in the dance. However, his Negras group, regarded as one of the four traditional groups in the city, continues to perform annually in the festival.

12. This and subsequent quotations from Donald Zepeda are from a personal interview, Masaya, July 4, 1991.

13. The practice of riding to the church on horseback borrows from an earlier town-center festival tradition, the Chinegros of Santiago, in which mounted, masked figures sang couplets in honor of friends whose names were Santiago. The tradition was abandoned probably after American adventurer William Walker burned the Santiago Church in the mid-1800s.

14. Kirshenblatt-Gimblett has provided a cogent overview of how such projection groups, which perform a variety of dances as national culture, homogenize local traditions and erase histories of conflict in an enactment of happy, healthy national unity (1998:17–78).

15. Palacios's group disbanded owing to the advanced age of several of its members.

16. In 2001, Montalván denied ever having danced with Bayardo González, now his principal rival. Chavarría also mentioned a group that went out from Monimbó in the 1970s, organized by Chilo Ruíz and Tito Rodriguez, as well as two other now defunct groups organized by the Castillo brothers and the Ortegas.

17. This and subsequent quotations from Omar Calero are from a personal interview, Masaya, July 19, 1991.

18. Jairo Arista, who later became the director of the Arista Bolaños group, was a teenager at the time. He had been trained in his aunt's mixed-sex Parejas group, which had been participating in the festival since the early 1970s.

19. Rigoberto Guzmán formed a family group in the early 1980s that was also regarded as traditional. He refused to become involved in the cultural politics of the period. Omar Calero split from Montalván in 1982 to form his own group. Because Calero also worked for the Ministry of Culture, his group achieved prominence during the Sandinista folklore revival in spite of its late formation.

20. From 1995 to 2000, the Patron Saint Festival Committee organized a closing activity for the Festival of Saint Jerome. All the dancers who had participated in the festival were invited to dance on stages set up at intervals along Masaya's central north-south thoroughfare. Organizers argued that the closing ceremony allowed outsiders the opportunity to see the dancers in a public space at a determined time. However, this activity never really attracted a large public and was finally abandoned.

21. In 2001, Centeno was finally recognized for his cultural contributions when he received a gold medal from the Masaya Office of Culture, a distinction he shared that year with Bayardo González.

Chapter 6. Masking and Unmasking Sexuality in the Dance

1. Edwin Sanchez, "Los travestís y la lupa social," *El Nuevo Diario*, December 30, 1999. The article takes the form of an interview with an Argentinean religious worker who assists transvestites in his own country. Thus, the Nicaraguan public discussion of transvestism seems to participate in a larger Latin American movement toward normalization of once stigmatized sexualities.

2. Howe (2003) provides an interesting discussion of similar drag performances in Managua. In this case, however, the organizing committee for the gay male pageants are lesbians, an inversion of the pattern in heterosexual pageants where female participants are sponsored, trained, and judged by male organizers (see Ballerino-Cohen, Stoeltje, and Wilk 1996). By the turn of the century, Howe reports, some Managua activists began to resist the association of transvestism with gay rights, and the Managua celebration replaced the beauty pageant with a choreographed dance show.

3. Edwin Somarriba, "Director de instituto escandalizado con Miss Gay," *El Nuevo Diario*, October 26, 2000.

4. This and subsequent quotations from Bayardo Cordoba are from a personal interview, Masaya, October 19, 2001.

5. Calero himself is related on his mother's side to the Cuadras, an important Nicaraguan family.

6. This and subsequent quotations from Alfredo Montalván are from a personal interview, Masaya, October 11, 2001.

7. See chapter 1, note 4, on Las Promesantes.

8. Cordoba takes out his Negras and Parejas groups in alternate years. In the Parejas, he dances with his wife.

9. The Nicaraguan verb used here, *arrecharse*, to be angry or excited, also carries a sexual connotation.

10. In contrast, Bayardo Cordoba asks his dancers to bring rum and covered dishes to the rehearsals so as not to overburden their host.

11. Arévalo is connected to Masaya's gay and indigenous communities. He once danced with Carlos Centeno's Negras group and continues to work with Centeno as a founding member of the Monimbó Association of Traditional Artists, a grassroots nonprofit that supports Monimbó cultural performances. Diabetes has prevented Arévalo from continuing to dance, but he regularly appears as an invited guest at Negras rehearsals.

12. On the zapateado doble, see chapter 5, note 6.

13. In his ethnographic study of working-class, Mexican American polka dancing in southern Texas, José Limón notes a similar tendency for the dancing couple to become one figure. He says, "Yet amid incipient violence, to watch a Cielo Azul couple on the floor at its best, to hear the sharp, well-formed class-consciousness of the *grito*, is to realize that, for a moment, some measure of artful control over these forces—some measure of victory—has been achieved in the never-ending struggle

against the choreography of race, class, and, one has to say gender. For transcending sexual intention on both sides, or, better still, sublimating it, the dance, in its best moment, even with the male in ostensible control, makes the couple look *como si fueran uno* (as if they were one). And, for a moment gender domination appears overcome . . . for a moment" (1994:165).

14. Contemporary Negras dancers provide a variety of explanations for the origins of the dance, yet all recognize that it initially developed as an Indian parody of Spanish authorities.

Chapter 7. The Neoliberal Religious Turn

1. In Monimbó, this festival runs from December 24 to Epiphany. It includes nightly prayers and singing to the altar of the Christ child and a procession on January 6 that includes an enactment of the popular drama *La Pastorela*, which depicts Joseph and Mary's search for hospice and the Three Kings or Wise Men on horseback.

2. In a comparative study of Latin American and European shrines, Nolan notes that relatively few shrines in Latin America that can be dated were established in the nineteenth century, whereas the sixteenth to eighteenth centuries and the twentieth century were periods of active shrine formation. We can postulate that if pilgrims were visiting Popoyuapa in the nineteenth century, the shrine had probably been formed one or more centuries earlier. Moreover, Nolan provides some comparative evidence that Jesus the Redeemer may reasonably be assumed to have had an indigenous predecessor. She notes that miraculous Christ figures are relatively rare in Europe and that important Christ cults in Guatemala and Mexico have identifiable pre-Columbian antecedents. Moreover, she says, "52 percent of the 73 shrines referred to in the available literature as traditional Indian pilgrimage centers are dedicated to Christ" (1991:31).

3. Reported in Euclides Cerda Calero, "Entusiasmo de feligreses en fiestas de Popoyuapa," *La Prensa*, March 27, 2001; and in Lourdes Vanegas López, "Comienza efervescencia por Jesús del Rescate," *La Noticia*, April 17, 2001.

4. Personal interview with Father Navas, Popoyuapa sanctuary, June 13, 2002.

5. Flor de María Palma, "Llegó Jesús del Rescate con ahogado y golpeado," *El Nuevo Diario*, April 7, 2001.

6. Lourdes Vanegas López, "Preparan celebración de Jesús del Rescate," *La Noticia*, February 28, 2001.

7. Socorro's farm is littered with unfinished development projects, testaments to the precarious nature of progress in Nicaragua. She and her husband were involved in a project to bring potable water to the area that stalled in the 1980s. They continue to distribute water to neighbors from large tanks that were built beside their house as a temporary measure pending the arrival of pipes. They also donated the land for a primary school and a chapel, both of which sit beside their farmhouse. The half-finished primary school was damaged by the 2000 earthquake, and

area children are currently using the chapel for classes. In the mid-1990s, affluent foreigners moved into the area and started an electrification project. They convinced all the residents of El Mojón to pay for the installation of electric lines and subsequently to pay the project committee for electric service. However, Socorro explained, the committee never paid the electric company, so six months after she began receiving electricity, her service was terminated, even though she had faithfully paid her monthly quota.

8. The exact date is uncertain. Socorro recalled that it was the year of the war, which may have been 1978 or 1979, but then gave the date 1980. In any event, what seems important for this analysis is that Socorro's experience occurred at the beginning of the revolutionary period, which was a time of both great confusion and general popular elation.

9. This and subsequent quotations from Socorro Ortíz de Vívas up to note marker 21 are taken from an interview conducted on March 23, 1991, at El Mojón. They represent excerpts from a continuous, uninterrupted response to my asking why Socorro started making the pilgrimage to Popoyuapa. Her narrative is an unusually long, elaborated, and tightly constructed example of miracle discourse, which provides much greater opportunity for analysis than the more common, fragmentary explanations of religious motivations for ritual practice I collected from other Monimboseños. I have inserted explanatory contextual information in brackets as needed. The full text in Spanish and English is printed in Borland 2003.

10. Other pilgrims condition their promises in similar ways. In the most extreme example of the flexible nature of a religious promise I encountered, Rosita Castillo, born in Matagalpa and now living in the United States, first attended the fiesta (by bus) in 1999 when she was in her seventies, fulfilling a promise that her mother had made when Castillo was a child, the obligation for which her mother passed to her when she died in 1998.

11. By 2001, wagon pilgrims recall that Concepción Torres died, and that's why Socorro assumed the mayordomía. His marital difficulties, related by Socorro in 1991, were thus no longer mentioned ten years later.

12. Flor de María Palma, "Padrinos recibieron carretas peregrinas," *Nuevo Diario,* April 4, 2001.

13. See, for example, Noelia Sánchez Ricarte, "Peregrinación por Jesús del Rescate en Rivas," *La Prensa,* April 2, 2001. Also, Flor de María Palma, "Padrinos recibieron carretas peregrinas," *El Nuevo Diario,* April 4, 2001.

14. This and subsequent quotations from Zulema Romero Mercado are from a tape-recorded interview, Masaya, November 2, 2001.

15. Munro observed the women's prayer in Honduras, but noted that the same custom extended throughout Nicaragua, wherever priests were in short supply.

16. Meanwhile, Bolaños's Sandinista opponent, Daniel Ortega, attended an evangelical service. Non-Catholic religious groups had become disaffected by neoliberal leaders' overwhelming support for the Catholic Church during the 1990s.

See Kendall (1991) for a discussion of the link between reactionary politicians and the pilgrimage to Esquipulas in Guatemala.

17. Socorro reports that since 1991 the Masaya wagon pilgrims have steadily grown in number, from seventeen wagons in 1991 to twenty-seven in 1992, twenty-three in 1993, twenty-seven in 1994, twenty-nine in 1995, thirty-one in 1996, thirty-three in 1997, thirty-nine in 1998, forty-one in 1999, and thirty-nine in 2000, but only twenty-three in 2001. The 42 percent drop in 2001 corresponds closely to the vote against the Liberal Party in the fall elections.

18. This and subsequent quotations from Juan Vívas are from a tape-recorded interview, El Mojón, November 1, 2001.

19. Juan's reasoning that the government should construct a wagon path from Masaya to Rivas is similar to that of Masaya dancers who believe the government should invest in promoting them by building a national dance academy and a museum in Monimbó because it values their practices as a national heritage.

20. Because the padrino/pilgrim pairs change each year, the brotherhood she refers to represents equality not personal relationship. Indeed, the important personal relationships for her are those cemented among Masaya pilgrims and mayordomía members.

21. This and subsequent quotations from Socorro Ortíz de Vívas from this point on are from a tape-recorded interview, El Mojón, November 1, 2001.

References

Abrahams, Roger D. 1981. Shouting Match at the Border: The Folklore of Display Events. In *"And Other Neighborly Names": Social Process and Cultural Image in Texas Folklore*, edited by Richard Bauman and Roger D. Abrahams, 304–21. Austin: University of Texas Press.

Adams, Richard N. [1957] 1976. *Cultural Surveys of Panama–Nicaragua–Guatemala–El Salvador–Honduras*. Scientific Publications No. 33. Washington, D.C.: Pan American Sanitary Bureau.

Alvarez, Sonia, Evelina Dagnino, and Arturo Escobar. 1998. The Cultural and Political in Latin American Social Movements. In *Cultures of Politics, Politics of Cultures: Re-visioning Latin American Social Movements*, edited by Sonia Alvarez, Evelina Dagnino, and Arturo Escobar, 1–29. Boulder, Colo.: Westview Press.

Annis, Sheldon. 1987. *God and Production in a Guatemalan Town*. Austin: University of Texas Press.

Appadurai, Arjun. 1996. *Modernity at Large: Cultural Dimensions of Globalization*. Minneapolis: University of Minnesota Press.

Arellano, Jorge E. 1986. *Breve historia de la iglesia en Nicaragua (1523–1979)*. Managua, Nicaragua: Editorial Manolo Morales.

———. 1990. *Nueva historia de Nicaragua*. Vol. 1. Managua, Nicaragua: Fondo Editorial CIRA.

Babb, Florence E. 2001. *After Revolution: Mapping Gender and Cultural Politics in Neoliberal Nicaragua*. Austin: University of Texas Press.

Bakhtin, Mikhail. 1984. *Rabelais and His World*. Translated by Helene Iswolsky. Bloomington: Indiana University Press.

Ballerino-Cohen, Colleen, Beverly Stoeltje, and Richard Wilk, eds. 1996. *Beauty Queens on the Global Stage: Gender, Contests, and Power*. New York: Routledge.

Bauman, Richard. 1977. *Verbal Art as Performance*. Rowley, Mass.: Newbury House.

Bauman, Richard, and Roger Abrahams. 1978. Ranges of Festival Behavior. In *The Reversible World: Inversion in Art and Society*, edited by Barbara Babcock, 193–207. Ithaca, N.Y.: Cornell University Press.

Bauman, Richard, and Beverly Stoeltje. 1989. Community Festival and the Enactment of Modernity. In *The Old Traditional Way of Life: Essays in Honor of Warren E. Roberts*, edited by Robert E. Walls and George Schoemaker, 158–71. Bloomington, Ind.: Trickster Press.

Beezley, William H., Cheryl English Martin, and William E. French, eds. 1994. *Rituals of Rule, Rituals of Resistance: Public Celebrations and Popular Culture in Mexico*. Wilmington, Del.: SR Books.

Bendix, Regina. 1989. Tourism and Cultural Displays: Inventing Traditions for Whom? *Journal of American Folklore* 102: 131–46.

———. 1997. *In Search of Authenticity: The Formation of Folklore Studies*. Madison: University of Wisconsin Press.

Bettelheim, Judith. 1998. Women in Masquerade and Performance. *African Arts* 31, no. 2: 68–71.

Beverley, John, and Marc Zimmerman. 1990. *Literature and Politics in the Central American Revolutions*. Austin: University of Texas Press.

Blaffler, Sarah C. 1972. *The Black-man of Zinacantan: A Central American Legend*. Austin: University of Texas Press.

Blandón, Erick. 2001. El torovenado: Un lugar donde pactar con el demonio o el cochón de la ciudad letrada. *Artefacto* 19: unnumbered pages.

Bobadillo, Fr. Francisco. [1527–29] 1998. Indígenas del Pacífico de Nicaragua. In *Culturas indígenas de Nicaragua*, 1: 173–89. Managua, Nicaragua: Editorial Hispamer.

Bolt, Alan. 1990. *El libro de la nación Qu*. Managua, Nicaragua: Vientos Del Sur.

Borland, Katherine. 1994. Performing Identities: The Politics of Culture in a Nicaraguan Community. Ph.D. diss., Indiana University.

———. 1996. The India Bonita of Monimbó. In *Beauty Queens on the Global Stage: Gender, Contests, and Power*, edited by Colleen Ballerino-Cohen, Beverly Stoeltje, and Richard Wilk, 75–88. New York: Routledge.

———. 2002. Marimba: Dance of the Revolutionaries, Dance of the Folk. *Radical History Review* 83: 77–107.

———. 2003. Pilgrimage to Popoyuapa: Catholic Renewal and Ethnic Performance in Neoliberal Nicaragua. *Journal of American Folklore* 116: 391–419.

Bourdieu, Pierre. 1984. *Distinction: A Social Critique of the Judgement of Taste*. Translated by Richard Nice. Cambridge, Mass.: Harvard University Press.

Bovallius, Carl. [1883] 1977. *Viaje por Centroamérica, 1881–1883*. Managua, Nicaragua: Fondo de Promoción Cultural, Banco de América.

Brandes, Stanley. 1988. *Power and Persuasion: Fiestas and Social Control in Rural Mexico*. Philadelphia: University of Pennsylvania Press.

———. 1998. The Day of the Dead, Halloween, and Mexican National Identity. *Journal of American Folklore* 111: 359–80.

Breso, Javier García. 1992. *Monimbó: Una comunidad india de Nicaragua*. Managua, Nicaragua: Editorial Multiformes.

Bricker, Victoria R. 1973. *Festival Humor in Highland Chiapas*. Austin: University of Texas Press.

———. 1983. The Meaning of Masking in San Pedro Chenalho. In *The Power of Symbols: Masks and Masquerade in the Americas*, edited by N. Ross Crumrine and Marjorie Halpin, 110–14. Vancouver: University of British Columbia Press.

Brinton, Daniel, ed. [1883] 1969. *The Gueguence: A Comedy Ballet in the Nahuatl-Spanish Dialect of Nicaragua.* New York: AMS Press.

Burns, E. Brandford. 1991. *Patriarch and Folk: The Emergence of Nicaragua, 1798–1858.* Cambridge, Mass.: Harvard University Press.

Butler, Judith. 1993. Gender Is Burning. In *Bodies That Matter: On the Discursive Limits of "Sex,"* 121–42. New York: Routledge.

Certeau, Michel de. 1988. *The Practice of Everyday Life.* Translated by Steven Randall. Berkeley: University of California Press.

Chance, John K. [1990] 1998. Changes in Twentieth-Century Mesoamerican Cargo Systems. In *Crossing Currents: Continuity and Change in Latin America,* edited by Michael B. Whiteford and Scott Whiteford, 214–25. Upper Saddle River, N.J.: Prentice-Hall.

Chapman, Anne M. 1974. *Los Nicarao y los Chorotega según los fuentes históricos.* Cuidad Universitaria: Publicaciones de la University de Costa Rica.

Chávez Metoyer, Cynthia. 2000. *Women and the State in Post-Sandinista Nicaragua.* Boulder, Colo.: Lynne Rienner.

Christian, William A., Jr. 1989. *Local Religion in Sixteenth-Century Spain.* Princeton, N.J.: Princeton University Press.

Clifford, James. 1988. *The Predicament of Culture.* Cambridge, Mass.: Harvard University Press.

Cofradía del Gran Torovenado del Pueblo. 2001. *40 aniversario Gran Torovenado del Pueblo "Elías e Israel Rodríguez Z." 1961–2001* (pamphlet). Masaya, Nicaragua: n.p.

Cohen, Abner. 1993. *Masquerade Politics: Explorations in the Structure of Urban Cultural Movements.* Berkeley: University of California Press.

Colburn, Forrest D. 1986. Foot Dragging and Other Peasant Responses to the Nicaraguan Revolution. *Peasant Studies* 3, no. 2: 77–96.

Cowan, Jane K. 1990. *Dance and the Body Politic in Northern Greece.* Princeton, N.J.: Princeton University Press.

Crumrine, N. Ross. 1983. Mask Use and Meaning in Easter Ceremonialism. In *The Power of Symbols: Masks and Masquerade in the Americas,* edited by N. Ross Crumrine and Marjorie Halpin, 92–100. Vancouver: University of British Columbia Press.

Dávila Bolaños, Alejandro. 1977. *Índice de la mitología nicaragüense.* Estelí, Nicaragua: Editorial La Imprenta.

Davis, Natalie Zemon. 1975. *Society and Culture in Early Modern France.* Stanford, Calif.: Stanford University Press.

De Caro, F. A., and Tom Ireland. 1988. "Every Man a King: Worldview, Social Tension, and Carnival in New Orleans. *International Folklore Review* 6: 58–66.

Degh, Linda. 2001. *Legend and Belief: Dialectics of a Folklore Genre.* Bloomington: Indiana University Press.

DeValle, Susana B. C. 1989. Discourses of Ethnicity: The Faces and the Masks. In *Ethnicity and Nation-Building in the Pacific,* edited by Michael C. Howard, 50–73. Tokyo: United Nations University.

Dore, Elizabeth. 1990. The Great Grain Dilemma: Peasants and State Policy in Revolutionary Nicaragua. *Peasant Studies* 17, no. 2: 96–120.

———. 1996. Patriarchy and Private Property in Nicaragua, 1860–1920. In *Patriarchy and Economic Development: Women's Positions at the End of the Twentieth Century*, edited by Valentine M. Moghadam, 56–79. New York: Oxford University Press.

———. 2000. Property, Households, and Public Regulation of Domestic Life: Diriomo, Nicaragua, 1840–1900. In *Hidden Histories of Gender and the State in Latin America*, edited by Elizabeth Dore and Maxine Molyneux, 147–71. Durham, N.C.: Duke University Press.

Dow, James. 1988. Sierra Otomí Carnival Dances. In *Behind the Mask in Mexico*, edited by Janet Brody Esser, 172–89. Santa Fe: Museum of New Mexico Press.

Durkheim, Emile. [1912] 1961. *The Elementary Forms of Religious Life.* Translated by Joseph Ward Swain. New York: Collier.

Eade, John, and Michael J. Sallnow. 1991. Introduction. In *Contesting the Sacred: The Anthropology of Christian Pilgrimage*, edited by John Eade and Michael J. Sallnow, 1–29. London: Routledge.

Eskorcia Zúniga, Avelino. 1979. *Crónica folklórica: Aspectos del torovenado en Masaya.* Masaya, Nicaragua: Editorial Magys.

Esser, Janet Brody. 1983. Tarascan Masks of Women as Agents of Social Control. In *The Power of Symbols: Masks and Masquerade in the Americas*, edited by N. Ross Crumrine and Marjorie Halpin, 114–27. Vancouver: University of British Columbia Press.

———, ed. 1988a. *Behind the Mask in Mexico.* Santa Fe: Museum of New Mexico Press.

———. 1988b. Those Who Are Not from Here: Blackman Dances of Michoacán. In *Behind the Mask in Mexico*, edited by Janet Brody Esser, 107–41. Santa Fe: Museum of New Mexico Press.

Field, Les. 1987. "I Am Content with My Art": Two Groups of Artisans in Revolutionary Nicaragua. Ph.D. diss., Duke University.

———. 1998. Post-Sandinista Ethnic Identities in Western Nicaragua. *American Anthropologist* 100, no. 2: 431–43.

———. 1999. *The Grimace of Macho Ratón: Artisans, Identity, and Nation in Late-Twentieth-Century Western Nicaragua.* Durham, N.C.: Duke University Press.

Gage, Thomas. [1648] 1958. *Travels in the New World.* Edited and with an introduction by J. Eric S. Thompson. Norman: University of Oklahoma Press.

Garber, Marjorie. 1992. *Vested Interests: Cross-Dressing and Cultural Anxiety.* New York: Routledge.

García-Canclini, Néstor. 1993. *Transforming Modernity: Popular Culture in Mexico.* Translated by Lidia Lozano. Austin: University of Texas Press.

Gilmore, David G. 1987. *Aggression and Community: Paradoxes of Andalusian Culture.* New Haven, Conn.: Yale University Press.

Gipson, Rosemary. 1971. Los Voladores, the Flyers of Mexico. *Western Folklore* 30: 269–78.

Gould, Jeffrey L. 1993. "Vana Ilusión": The Highland Indians and the Myth of Nicaragua Mestiza, 1880–1925. *Hispanic American Historical Review* 73, no. 3: 393–431.

———. 1998. *To Die in This Way: Nicaraguan Indians and the Myth of Mestizaje 1880–1965*. Durham, N.C.: Duke University Press.

Guss, David M. 2000. *The Festive State: Race, Ethnicity, and Nationalism as Cultural Performance*. Berkeley: University of California Press.

Hagedorn, Katherine J. 2001. *Divine Utterances: The Performance of Afro-Cuban Santería*. Washington, D.C.: Smithsonian Institution Press.

Halpin, Marjorie. 1983. The Mask of Tradition. In *The Power of Symbols: Masks and Masquerade in the Americas*, edited by N. Ross Crumrine and Marjorie Halpin, 214–21. Vancouver: University of British Columbia Press.

Harris, Max. 2000. *Aztecs, Moors, and Christians: Festivals of Reconquest in Mexico and Spain*. Austin: University of Texas Press.

Hatton, Joshua P. 2000. Las raíces indígenas de la peregrinación de Jesús del Rescate en Popoyuapa, Rivas. Unpublished paper.

Hennen, Peter. 2001. Powder, Pomp, Power: Toward a Typology and Geneology of Effeminacies. *Social Thought and Research* 24: 121–44.

Hodges, Donald C. 1986. *Intellectual Foundations of the Nicaraguan Revolution*. Austin: University of Texas Press.

Howe, Alyssa Cymene Mathilde. 2003. Strategizing Sexualities, Re-imagining Gender, and Televisionary Tactics: The Cultural Politics of Social Struggle in Neoliberal Nicaragua. Ph.D. diss., University of New Mexico.

Hutcheon, Linda. 2000. *A Theory of Parody: The Teachings of Twentieth-Century Art Forms*. Urbana: University of Illinois Press.

Incer, Jaime. 1990. *Crónicas de viajeros: Nicaragua*. Vol. 1. San José, Costa Rica: Libro Libre.

Kendall, Carl. 1991. The Politics of Pilgrimage: The Black Christ of Esquipulas. In *Pilgrimage in Latin America*, edited by N. Ross Crumrine and Alan Morinis, 139–56. New York: Greenwood Press.

Kinser, Steven. 2003. Downfall in Nicaragua. *New York Review* (July 17): 39–40.

Kirshenblatt-Gimblett, Barbara. 1998. *Destination Culture: Tourism, Museums, Heritage*. Berkeley: University of California Press.

Kugelmass, Jack. 1991. Wishes Come True: Designing the Greenwich Village Halloween Parade. *Journal of American Folklore* 104: 443–65.

Kunzle, David. 1995. *The Murals of Revolutionary Nicaragua 1979–1992*. Berkeley: University of California Press.

Lancaster, Roger N. 1988. *Thanks to God and the Revolution: Popular Religion and Class Consciousness in the New Nicaragua*. New York: Columbia University Press.

———. 1992a. Skin Color, Race, and Racism in Nicaragua. *Ethnology* 30: 339–53.

———. 1992b. Subject Honor and Object Shame: The Construction of Male Homosexuality and Stigma in Nicaragua. In *Ethnographic Studies of Homosexuality*, edited by Wayne R. Dynes and Stephen Donaldson, 289–303. New York: Garland.

———. 1995. "That We Should All Turn Queer?" Homosexual Stigma in the Making of Manhood and the Breaking of a Revolution in Nicaragua. In *Conceiving Sexuality: Approaches to Sex Research in a Postmodern World*, edited by Richard G. Parker and John H. Gagnon, 135–56. New York: Routledge.

———. 1997. Guto's Performance: Notes on the Transvestism of Every-Day Life. In *The Gender Sexuality Reader: Culture, History, Political Economy*, edited by Roger N. Lancaster and Micaela Di Leonardo, 559–70. New York: Routledge.

Largey, Michael. 1991. Musical Ethnography in Haiti: A Study of Elite Hegemony and Musical Composition. Ph.D. diss., Indiana University.

Lechuga, Ruth D. 1988. Carnival in Tlaxcala. In *Behind the Mask in Mexico*, edited by Janet Brody Esser, 143–71. Santa Fe: Museum of New Mexico Press.

León-Portillo, Miguel. 1972. *Religión de los Nicaraos: Análisis y comparación de tradiciones culturales Nahuas*. Mexico City: Universidad Nacional Autónoma de México, Instituto de Investigaciones Históricos.

Lévy, Pablo. [1873] 1976. *Notas geográficas y económicas sobre la República de Nicaragua*. Managua, Nicaragua: Fondo de Promoción Cultural, Banco de América.

Limón, José E. 1994. *Dancing with the Devil: Society and Cultural Poetics in Mexican-American South Texas*. Madison: University of Wisconsin Press.

Lindahl, Carl. 1996. Bakhtin's Carnival Laughter and the Cajun Country Mardi Gras. *Folklore* 107: 49–62.

Lombardi-Satriani, Luigi María. 1974. Folklore as Culture of Contestation. *Journal of the Folklore Institute* 11: 99–122.

———. 1978. *Apropriación y destrucción de las clases subalternas*. Sacramento, Mexico: Editorial Nueva Imagen.

Mace, Carroll Edward. 1970. *Two Spanish-Quiché Dance-Dramas of Rabinal*. Tulane Studies in Romance Languages and Literature. New Orleans: Tulane University.

Magliocco, Sabina. 1988. The Two Madonnas: Festivals and Change in a Sardinian Community. Ph.D. diss., Indiana University.

———. 1993. *The Two Madonnas: The Politics of Festival in a Sardinian Community*. New York: Peter Lang.

Martin, Randy. 1994. *Socialist Ensembles: Theater and State in Cuba and Nicaragua*. Cultural Politics no. 8. Minneapolis: University of Minnesota Press.

Marzal, Manuel María. 1992. Daily Life in the Indies. In *The Church in Latin America: 1492–1992*, edited by Enrique Dussel, 69–80. Maryknoll, N.Y.: Orbis Books.

Membreño Idiaquez, Marcos. 1994. *Las estructuras de las comunidades étnicas*. Managua, Nicaragua: Editorial Envío.

Mendoza, Zoila S. 2000. *Shaping Society Through Dance: Mestizo Ritual Performance in the Peruvian Andes*. Chicago: University of Chicago Press.

Molina Argüello, Carlos. 1957. *Misiones nicaragüenses en archivos europeos*. Mexico City: Instituto Panamericano de Geografía e Historia.

Monaghan, John. 1990. Reciprocity, Redistribution, and the Transaction of Value in the Mesoamerican Fiesta. *American Ethnologist* 17: 758–74.

Mora Castillo, Luis. 1991. La organización comunal y la participación popular en la construcción de la democracia en Nicaragua (1979–1991). Unpublished paper.

Morel de Santa Cruz, Antonio. 1962. Informe al rey de Expaña del Obispo de Nicaragua. *Cuadernos Universitarios* 20 (León): 30–35.

Munro, Dana G. 1983. *A Student in Central America, 1914–1916*. Middle American Research Institute no. 51. New Orleans: Tulane University.

Nájera-Ramírez, Olga. 1989. Social and Political Dimensions of Folklorico Dance: The Binational Dialectic of Residual and Emergent Culture. *Western Folklore* 48, no. 1: 15–32.

———. 1997. *La Fiesta de los Tastoanes: Critical Encounters in Mexican Festival Performance*. Albuquerque: University of New Mexico Press.

Nash, June. 1970. *In the Eyes of the Ancestors: Belief and Behavior in a Maya Community*. New Haven, Conn.: Yale University Press.

Ness, Sally Ann. 1992. *Body, Movement, Culture: Kinesthetic and Visual Symbolism in a Philippine Community*. Philadelphia: University of Pennsylvania Press.

Newson, Linda. 1987. *Indian Survival in Nicaragua*. Norman: University of Oklahoma Press.

Nolan, Mary Lee. 1991. The European Roots of Latin American Pilgrimage. In *Pilgrimage in Latin America*, edited by N. Ross Crumrine and Alan Morinis, 19–52. New York: Greenwood Press.

Noyes, Dorothy. 1997. New Books on Festival, Part Two: Powers and Peripheries. *Journal of Folklore Research* 34, no. 2: 139–51.

———. 2003. *Fire in the Plaça: Catalan Festival Politics after Franco*. Philadelphia: University of Pennsylvania Press.

Nunley, John W., and Judith Bettelheim. 1988. *Caribbean Festival Arts*. Seattle: University of Washington Press.

Orso, Ethelyn G. 1990. Folklore as a Means of Getting Even. *Southern Folklore* 47: 249–60.

Oviedo y Valdez, Gonzalo Fernández. 1976. *Nicaragua en los cronistas de Indias: Oviedo*. Edited by Eduardo Pérez Valle. Managua, Nicaragua: Banco de América, Fondo Cultural.

Paige, Jeffery M. 1997. *Coffee and Power: Revolution and the Rise of Democracy in Central America*. Cambridge, Mass.: Harvard University Press.

Palma, Milagros. 1984. *Por los senderos de los mitos de Nicaragua*. Managua: Nueva Nicaragua.

———. 1988. *Nicaragua: Once mil virgenes: Imaginario mítico-religioso del pensamiento mestizo nicaragüense*. Bogotá, Columbia: Tercer Mundo Editores.

Paredes, Americo. 1971. Mexican Legendry and the Rise of the Mestizo: A Survey. In *American Folk Legend: A Symposium*, edited by Wayland Hand, 97–108. Berkeley: University of California Press.

Peña, Ligia María. 1998. Las cofradías indígenas en Nicaragua 1730–1812. Master's thesis, Universidad Centroamericana.

Peña Hernández, Enrique. [1968] 1986. *Folklore de Nicaragua.* Guatemala City: Talleres Piedra Santa.

Pérez, Jerónimo. 1977. *Obras historicas completas.* Managua, Nicaragua: Fondo de Promoción Cultural, Banco de América.

Remesal, Fray Antonio de. 1964. *Historia general de las Indias Occidentales y particular de la gobernación de Chiapa y Guatemala.* Edited by P. Carmelo Saenz de Santa María. Madrid: Atlas.

Rice, Eugene F., Jr. 1985. *Saint Jerome in the Renaissance.* Baltimore: Johns Hopkins University Press.

Rist, Gilbert. 1997. *The History of Development: From Western Origins to Global Faith.* New York: ZED Books.

Rizo, Mario 1999. *Identidad y derecho: Los títulos reales del pueblo de Subtiava.* Managua, Nicaragua: IHNCA-UCA.

Roach, Joseph. 1996. *Cities of the Dead: Circum-Atlantic Performance.* New York: Columbia University Press.

Robe, Stanley L. 1971. Hispanic Legend Material: Contrasts Between European and American Attitudes. In *American Folk Legend: A Symposium*, edited by Wayland Hand, 109–20. Berkeley: University of California Press.

Romero Vargas, Germán. 1988. *Las estructuras sociales de Nicaragua en el siglo XVIII.* Managua, Nicaragua: Editorial Vanguardia.

Rosaldo, Renato. 1995. Forward. In *Hybrid Cultures: Strategies for Entering and Leaving Modernity*, by Nestor García-Canclini, translated by Christopher L. Chiappari and Silvia L. López, xi–xxi. Minneapolis: University of Minnesota Press.

Rowe, William, and Vivian Schelling. 1991. *Memory and Modernity: Popular Culture in Latin America.* New York: Verso.

Ryan, John Morris, et al. [other authors not listed]. 1970. *Area Handbook for Nicaragua.* Washington, D.C.: U.S. Government Printing Office.

Saldana-Portillo, María Josefina. 1997. Developmentalism's Irresistible Seduction: Rural Subjectivity under Sandinista Agricultural Policy. In *The Politics of Culture in the Shadow of Capitalism*, edited by Lisa Lowe and David Lloyd, 132–72. Durham, N.C.: Duke University Press.

Sallnow, Michael J. 1991. Pilgrimage and Cultural Fracture in the Andes. In *Contesting the Sacred: The Anthropology of Christian Pilgrimage*, edited by John Eade and Michael J. Sallnow, 137–53. London: Routledge.

Santino, Jack. 1995. *All around the Year: Holidays and Celebrations in American Life.* Carbondale: University of Illinois Press.

Sawin, Patricia E. 2001. Transparent Masks: The Ideology and Practice of Disguise in Contemporary Cajun Mardi Gras. *Journal of American Folklore* 114: 173–203.

———. 2002. Performance at the Nexus of Gender, Power, and Desire: Reconsidering Bauman's Verbal Art from the Perspective of Gendered Subjectivity as Performance. *Journal of American Folklore* 115: 28–61.

Schechner, Richard. 1993. *The Future of Ritual: Writings on Culture and Performance.* New York: Routledge.

Scott, James C. 1985. *Weapons of the Weak: Everyday Forms of Peasant Resistance.* New Haven, Conn.: Yale University Press.

———. 1990. *Domination and the Arts of Resistance.* New Haven, Conn.: Yale University Press.

Scruggs, Thomas Mitchell. 1994. The Nicaraguan *Baile de la Marimba* and the Empowerment of Identity. Ph.D. diss., University of Texas, Austin.

———. 1998. Cultural Capital, Appropriate Transformations, and Transfer by Appropriation of the *Baile de la Marimba* in Western Nicaragua. *Latin American Music Review* 19, no. 1: 1–30.

———. 1999. "Let's Enjoy as Nicaraguans": The Use of Music in the Construction of Nicaraguan National Consciousness. *Ethnomusicology* 43, no. 2: 297–321.

———. 2002. Socially Conscious Music Forming the Social Conscience: Nicaraguan *Música Testimonial* and the Creation of a Revolutionary Movement. In *From Tejano to Tango: Latin American Popular Music,* edited by Walter Aaron Clark, 41–69. New York: Routledge.

Smith, Robert J. 1975. *The Art of the Festival, as Exemplified by the Fiesta to the Patroness of Otuzco: La Virgen de la Puerta.* Publications in Anthropology no. 6. Lawrence: University of Kansas.

Smith, Waldemar. 1977. *The Fiesta System and Economic Change.* New York: Columbia University Press.

Squier, Ephraim G. 1852. *Nicaragua: Its People, Scenery, Monuments, and the Proposed Canal.* 2 vols. New York: D. Appleton.

———. [1853] 1990. *Observations on the Archeology and Ethnology of Nicaragua.* Culver City, Calif.: Labyrinthos.

Stanlislawski, Dan. 1983. *The Transformation of Nicaragua: 1519–1548.* Berkeley: University of California Press.

Taussig, Michael. 1987. *Shamanism, Colonialism, and the Wild Man: A Study in Terror and Healing.* Chicago: University of Chicago Press.

Taylor, Diana. 1998. A Savage Performance. *TDR: The Drama Review* 42, no. 2: 160–76.

Thompson, Michael. 1979. *Rubbish Theory: The Creation and Destruction of Value.* Oxford: Oxford University Press.

Trexler, Richard C. 1984. We Think, They Act: Clerical Readings of Missionary Theatre in Sixteenth Century New Spain. In *Understanding Popular Culture: Europe from the Middle Ages to the Nineteenth Century,* edited by Steven L. Kaplan, 189–227. New York: Mouton.

Tünnerman Bernheim, Carlos. 1980. *Hacia una nueva educación en Nicaragua.* Managua: Edicíones Distribuidora Cultural, S.A.

Turner, Victor. 1974. Pilgrimages as Social Processes. In *Drama, Fields, and Metaphors: Symbolic Action in Human Society,* 166–230. Ithaca, N.Y.: Cornell University Press.

————. 1986. *The Anthropology of Performance.* New York: PAJ.

Van Young, Eric. 1994. Conclusion: The State as Vampire: Hegemonic Projects, Public Ritual, and Popular Culture in Mexico, 1600–1990. In *Rituals of Rule, Rituals of Resistance: Public Celebrations and Popular Culture in Mexico,* edited by William H. Beezley, Cheryl English Martin, and William E. French, 343–74. Wilmington, Del.: Scholarly Resources.

Vilas, Carlos M. 1992. Family Affairs: Class, Lineage, and Politics in Contemporary Nicaragua. *Journal of Latin American Studies* 24: 309–41.

Vogt, Evon Z. 1955. A Study of the Southwestern Fiesta System as Exemplified by the Laguna Fiesta. *American Anthropologist* 57: 820–39.

Walker, Thomas W. 2003. *Nicaragua: Living in the Shadow of the Eagle.* Boulder, Colo.: Westview Press.

Walsh, Michael, ed. 1991. *Butler's Lives of the Saints.* San Francisco: Harper San Francisco.

Ware, Carolyn. 1995. "I Read the Rules Backward": Women, Symbolic Inversion, and the Cajun Mardi Gras Run. *Southern Folklore* 52: 137–60.

————. 2001. Anything to Act Crazy: Cajun Women and Mardi Gras Disguise. *Journal of American Folklore* 114: 225–47.

Warren, Kay B. 1978. *The Symbolism of Subordination: Indian Identity in a Guatemalan Town.* Austin: University of Texas Press.

Wellinga, Klaas S. 1994. *Entre la poesía y la pared: Política cultural Sandinista 1979/1990.* Amsterdam: Thela.

Whisnant, David E. 1995. *Rascally Signs in Sacred Places: The Politics of Culture in Nicaragua.* Chapel Hill: University of North Carolina Press.

White, Steven. 1986. *Culture and Politics in Nicaragua: Testimonies of Poets and Writers.* New York: Lumen Books.

Index

About the Author

Katherine Borland is associate professor of comparative studies in the humanities at Ohio State University, Newark, where she teaches folklore, world literature, and postdevelopment theory. She has conducted fieldwork among Spanish-speaking people in Spain, Nicaragua, Miami, Florida, and Delaware. Her published work includes articles in *Radical History Review* and *Journal of American Folklore*, chapters in edited collections, and one book, *Creating Community: Hispanic Migration to Rural Delaware* (2001), for the Delaware Heritage Commission. She is currently studying the relation between feminist ethnography and decolonizing methodology as she collaborates in a team project to collect the life stories of American Indians living in Ohio. Dr. Borland returns to Masaya regularly in her work as director of an international service-learning program that takes Ohio student groups to Nicaragua to participate in grassroots community-development projects. Outside the academy, she has worked as a public folklorist and directed an educational non-profit organization for five years.